OP

3—

RELIG

JAMES PARKES

PRELUDE TO DIALOGUE

Jewish-Christian relationships

A

JAMES PARKES

PRELUDE TO DIALOGUE

Jewish-Christian relationships

With a foreword by Professor A. J. Heschel

VALLENTINE, MITCHELL

First published in Great Britain by
Vallentine, Mitchell & Co. Ltd.,
18 Cursitor Street, London, E.C.4.

SBN 85303 020 0

****

Contents

****

III

Israel

IV

Theological Foundations

vi

FOREWORD

THE WORLD WE live in has become a single neighbourhood, and the role of religious commitment, of awe and compassion, in the thinking of our fellow-men, is becoming a domestic issue. What goes on in the Christian world affects us deeply. Unless we learn how to help one another, we will only weaken each other.

Our society is in crisis not because we intensely disagree but because we feebly agree. "The clash of doctrines is not a disaster, it is an opportunity."

The survival of mankind is in the balance. One wave of hatred, callousness or contempt may bring in its wake the destruction of all mankind. Vicious deeds are but an aftermath of what is conceived in the hearts and minds of man. From the inner life of man and from the articulation of evil thoughts evil actions take their rise. It is therefore of extreme importance that the sinfulness of thoughts of suspicion and hatred and particularly the sinfulness of any contemptuous utterance, however flippantly it is intended, be made clear to all mankind. This applies in particular to thoughts and utterances about individuals or groups of other religions, races and nations. Speech has power, and few men realise that words do not fade. What starts as a sound ends in a deed.

In an age when the spiritual premises of our existence are both questioned and even militantly removed, the urgent problem is not the competition among some religions but the condition of all religions, the condition of man.

The world is too small for anything but mutual care and deep respect ; the world is too great for anything but responsibility for one another.

James Parkes has made distinguished contributions toward such a goal. A man of deep concerns, with a vast range of learning at his disposal, he is a pioneer in this field.

He regards his task as the attempt to reverse a stream which has flowed in the wrong direction for 1900 years ; " to enable the relationship between Jews and non-Jews to be free from centuries of ignorance and prejudice and to find its own proper level."

It is a noble cause which James Parkes serves with high distinction.

January, 1968.   Abraham J. Heschel.

INTRODUCTORY NOTE

As the Table of Contents shows, this *Prelude to Dialogue* consists of papers and articles delivered over a number of years, but with the common factor that all were delivered on a background of the Jewish-Christian relationship, and the relation of Jews, Judaism and Israel to the outside world. This method of presenting what I wanted to say had the advantage that over a very wide range of subjects I could express a more concentrated point of view than would have been easy in a book where a coherent thesis had to be built up in a series of connected chapters. It has the disadvantage—for which I apologise—that there is a certain amount of repetition. Only a passion for mechanical consistency—which I do not possess—would have justified scrutinising each paper or lecture to avoid this. The essays stand here as they were originally produced. In particular I feel no apology is needed for a repetition in the first two essays of the exquisite explanation of the meaning of the *lulav*. As Ruth Draper remarked in one of her impersonations—it cannot be said too often.

I hope that in all the cases where it was necessary I have received permission for the publication of these papers and articles. If in any case I have slipped up, I trust that my apologies for my inadvertence will be accepted.

The idea of publication in a permanent form of what had been pamphlets, articles and lectures, began while my wife and I still ran an active institute at Barley; its realisation has taken place after our retirement, when most of our archives have joined the Parkes Library at Southampton University.

James Parkes.
August, 1968.

Iwerne Minster,
Blandford,
Dorset.

****

To Pioneers in the Field of Dialogue:
Peter, Zwi, and the Rainbow Group in
Jerusalem,
Roland, Stuart, and the Toronto Dialogue,
and
Marc, Roy and Edward in the U.S.A.

****

I

****
The Nature of Judaism
****

1

The Nature of Judaism

1

A REAPPRAISAL OF THE CHRISTIAN ATTITUDE TO JUDAISM

It is now more than thirty years since I was plunged unexpectedly into a close study of European academic antisemitism. It would have surprised me greatly at that time to have been told that these studies of a contemporary social evil would lead me through history into theology, and into the reappraisal of theological statements which I had previously seen no reason to question. But I soon found that contemporary antisemitism was incomprehensible without a knowledge of Jewish history, and that there was no clue to Jewish history without an understanding of Judaism. As I began to understand historic Judaism, I began also to realise that it impinged far more deeply and disturbingly on my Christian preconceptions of its nature than I had ever expected. The whole issue of our relations with it demands a thorough re-examination, though I would emphasise that everything which I am seeking to put forward in this paper is tentative, and that I claim for it no final authority. Nevertheless, these are conclusions which have emerged from the study and experience of thirty years, in which I have had quite unusual contacts with every aspect of our relationship with Jews and Judaism, and which I originally approached with a singularly open—indeed empty—mind, since I had never met in my youth either Jews or the missionaries to them. Neither were to be found in my native Guernsey.

No one will question the statement that the relations between Judaism and Christianity are so intimate, and the traditional position taken by the Christian churches so unanimous and categoric, that to disturb either is bound at some point to cut extremely deeply into the traditional expression of our theology. The verdict which we pass upon the people and religion in which Jesus of Nazareth was born cannot be a matter of peripheral interest; and our claim to the inheritance of the promises of the Old Testament has involved an attitude to Jews who have remained faithful to Judaism on which they have every right to challenge us to the clearest and most unequivocal justification. They are, in fact, beginning to do so, as a number of books bear witness.

I have said "Christian churches" advisedly, for in their attitude to pre- and post-Christian Judaism the Eastern churches, the great Western tradition and the Reformed churches exhibit an unusual unanimity; and the extremists have come from east and west, medieval and post-medieval alike.

The violence of the eight infamous sermons which John Chrysostom preached at Antioch in A.D. 387 is balanced by the equal violence and obscenity of Martin Luther's *Die Juden und Ihre Lügen*. Moreover, quite apart from extremists, no ordinary Christian writer or preacher seems to feel it necessary to guard his words or pull his punches in making abusive and derogatory remarks about Judaism and even Jews. When one has become sensitive to such remarks, as I have inevitably become, it is really horrifying from what gentle lips and with what sweet insouciance words can issue which I know to be factually untrue and grossly libellous. An excellent example is the constant repetition from pulpit and religious press of the supposed contrast in the field of law between the harsh Jewish enforcement of the *lex talionis* and the soul-winning Christian doctrine of love. But the *lex talionis* had been abolished in Judaism some generations before Jesus was born, whereas the record of all the Christian churches in the enforcement of laws supposed to be verbally inspired in the Old Testament is, right up to the nineteenth century, uniformly bad. Even today members of the Dutch Church in South Africa give the biblical condemnation of Ham, the son of Noah, as justification for its policy of apartheid.

The unanimity of this traditional attitude to Judaism has

4

been rooted in two interpretations of history, both of which have been intimately entwined with Christian beliefs. It is for this reason that any reappraisal cuts so deep into our theological assumptions.

The first root is the delineation of the period between the return from the Babylonian exile and the Incarnation as one of continuous spiritual decline. Such a delineation is fortified in turn by two suppositions: that the clue to the understanding of the spiritual values of the period is provided by the doctrine of the faithful remnant, and that the immediate background to the mission of Jesus is provided by apocalyptic eschatology.

In amplification of the idea of the faithful remnant a picture is often drawn of fidelity to the divinely given covenant narrowing down to a tiny group on the fringes of a mass of national rigidity and infidelity, until the remnant came to be represented only by the twelve disciples. When these deserted Jesus in Gethsemane, then Christ upon the cross remained the sole link between the ancient covenant people and the new. As George A. Knight says in the most recent exposition of *A Christian Interpretation of the Old Testament*: "Christ is the remnant of Israel in himself" (p. 350). A further example of the consequences of this emphasis on a remnant might be drawn from an important recent American work, *The History of New Testament Times, with an Introduction to the Apocrypha*, by Robert H. Pfeiffer. In a book of 560 pages, the "religious history" of Palestinian Judaism from 200 B.C. to A.D. 200 occupies fourteen pages, and of that as many pages are given to messianic expectations as are sentences to the development of rabbinic Judaism.

This allocation of space faithfully reflects the supposition that the emergence of apocalyptic eschatology was the central religious event of these centuries; and that in this type of writing the coming of "the fullness of time" is to be seen, and the conditions prepared for the Incarnation. Such a supposition naturally views the Incarnation itself as an eschatological and not as a seminal event; and this is certainly in line with most current schools of New Testament interpretation. For they assume that the apocalyptists held tenuously to the spiritual inheritance of Israel, while the overwhelming majority of the nation fell away to the arid legalism of increasing subservience to priest and Pharisee. The remnant was composed of those who proclaimed an eschatological view of history.

The second root is the conviction that post-Christian Judaism is without independent spiritual dynamic or vitality. Those New Testament scholars and theologians who feel that anything more is needed than the bare statement of an obvious fact have no difficulty in producing quotations from the more congested pages of the Talmud (and there are many) to demonstrate this. I remember that in my Oxford days it was popular to place the highest spiritual duty of a rabbinic Jew in the detection of eggs laid on the Sabbath. Even when the bare bones of this view were somewhat clothed in respect for the piety of such men as Hillel or Gamaliel, it would probably be fair to say that this was thought of as the reflection of an atmosphere surviving from a nobler period, but which, so far as the first century of the present era was concerned, was already better exemplified in Christianity. Hillel and Gamaliel were not thought of as early examples of a type of spiritual dynamic and personal piety which had survived and was continued in post-Christian Judaism. In fact, we have coined the word *Spät-Judentum, bas-Judaïsme,* or Late Judaism to imply that we considered that Judaism had already passed its zenith some centuries before they were born.

On such a background a picture was drawn of the process of history which likened it to two cones, meeting at their points, which point of meeting was Christ upon the Cross. All history before him looked forward to that event ; all subsequent history looked back to it. The action of God in history was thus entirely Christo-centric. As a natural corollary to this belief it is assumed that everything which was valid in the previous revelation of Sinai was taken over and incorporated into the life of Jesus and so into the life and doctrine of the Christian Church. Thus, had post-Christian Judaism retained any validity, it could, theologically, be only as a pale shadow of what was actually better present in Christianity, implicitly, if not explicitly.

6

A REAPPRAISAL OF THE CHRISTIAN ATTITUDE TO JUDAISM

And here is my problem. As I progressed more in the study and understanding of my subject, I came more and more clearly to recognise that on every point our interpretation of the period between Ezra and the Incarnation was demonstrably false; and good theology cannot be built on bad history. The spiritually-minded remnant, withdrawn from the main stream of national life, is a figment of Christian imagination. Apocalyptic eschatology, in spite of popular appeal at different moments of Jewish history, is a movement which was never of religious importance or distinguished for spirituality. Finally, the Judaism of these centuries is not *Spät-Judentum*, but early Judaism, leading to the establishment of a fully developed ortho*praxy*, in just the same centuries as Christiantiy was reaching its fully developed orthodoxy. Rabbinic Judaism is not a predecessor of Christianity ; it is a contemporary.

The trouble begins with our estimate of the work of Ezra and his successors. They were not narrow legalists from whom a spiritually-minded remnant had to withdraw. They ushered in one of the most remarkable periods in the spiritual Odyssey of humanity. They came back from Babylon convinced that defeat and exile had been just punishments for the sins of the nation, especially for its idolatry and its social malpractices. The redemption of the nation as a whole was therefore the constant object of their thinking. To achieve it they set themselves a double task. The worship of the nation, centred in the Temple, had to be purified from any stain of syncretism or worship of idols ; and the whole nation had to be taught what God demanded of it in terms of constant obedience to his revealed will in every act of ordinary daily living. That within less than five hundred years " the fulness of time " had come, and Jesus of Nazareth was born, is a tribute alike to their just understanding of the spiritual need, and to the propriety of the measures which they took to meet it.

These measures were manifold. But at the heart of them was the absolute conviction that the *whole* people was involved in their fulfilment. This was no palace reform, depending on one good king ; no setting-up of a standard of holiness only to be achieved by withdrawal from the common life. It was the emergence of something much greater and much more permanent. The pre-exilic prophets had proclaimed that God was concerned with the conduct of ordinary men and with the true living of ordinary life. Ezra and his successors created the machinery by which alone the ideals of the prophets could become a reality.

From the very beginning it was planned that the Torah should be regularly read and expounded to the people. It was so read and expounded in every Jewish settlement twice a week ; and those who read it were trained in the performance of their task. At first it seems that they were drawn from the lesser priestly families, but later a special class of " scribes " emerged who took their name from the fact that they copied the scrolls of Torah as well as expounded them. Thus literacy and the local possession and knowledge of the Bible became common in the Jewish world.

That religion contained something to be taught was only part of their revolution. Though they laid great stress on the exact performance of the ritual of the Temple at Jerusalem, the group surrounding Ezra made a far more fundamental contribution to religious history by their enrichment of an exilic development. For in the exile there grew up the tradition of the local congregation meeting regularly for worship as well as for instruction. The synagogue became the centre of every Jewish community, in Palestine as well as abroad ; and the synagogal liturgy, with its combination of prayer, praise and thanksgiving, is the model on which the services of the Church are built.

For both teaching and worship there was immense value in an agreed collection of sacred Scriptures, which should be authoritative and serve to unite a people already widely scattered. It is not surprising that the essential steps to the formation of the canon were taken during these centuries.

Their final contribution lay in the progress made in the understanding of man as person, as a child of God, unique in himself and with his own unexchangeable destiny. To this period belongs the exquisite devotion of much of the Psalter ; and the post-exilic psalms alone should convince us of the unreality of separating the spiritual leadership of the nation from the teaching of Torah. For delight in the Law

is writ large upon these psalms, and it is a delight which is
neither external nor superficial, but of the very stuff of
personal piety and devotion. It is from this period that we
get the two stories of the lives of individuals included in the
canon, the books of Ruth and Jonah. The books of apothegms
or proverbs, within and without the canon, reflect much of
the interest in man as an individual. Ecclesiastes is an
individual philosophy of life, perhaps the most surprising
inclusion in Holy Scripture. Above all the book of Job saw
the light in this period, and the author dared to pose the
question of individual destiny with a profound perplexity
which at that time there was not the material to resolve.
Underlying all this is the strangely slow beginning of a belief
in personal and conscious survival, mostly in the form of the
resurrection of the soul and body.

When we look at all this solid achievement, and contrast
it with the shallow tinsel of the world of illusion in which
apocalyptic eschatologists elaborated their politico-religious
pamphlets, we cannot but be astonished that the mere
coincidence of a quotation or two and a title or so, should
make scholars see in them, and not in the teachers of Torah
and their successors, the *preparatio evangelica* which made
possible the Incarnation of the Son of God. The teaching
and life of Jesus, and the establishment of the Christian
Church, grow right out of the heart of post-exilic Judaism,
and not on the periphery, where the dreams of the apocalyptists were leading men into the dangerous fantasies of
zealotry, war and political assassination. Not only because
of the content of their teaching, but because of the techniques which they had evolved of the religious school, the
synagogue, and the agreed Scriptures, the spread of
Christianity is inconceivable without the work which they
had done.

At this stage of my presentation it could be claimed that
all that I was advocating was that we should see the source
—humanly speaking—of "the fulness of time" in one aspect
of Jewish history and not in another. So far as our relations
with the surviving Judaism are concerned, it might appear
that to say that Christianity came out of the heart of it, and
not from some peripheral movement, was even to take away

such reason as might otherwise exist for its independent survival. But this is just what, as an historian, I find it quite impossible to do.

It does not correspond to well-known, well-authenticated and easily established facts about post-Christian Judaism. The position has been somewhat obscured by the convention of speaking of post-exilic Judaism as " a Church." The phrase goes back to Dean Prideaux, though I do not know whether it originated with him. But the ascription of the word is quite misleading. The task undertaken by Ezra was not to found a Church. There is no sense in which it would be true of his work to say that he was " calling out " one Jew from amidst other Jews, or regarded one group of Jews as *the elect* as distinct from other Jews. His mission was conceived to be, and was successful in being, a call to the whole people. He secured from *the people* the repetition of the Sinaitic acceptance: " All that the Lord has spoken we will do," and on that basis he planned his campaign to teach Torah to the whole people.

In distinction from all this, the followers of Jesus had no doubt whatever that he was calling men, by personal repentance and conviction, " out " from the midst of the world, whether they were Jew or Greek. The period during which they expected a total acceptance from all Israel was a very short one. Today we are repeating the error of Prideaux in a new way by saying that " Jesus did not found the Church ; it had been in existence since Abraham." This could not be so. It is surely contrary to all that we have learned from anthropological study to believe that the Divine call to man as person came before the Divine call of Sinai to a whole people. The Incarnation is rooted in previous history. But it is itself a *new* Divine initiative, and the continuing product of that initiative is a *new* creation, the Church.

Thus, whether post-Christian Judaism be right or wrong, it is clear that Christianity has not absorbed its values, but created *new* ones. Judaism and Christianity are different kinds of religion and neither is an imperfect form of the other. Not only do both claim a Divine origin on the same basis, but, from a human point of view, both are reasonable growths from their different foundations. Both accept the proposition that God chooses agents through whom His will is known and His work is done throughout His creation. Christianity sees those agents gathered in the Church as "the elect from every nation." Judaism sees them gathered in the synagogue as an "elect nation." It is foolish for either to reproach the other with selfishness, for it is the best teaching of neither that any benefits which God may bestow upon them should be kept to themselves.

PUT IN ITS simplest form the result has been that Christianity as an historical religion has clearly found its human centre in man as person, and we have shown how this is rooted in the previous half millennium. Judaism, equally obviously, has its centre in man as social being, as member of a natural community—a "people"; and this is equally genuinely and unmistakably rooted in the developments of the same period.

It is important to emphasise that to say that Christianity is rooted in man as person is not the same as saying that it is rooted in the individual. Christianity does not see the world atomised into millions of individuals. Man as person has both a corporate and a singular existence, as the Church bears witness. But this corporate existence is something new, something growing out of the Incarnation.

The dilemma would be solved if we could accept the idea, which we find already in the New Testament, that the Church, that is a selected community, was identical with the natural community on which Judaism rests. The dilemma would be equally solved if we could argue that the history of the last two millennia showed that the natural community, now the nation State, was clearly passing away, and that the Church was ready and well equipped to replace it on the world stage. Unfortunately, natural and selected communities are not identical; the State is not withering away but becomes every day a more inescapable part of the organisation of human life; and in no field does the trumpet of the churches give forth more uncertain sounds than in the realms of national and international politics.

I am, I know, making cut and dried statements in fields

11

where there is much variety, and adducing black and white where there is an infinity of nuances. Churches *have* spoken in politics, Judaism regards the individual as a person and not as a robot; the Christian tradition is well aware that man cannot live alone . . . and so on. Yet the difference between Christianity and Judaism is a real one. I think that I can show it by two quite fair illustrations.

The traditional ideal of a Jewish rabbi does not include a pastoral vocation " to seek and save those who are lost"; and the evangelistic mission, in the form in which Christianity has developed it, plays no part in Jewish history. This must be said with great delicacy, for both Christianity and Islam have made conversion to Judaism a capital offence, and Jews are not to be blamed for an isolation, and concentration on their own community, which we have imposed upon them. But I think that I am legitimately citing the experience of those centuries when Jews could and did make converts. They were made by the attractive power of the local synagogue, not by trained missionaries going out singly or in groups to cities and regions where settled Jewish communities did not exist. Christianity, on the other hand, cannot but be a missionary religion; and that mission must, as Paul realised at the beginning, take no account of bond or free, man or woman, or, as I am sure he would add if he were preaching now, white or coloured.

My other illustration is taken from a midrash explaining why Jews, at the Feast of Tabernacles, hold in one hand a sweet-smelling citron and in the other the *lulav*, a spray of the palm, the myrtle and the willow bound together. The explanation is this:

" The fruit of the Hadar tree symbolises Israel: just as the citron has taste as well as fragrance, so Israel have among them men who possess learning as well as good deeds. Branches of palm tree, too, applies to Israel: as the palm has taste but no fragrance, so Israel have among them such as possess learning but not good deeds. And boughs of the thick trees likewise applies to Israel: just as the myrtle has fragrance but no taste, so Israel have among them such as possess good deeds but not learning.

And willows of the brook also applies to Israel: just as
the willow has no taste and no fragrance, so Israel have
among them such as possess neither learning nor good
deeds. What then does the Holy One, blessed be He, do
to them ? To destroy them is impossible. But, says the
Holy One, blessed be He, let them all be tied together in
one band, and they will atone, one for another. And in
that hour the Lord is exalted."

Broadly speaking the willow is not bound into the Christian
lulav, and in saying this I am not ignoring the outpouring
century by century of the love of Christ in the haunts of
ignorance and vice of a fallen world. The willow represents
those who are outside the Church, those who, in any
predestinarian theology, would have been ear-marked for
damnation. Less rigid theologies may deal with them more
tenderly, but the basic fact would be the same: such may
be within the sphere of the Church's redemptive activity,
but they would not provide cause why the Church should
modify its theology. There is nothing comparable in the
Christian tradition to the constant Jewish feeling that
demands must not be made upon the people which it is not
possible for them to obey.

This is a fundamental difference between a religion whose
members enter it by choice, whether of God or man, and a
religion whose members are there by the simple fact of
birth, a difference not eliminated by the Christian adoption
of infant baptism. Running all through Jewish thought is
insistence that what is asked for is attainable in the ordinary
paths of life. "It is not too hard for you, neither is it far
off. . . . But the word is very near to you, in your mouth and
in your heart, so that you can do it" (Deut. xxx, 11-14).
Running all through Christianity is an equally clear insistence on the unattainable, on the perfection striven for but
not reached—"here we have no abiding city."

Now it is true that Christian polemicists have sneered at
Judaism because they have regarded this Jewish characteristic as implying superficiality; and Jewish polemicists have
likewise spoken of Christianity as out of this world. When
we ignore the fact that in the history of each there are

weaknesses connected with these two emphases, and seek to understand the two emphases themselves, then I think that we are forced to the conclusion that each is right according to its premises, and that its premises rest securely upon actual facts of human experience.

If a nation is to have a religion guiding its political, social and international conduct, then there must be constant care for the willow in its *lulav*. It is not the task of its religious leaders to concentrate only upon what can be achieved or understood just by a few—though, of course, there is place within a nation for those few—but is unattainable by those who must do its daily and ordinary work. Their main task is to set before the nation that which is attainable by their society as it actually exists at the given moment; and constantly to renew the techniques which will most help ordinary men and women to bend their lives to that goal. Except in very unusual circumstances, nations do not repent. But they can change their objectives. Nations are not made virtuous by regulations which go beyond their willingness to be regulated—witness the tragic failure of prohibition in the United States. But they can change their habits. They cannot always be made good. But they can be safeguarded from foreseeable temptation. It is wise to build a fence about their Torah.

The situation is quite different when one considers man as person. It is impossible to imagine a Christian Church setting before its congregation an attainable goal of righteousness; and it is right, within the body of a Christian Church, to have a place—a central place—for the mystic and the ascetic, for the cloister and the life of dedicated prayer and poverty. For the Church as a community is not the nation as a community. It is the body of Christ.

Here, then, is the dilemma. It would be intolerable that Christianity should clothe itself in the garb of Judaism. But I cannot, as do most of my fellow-Christians, thereby relegate Judaism to the limbo of outworn creeds. For I am bound as an historian to say that the same is true of post-Christian Judaism. It is no part of its task to clothe itself with the ethos and activity of Christianity. A religion designed, as the recipients of the Sinaitic revelation rightly

14

understood it to be, to create a holy nation, must take into account the way in which a nation changes. It must be perpetually conscious of the need to keep the willow bound within its *lulav*. And, as nations are permanently with us, can it not be that Judaism is still divinely intended to show the way towards a nation's holiness ?

Before I pass to a further point, I want for a moment to touch on one of the peculiar difficulties of this whole endeavour. The Jews have been subjected to a history so full of persecution, restriction and distortion, that their Judaism is inevitably affected. The miracle is that it has survived at all. But both in Orthodoxy and in Reform, Judaism shows weaknesses which can be easily exploited. Excessive rigidity on the one hand, and excessive vagueness on the other, can obscure the basic character of the Sinaitic faith to an unsympathetic outsider. But in its essence, that faith is, as the faith of a nation must be, astonishingly flexible and astonishingly positive.

We have only to reflect on that history to confirm this description. The rabbinic academies of Palestine and Babylon evolved a way of life which was identifiable from China to the Atlantic through a thousand separate autonomous communities, and which endured century after century the seduction of the differing environments of all the world's major faiths, without apostasy and without schism, and yet without compulsion and without any central authority.

I would return now to a second point. It is the fashion of some schools of contemporary theology to sneer at "moralism," and they are happy to dismiss the Hebrew prophets under this cliché. But a delicate sense of the moral, and an extended use both of law and custom and of the right and duty to interpret them, is the quite inevitable way in which to approach the transformation of man's daily life into the conscious service of God. Be it noted that the ordinary Jewish prayer book contains six pages devoted entirely to the benedictions appropriate to every joy and sorrow of life. Everything is a gift of the Creator, and He asks of man only that in using it he gives thanks. A Jew can, of course, say grace in as slovenly and mechanical a fashion as a Christian. But Judaism has continuously

15

emphasised that "the trivial round, the common task, can furnish all we need to ask." That is also the way to a nation's holiness.

Thus we have come to the heart of the problem. Because the same man is both a person in himself and a member of a natural community, does he not need the insights of both Judaism and Christianity? Not only has Christianity not absorbed Judaism, historically speaking; but, theologically speaking, it would not have absorbed it if all Jews individually accepted baptism in the different existing Christian churches. They would have gained Jews, but they would have lost Sinai.

I am often accused of saying that I regard Judaism and Christianity as equally legitimate alternatives, so that it is a matter of indifference which of the two a man might accept for himself. This is not my position at all. The conclusion to which I find myself forced is the apparently absurd proposal that man needs both.

It will help at this stage to turn from the consideration of the two religions to look at the world in which they are operating. We see that it is an inescapable destiny of man to be both person in himself and member of a natural community; and that it is inherent in the very nature of the world that these two qualities should often be in tension, even in opposition, to each other. The government of a nation must act differently towards its stewardship of national affairs from an individual dealing with his own property and relationships. Any public official, from judge to member of the parish council, must be able to set aside personal predilections to consider what can be publicly achieved, or what is the public good. One could multiply examples, but the point is too obvious for it to be necessary; and it is more important to seek the interpretation.

I believe that we would all accept the view that this tension is part of God's creation, and will endure while this Age endures. The argument between the individual and society is permanently and intentionally insoluble. True community must consist of free persons, and personality cannot reach its fulfilment except in community. With this

16

in mind, I cannot escape the conviction that the historical
evidence shows clearly that each religion has, as it were,
backed one side of the equation. Each can offer evidence
that it has channelled the power of God into human lives.
But differently. They are neither identical nor interchangeable, so that neither can be said to be superfluous. Moreover,
is it not reasonable to add that God would prefer that His
power should be channelled equally to both sides of the
equation ? Are there not vast reserves of Divine power
which Christians do not tap, because we insist that God
deals *directly* with man as person but *only indirectly* with
man as citizen ? I remember Father E. K. Talbot arguing
passionately with me that, when you had a banker who was
a regular communicant, there you had the Church in
banking. But would not God like also that the banker should
expect to meet Him directly in the bank, and to receive His
guidance in the problems of his bank ?

At first it seems fantastic in any way to equate God
speaking at Sinai with God acting upon Golgotha. But I am
puzzled as to whether the shock is not emotionally natural
rather than intellectually justifiable. Because I am a
Christian talking to a Christian audience, I have been
stressing the positive contribution of Judaism. But I have
not been denying the positive values of Christianity. Nothing
that I have found in my studies lessens my belief in Christ
as " God of God, Light of light, very God of very God."
Nothing lessens my belief in the Incarnation or the Atonement, nothing has made the Christian Church less the
continuation of that Incarnation. What puzzles me is not
something to be taken away, but something to be added.

As to the shock of which I have spoken, is not the answer
that God would in these supreme moments of revelation
choose the channel natural and appropriate to His purpose ?
All that we know of the natural community suggests that
the revelation of God's purpose to it should be addressed,
not to the heart, but to the intellect and the reason. But that
does not mean that it is less important. After two world
wars, in the middle of the cold war, and with the evidence
of the power over man as person of brainwashing, mass
propaganda, and torture, it is difficult to say that man as

17

social being is evidently less important to God than man as person.

I do not know the answer to all the questions which I have asked. I am sure that it involves more than adding another cardinal to the Vatican, drafting another resolution for the World Council of Churches, or laying another burden on the backs of the parochial ministry of all denominations. Likewise it does not mean the Christian adoption of all the multiple orthopraxis of Jewish life. But I do not think that we shall find out what it does mean until we begin to sort out the implications of such things as I have been saying in this paper.

2

THE CONCEPT OF A CHOSEN PEOPLE IN JUDAISM AND CHRISTIANITY

IN 1948 THE University of Chicago Press published under the title *Judaism and Christianity* the lectures which, as Charles William Eliot Lecturer, I had given at the Jewish Institute of Religion during the session 1946-47. It is therefore fitting that it should be at Chicago that I should make this further statement of the position which I have reached after six more years of study; and I am profoundly grateful to the University and to the Hillel Foundation for their invitation to deliver the annual Charles W. Gilkey Lecture under their auspices on this occasion.

We can rejoice that understanding between the two religions is growing in many circles, but there is still a long way to go, even among those who are possessed with a spirit of goodwill on both sides. Let me illustrate this by two questions which I have been asked during the lecture tour on which I have been engaged during the past two months in the United States. One questioner asked me whether I did not agree that the New Testament was almost entirely *haggadic* and contained very little *halacha*. From the traditional Jewish point of view, *halacha*, that is express commandment, is the core of religion. *Haggada*, or moral commentary on *halacha*, is much less important. But the question implied that the New Testament, and therefore Christianity, could be assessed by its conformity with the values appropriate to Judaism, whereas no Christian scholar would approach any New Testament book on the basis of the relative proportions of *halacha* and *haggada* which it contained. Another person asked this question: " In

19

Christianity we know that we are saved in the name of Jesus Christ. In what name does Judaism offer salvation ? " Here the situation is exactly reversed. The questioner assumes that Judaism is to be judged by the Christian standard of its efficacy in securing personal salvation. But no Jew would judge Judaism by this test: for Judaism does not offer a way of personal salvation, but a way of living for men in community. That is why its traditional emphasis is on *halacha*.

Let me emphasise still further current conceptions of the relations between the two religions by giving two interpretations which have been put on the special task I was invited to this country to undertake. I was invited by the Union of American Hebrew Congregations to address my fellow Christian clergy on the nature of Judaism, at the " institutes " which they hold annually in many centres for that purpose ; but to which they had previously always invited a Rabbi as lecturer. I have met in this country a number of fine, broad-minded Christian leaders from my own Church, the Anglican communion ; but all of them, when I explained my task, assumed it to be legitimately re-expressed as the Jewish *background* of Christianity. Likewise on the Jewish side it was frequently understood to be a " goodwill " mission, based on the conception that all religions were essentially identical, and each should live in full acceptance of the other without interference.

I do not want for a moment to belittle the sincerity of my questioners or interpreters, or to deny the value of the open minds with which they are seeking a deeper understanding of the relations between the two faiths, and the positive values inherent in each of them. Indeed, although my task is different, and, in the end, I think gets nearer to fundamentals, I would like to pay tribute to the importance of Jewish-Christian co-operation in the goodwill movement. Not only is it an essential method of overcoming the blind ignorance which so easily leads to antisemitism and group prejudice, but there is a vast field of social relations in which Jews and Christians can serve both their own faiths and the community at large by the fullest and most uninhibited joint activity.

20

My own task I would explain by going back to the assumption I have already quoted, that the natural—or indeed, sole—interest of a Christian in Judaism is in studying the background of his own faith. If by Judaism we mean the religion and worship of the Synagogue, then the statement is just historically untrue. For the centuries in which the religion of the Synagogue took its definite shape are not even pre-Christian. They are identical with those in which the Church, also, was assuming its distinctive theology and institutional forms, i.e., from the first through the fourth century of the Christian era. Moreover, they were centuries during which mutual relations between the two religions became almost non-existent.

The real position is that historically both Christianity and Judaism stem from the experience of the people of Israel, as it developed from the time of the call of Abraham, through the experience of Sinai, down to the Herodian period. For both religions the books in which this experience is embodied are "Holy Writ," whether with the Jews we entitle them *The Scriptures,* or with Christians, *The Old Testament.* But we interpret them differently, and it is from our different interpretations that arise the profound and fascinating differences between our two faiths, as they have developed and been moulded by nearly two thousand years of history.

The Christian, viewing the experiences of the Israelite or Hebrew nation, sees a gradual but narrowing development from the call to the whole people at Sinai and the giving of the Law, to the concentration on the faithful remnant spoken of by Isaiah and other prophets, and so to the individual Messiah, Jesus of Nazareth. Then comes the Church, the New Israel, in which the Divine call broadens out again to assume world-wide dimensions. The Christian contrasts the large element of ritual and ceremonial in the Law with the call of the prophets to " do justly, love mercy, and walk humbly with thy God." He notes the continual rebuke and rejection of the nation with which the writings of the prophets are filled, and he contrasts the sinful nation with the righteous remnant, the servant expiating the sins of his people. Likewise his interest in the Messianic prophecies is concentrated on the person of the Messiah and

21

the new summons to the Gentiles, while he relegates the Messianic Age of universal righteousness and peace to a distant future, or even to another world.

The first point at which the Jew would express his disagreement lies in the word "law." Even if the Christian is aware that the Hebrew word "Torah" has a somewhat wider meaning than the modern word "law," yet law seems to him to give an adequate description of what is to be found in the first five books of the Bible. He is satisfied to accept the prophets as critics and successors to the lawgivers, whether he attributes all the law to one period or regards it as having been continually edited by another class whom he willingly contrasts to their detriment with the prophets, i.e., the priests.

But to the Jew the word Torah does not mean law, but something very much fuller and deeper, and unless we can understand this Jewish meaning of Torah, we shall never understand Judaism. The great American scholar, George Foot Moore, speaks thus of Torah (*Judaism*, Vol. I, p. 163): "It is a source of manifold misconceptions that the word is customarily translated ' law,' though it is not easy to suggest any one English word by which it would be better rendered. 'Law' must, however, not be understood in the restricted sense of legislation, but must be taken to include the whole revelation—all that God has made known of His nature, character and purpose, and of what He would have men be and do. The prophets call their own utterances Torah, and the Psalms deserve the name as well. . . . In a word, Torah in one aspect is the vehicle, in another and deeper view it is the whole content of revelation." Another scholar, Travers Herford, says bluntly : "It does not, and never did, mean law. It means and always has meant ' teaching.'" (Talmud and Apocrypha, p. 7.) If we think of the way in which human societies have evolved, we shall see that these two statements are not so disparate as they appear.

In the gradual evolution of social order men first learned to obey tabus, because they were told that these were of Divine origin—whatever the concept of divinity involved. The same Divine sanction remained, as tabu came to have an ethical content, and as the religious myth and legend which were intertwined with the origin of tabus were woven into the ever-lengthening histories of human societies. The transmission of this corpus of experience and interpretation of the nature and meaning of life, and of the way in which to please divinity, was an essential task of each generation. Hence the emphasis on teaching in the definition of Travers Herford. Thus, as the people of Israel gradually came to the belief in One God, whose sway was universal, who was the Lord of history, and who had comprehensive moral demands to make upon His children, so the totality of this belief and its consequences were embodied in the one word "Torah." It was at once the content, the vehicle, and the transmission from generation to generation, of a complex unity of Divine truth and inspired interpretation.

From this standpoint the whole of the Scriptures is concerned with Torah. There is no antithesis between "law" and prophets. Prophet and priest alike are, just as are lawgivers, interpreters of Torah. But likewise from this standpoint there is no narrowing down from a national call to a faithful remnant. Throughout the Scriptures the whole people is involved, just as in the Messianic prophecies the personal Messiah is inseparable from the Messianic Age involving all peoples.

We can, of course, reject both views as superstition. But if we accept that the Christian interpretation is a legitimate one, then I find it difficult, especially as a historian, to deny equal validity to the Jewish. They differ, but they are not necessarily mutually exclusive. The history of the two religions reflects the natural consequences of the two interpretations, but if the hand of God is in the one, it is equally clear in the other.

Both religions draw from their interpretation belief that God has chosen from humanity certain men as vehicles of His universal purpose and design. Neither—at its best—considers the choice a privilege ; both regard it as a responsibility. If the weaker brethren have at times tended to regard those outside the choice with disdain, this is also true of both religions. But for our purposes we can ignore these evidences of human weakness and attempt to see both religions at their best, and accept for our purposes the deepest and most spiritual interpretation of this Divine choice, as it is expressed in each. But, since Christians are apt to think that the Jewish conception of being a chosen people sets Jews apart, and narrows their religion down to tribalism, it is perhaps well to emphasise that the original word for the Church, the Greek word *ecclesia,* means those who are called out from among others, or chosen, and that the Latin word, *electi,* the elect, a favourite title for a Christian community, means just the same thing. Christians, as much as Jews, believe themselves subjects of a Divine choice.

Christianity, however, sees the Divine choice enshrined in the Biblical story narrowing down to the single figure of Jesus the Messiah, then, after His Incarnation, it sees this same choice widening out again to embrace mankind, without distinction of Jew or Greek, bond or free, or, one may add, white or coloured. But within boundaries limited only by mankind, it still holds that only some are chosen, chosen as the " elect from every nation," to receive the mystery of salvation, and to become, in the words beloved of St. Paul, " new men in Christ," the new Israel, the new chosen people.

To Judaism it is the whole of one people which is chosen for a Divine responsibility, chosen as it now is, in its present condition, with its imperfections and its good and bad members. This is not tribalism as opposed to universalism ; for the choice is to responsibility, not to privilege, and is related to the same assertion of the universal dominion of God, and of the ultimate responsibility of those He has chosen towards the whole of His creation.

Both religions, then, rest on the idea of choice. Both see that choice within a universal framework. But the result of these two different conceptions of the nature of the choice has been quite naturally and logically to make the two religions differ in almost every conceivable emphasis and interest.

Both religions started with the acceptance of the Divine authority of certain written Scriptures, but their differences begin in the two attitudes developed to these Scriptures. The Judaism which survived the destruction of Jerusalem, of the Temple, and of the whole apparatus of sacrifice, drew its inspiration from the Pharisaic doctrine of interpretation—a doctrine most frequently misunderstood by New Testament scholars. The Rabbis, who were the successors of the Pharisaic scribes, saw in the written Torah the focusing point through which the infinity of God's wisdom and design in creation reached out to meet the infinity of men's needs as generation succeeded generation in a never static world. Each generation had the task of interpreting it anew, in terms of its own needs ; and an interpretation once accepted by the scholars of a generation had the same Divine authority as the original. In a sense it had more, for they regarded it as a greater sin to deny that God was continuously speaking to man, than to deny that He had once so spoken at Sinai.

Christianity made a sharp distinction between the Old and the New Testament, and interpreted the former only in terms of its fulfilment in the latter. The main interest in the Old Testament of the Church Fathers was as a quarry of proof texts that Jesus was the Christ foretold by the prophets. They had no conception of its unity comparable to the Jewish doctrine of Torah, and no doctrine of its interpretation. Where they used it, they used it in its literal sense, often with unhappy results, especially on the development of law and the justification of wars. From a doctrinal point of view the only sphere in which they regarded it as a focusing point between two infinities was in the development of Christological doctrine. And here we must come back to the two conceptions of a chosen people.

The development of Judaism was determined by the belief that a Divine way of life was set before a whole people, here and now ; and that its primary mission, and its primary contribution to mankind, was to explore, understand and express in every aspect of its daily life that Divine plan for a whole community. In the literature of rabbinic Judaism there is to be found practically no interest in theological speculation, and nothing which could be called a systematic theology. Having accepted the existence and the unity of God without hesitation, the Rabbis concentrated all their practical interest on His activities in creation, as they were to be embodied in the living of the chosen people. A number of consequences flowed from this determination of interest.

In the first place it demanded a strong emphasis on education, for *understanding* occupies in Judaism the same key place as *faith* in Christianity. In the second place it put an end to the reasons for the existence of a clerical or priestly hierarchy. The priesthood disappeared with the Temple, except for some trifling concessions to past prestige. The Judaism which grew in the second century was a religion of educated laymen. Moreover, it was a religion whose details were worked out by men following every occupation open to the community. The Rabbis of the Talmudic period were not merely not priests: they were not even in the modern sense "professionals." If some gave almost the whole of their lives to study, they did it for love of Torah, not because they were salaried or held official posts. Some were wealthy landowners, some were merchants, some were artisans taking only such time off from their studies as would ensure the most meagre and frugal existence.

Because they represented every aspect of the life of the community, they dealt freely with every aspect. Their discussions of education, of economics, of agriculture, of family life, of social relations, of communal responsibilities, in spite of the curious techniques which they employed, were infused with an astonishing realism, just because they knew what they were talking about from experience. This realism reached its culmination in their conceptions of the functions of a law court, since it was an obligation of a scholar to be ready to judge in disputes. It is important to emphasise this point, since Christian scholars are so apt to assume that "Jewish" conceptions of justice are still based on the more primitive sections of the Pentateuch. I have again and again seen Christian and Jewish attitudes compared by contrasting "the law of love of the Gospel" with "the Jewish belief in an eye for an eye." In fact, it is only in some parts of the Christian world, and in the nineteenth and twentieth centuries, that Christian justice has begun to approximate to the sensitivity and compassion of Jewish rabbinical courts fifteen hundred years earlier.

Finally, the Rabbis, in their perpetual concern with interpretation, were constantly conscious of the fact that it was a whole community, not a select body of saints, with which

26

they were dealing. This concern is charmingly illustrated by a Midrashic interpretation of the reason why, at the Feast of Tabernacles, Jews hold a sweet-smelling citron, and wave the *lulav*, a nosegay with twigs of palm, myrtle and willow (Lev. xxiii, 40 in Midrash Rabba on Lev. xxx, 12). " The fruit of the Hadar tree symbolises Israel: just as the citron has taste as well as fragrance, so Israel have among them men who possess learning as well as good deeds. Branches of palm tree, too, applies to Israel: as the palm has taste but not fragrance, so Israel have among them such as possess learning but not good deeds. And boughs of the thick trees likewise applies to Israel: just as the myrtle has fragrance but no taste, so Israel have among them such as possess good deeds but not learning. And willows of the brook also applies to Israel: just as the willow has no taste and no fragrance, so Israel have among them such as possess neither learning nor good deeds. What then does the Holy One, blessed be He, do to them ? To destroy them is impossible. But, says the Holy One, blessed be He, let them all be tied together in one band, and they will atone, one for another. And in that hour the Lord is exalted."

This tenderness for " willow in the *lulav* " runs all through their activities. They were concerned with the attainable. They certainly did not make Judaism a soft religion, but they were concerned that men should not fail and fall away through despair of ever attaining a loyal conformity to the will of God for their lives ; and to this end they made " a fence about the Torah " by which men could be aided in their daily loyalty. Sometimes the fence may seem to us too high, or the bricks of which it is composed too small ; but its provision was, in modern terms, good psychology and wise therapeutics. For Christendom and Islam saw to it that a Jew should have every temptation to be disloyal, and to desert his ancestral faith. The fence was not the core of Judaism, but it kept the core inviolate through nearly two thousand years of unparalleled external pressures.

The Christian conception of a chosen people was no less profound than the Jewish, no less universal in its implied responsibilities, but it rested on the idea that men were chosen individually and personally to receive salvation in Christ without regard to their race or status—without regard, indeed, even for their family ties. As the Church soon discovered, once the apostles had begun their preaching, this conception could easily be abused. Men could and did arise, falsely proclaiming that they held the key by which the longed-for salvation could be assured. Men could and did so fashion Redeemer Christs that they fitted into the pattern of every Eastern mysticism and occult cult. The insistence on the finality and fulness of the Divine choice could lead to even darker consequences; and men could proclaim a rigid predestinarianism, and even that, once saved, there was no indulgence of the flesh which need be avoided, since to wallow in sin only exalted the Divine mercy and the wonder of the choice. In such a situation Christianity emphasised the unattainable as rightly as Judaism was emphasising the attainable. To human duty to love God and to love men, neither religion set any limits. But a religion calling on men to be "saved" had always to remind them that salvation was a beginning not an end, lest they should believe that no further spiritual growth was required, or that faith had no further experience to offer.

This totally different picture was reinforced by the fact that, while Judaism was coping with the appallingly difficult problem of finding a new centre for the survival of a people whose every natural insignia—government, land, public religious centre—had been destroyed, Christianity, proclaiming that the saved were from every people and nation, had to struggle to maintain its proclamation in competition with the religions, philosophies, temptations and peculiarities of every people and nation. And so it became an intensely theological religion. It created, and strictly determined, its official interpreters in a clerical hierarchy geographically covering every Christian community. Above all, it built around the person of the Redeemer and Saviour a fence of Christology as high, and with bricks as small, as that of the Rabbis about the Jewish way of living; and with the same justification, and the same vindication by history.

It is only as we contemplate the task which was set to the Christian Church by its chosenness that we can understand

28

sympathetically the bitter heresy hunts, the condemnation of men of the most upright and sincere belief for false views on what may seem to us academic trifles, and the long story of schism and excommunication which mars Christian history. For, just as the Rabbis knew that it was vital to safeguard their way of life, so the theologians knew that it was vital to safeguard the historic Jesus of the Gospels, the historic crucifixion and resurrection, against interpretations which might deny the unity of God, or the true humanity of Jesus, which might take Jesus out of actual history or God's activity out of the world He had created. Credal definition and credal conformity had as natural a place in Christianity as the Sabbath and *kashrut* in Judaism. Christianity was as naturally a faith directed by educated clergy as Judaism a practice directed by educated laymen.

It has already been said that in each religion the belief that God had chosen a certain group out of all His children for a special relationship with Himself was accompanied by the recognition that this choice involved obligations to the whole of humanity. It is, of course, true that there is plenty of evidence to be culled from either religion of intolerance and disdain towards those outside, and of narrowness and self-conceit in the assertion of privileged positions. Since both religions dwell in an imperfect world, this is to be expected.

At a deeper level we must not expect an immediate or early recognition on the part of either religion that *all* men will ultimately achieve the perfection for which God designed His creation. In fact, universal salvation is not yet an official doctrine of any Church or Jewish congregation. Both are willing to believe that ultimately some substantial portion of humanity will be denied ultimate bliss. On the whole, the Christian record is the more gloomy one. While Judaism contented itself with denying the ungodly a place in the world to come, some Churches, modern as well as medieval, have delighted to paint the terrors and pains of Hell, and even to make them an exemplary part of their preaching. But this again can be explained by the different emphases of the two faiths. Judaism has always been mainly interested in the fulfilment of God's will in this world, while not denying the world to come ; Christianity has placed

29

its centre in the future life, while not denying that Christians have duties here " below."

Apart, however, from differences of attitude towards the destiny of those outside the Divine choice in the world to come, the two religions differ to such a degree in the form of missionary activity natural to their particular responsibilities that most Christians, and even many Jews, are convinced that Judaism is not a missionary religion at all. A monotheistic religion must be either a missionary religion or perish of degeneration and atrophy of the soul. Where there is no responsibility to the world outside, choice becomes privilege, and God, from being universal, becomes tribal. But it still remains true that the form in which Judaism naturally and properly expresses its missionary responsibilities is quite different from that equally natural to Christianity.

From the very earliest days of the Church the vocation to go out among non-believers and bring to them " the new life in Christ " has received the highest honour. A Church which has no missions is a dead Church. But it is a mistake to assume that this is the only way in which a missionary obligation can be met. As the Christian community seeks to win men outside its fold to surrender to Jesus Christ, so the Jewish community seeks to bring its non-Jewish environment one stage nearer to the concept of the righteous community embodied in the Torah.

The missionary enterprise in Judaism is communal and social. Only in small measure has it been actually concerned to bring Gentiles within the covenant relationship by circumcision and full admission to the Jewish congregation. But wherever it has had the opportunity to do so it has been active in bringing men within the influence of Torah, and in bringing before societies in which Jews are allowed to exercise the responsibilities of citizenship, the challenge of ever deepening and broadening mutual responsibility, justice and righteousness in the whole life of the community.

There is no subject on which a Christian should speak with more restraint and delicacy. For we must remember that the first law of the Roman Empire in which we can trace the influence of the Christian Church is a law of

Constantine which attached the death penalty to conversion to Judaism, and a like penalty to the Jew who did the converting. The last man to die in England for his religion was burnt because he proclaimed the truth of Judaism. Fourth-century Christendom deprived Jewry of the power to exercise any influence on its environment, and Islam followed suit. It was only the secular ideology of the eighteenth century which led to the emancipation of the Jews. But looking before and after this long and tragic period, we should remember that the Gentile Church itself was built on foundations laid by the synagogues of the Hellenistic world, and that in the nineteenth century those countries in which Jews were citizens will find among those prominent in every endeavour for liberalism and democracy, for deeper social justice, better education, more humane public health services, Jewish names out of all proportion to their number in the community. These are the ways in which Judaism exercises its mission, and history has not yet given any evidence that Jews have abandoned it.

This conception of the Jewish mission as a continuing and gradual process of permeation by ideas which slowly change society is in its nature appropriate to the conception of history which underlies every aspect of the Jewish consciousness. It is generally recognised that Christendom owes its sense of the meaning of history to Judaism, and not to either Greece or Rome. But Christianity has absorbed the sense of the reality of history into its being to a far lesser extent than Judaism, while, on the other hand, the Johannine concept of the unity of the here and the hereafter is peculiar to Christianity.

In the period before the separation between the two religions, Judaism contained a number of apocalyptic sects, sects which in one way or another expected the present Divine activity in creation, as well as the present " earth," with its present values and disciples, to be replaced by a " new heaven and a new earth." It is interesting that the whole of the extensive literature of these Jewish sects has been preserved by Christian churches, and not by Judaism. For rabbinic Judaism rejected this development, and restored history to its place as the scene of the working out of God's

31

purpose in creation. Though from time to time, and under the stress of persecution, apocalyptic elements re-entered Judaism, and produced a number of false Messiahs, yet basically Judaism never accepted the easy alternative which apocalyptic offered. It was in history, and not in the over-throw of history, that God's design would ultimately be manifested.

It was in history, therefore, that the judgement of God's moral order was perpetually manifest, and God's moral laws were perpetually operative. To an astonishing extent Jews regarded even the most brutal and unjustified sufferings inflicted by Christendom or Islam upon them, as God's legitimate punishment for their lack of faith in Him, and their failure to live according to His divinely revealed pattern of life. They did not take the facile line of escape of proclaiming that the world itself was evil, or under the power of evil, a temptation into which too often Christian Churches have fallen, and, indeed, are falling in our own day.

In the basic Christian tradition God's judgement is revealed only at the end of time ; and Christians, conscious of how far short this world has fallen of what it could have been, have always pictured that final consummation in words of gloom and terror. A synonym for the last judgement is " doom." The most famous liturgical hymn describing it opens with the words *Dies Irae*—Day of Wrath. In every medieval church, worshippers were confronted, every time they entered the building, with a horrific picture. It was in the most prominent position in the church, that is, over the arch separating the congregation from the sanctuary. In the centre was a stern Christ sitting in judgement. On the left were the happy souls—often few in number, being received by angels into eternal bliss. But on the right was the open mouth of hell, through which horned and tailed devils of horrific appearance were shovelling an innumerable host, including popes, kings, bishops and monks, into the flames of eternal punishment.

Jewry, by contrast, held firmly to the conviction that they were passing through the fires of judgement all through their long and painful pilgrimage within history, and so they pictured its consummation in terms of reconciliation, of justice and of peace. No body of men has ever chastised the sins of their contemporaries with such vigour or such insight as the Hebrew prophets. Yet, even when they told them that all that they could expect to survive would be comparable to the fragments of its victim which could be rescued from a bear or a wolf, they were still convinced that at the end there would be reconciliation, justice and peace.

It is in this belief that Jewish Messianic hopes are firmly grounded. Traditionally, Judaism certainly believed in a personal Messiah, and there were many interpretations of his role. Today, because many Jews have abandoned that belief, Christians are apt to assume that they have automatically abandoned their Messianic hopes. But this is not so. For, even where belief in a personal Messiah was held, the Messiah was inseparable from the Messianic Age. He was its herald. After the loss of the land of Israel, his function was almost wholly confined to the task of restoring the Jews to their ancient home from all the corners of the earth to which they had been exiled. But the central core of the belief was nothing comparable to the Christian doctrine of a Saviour and Redeemer from a sinful world. That central core was the consummation of history, the Messianic reign of righteousness, justice and peace—the three ideas on which creation itself rested, and which it would then see fulfilled. Only after its fulfilment within history did creation pass from this world to the world to come.

That world to come, and its implications in personal immortality, Judaism has, since the disappearance of Sadducism, universally accepted. But it has played very little part in shaping Jewish life or thought, nothing certainly comparable to the proportion which it occupies on the Christian canvas ; and this again is to be expected when we consider the implications of the two ideas of chosenness which underlie the growth of the two religions, and have shaped their characteristics. The mutual relations of a community are more visibly of this world than the short life of an individual person.

Within the compass of a single lecture I have inevitably spoken of the two religions in monolithic terms. I have traced what seem to me to be the central lines of development that sprang naturally from the root ideas from which each religion grew. The belief in a chosen people had consequences as inevitable as the belief in a new people —a church—chosen from among all peoples. There were differences in the nature of the choice, and in the understanding of the purpose of the choice. If I had time I could take you into innumerable bypaths within the main story of each, which would show that the two have not grown entirely separately, that the common origin of each in the history of the people of Israel has produced common features, sometimes where we would least expect them. Some churches have been more affected by the Judaic inheritance than others ; some, in their organisation, reflect the Judaic pattern more than others. Likewise, on the Jewish side, some growths within the synagogue, especially in modern times, owe much to their non-Jewish environment.

There are whole subjects within each faith on which I have not touched at all, where similar pictures of fascinating and creative differences could be drawn, but I believe that I have traced enough for the main lines of the picture to emerge, and at this point I believe that it would be right for me to emphasise that I have been speaking as a Christian. For I have no right to pass judgement from the Jewish side, especially as so many of the faults and limitations in Jewry, on which many of my fellow-Christians are far more expert than I, stem from Christian persecution, from the consequences of a life restricted and insecure, which Christendom imposed on Jewry for as long as it had the power to do so.

From the Christian side, then, I believe that the central consequence of what I have been saying, if it is accepted as broadly true, is the abandonment of the belief that Judaism existed merely as a preliminary to Christianity ; or just exists side by side with Christianity, exhibiting in incomplete form qualities whose full expression is only to be found within the Christian Church.

Here let me repeat what I said earlier. It is, of course, possible to dismiss both religions as superstition, as merely milestones on the path to human control of human destiny, and human perfection achieved by human means. But if we accept the belief of a God working in history, then I cannot see any basis on which we can claim that He has worked in the one and not in the other. Every argument we could adduce to exemplify the truth of our own faith is equally applicable as an argument for the truth of the other. Either both religions carry into the life of men a Divine imperative and a Divine power, or neither does. If history shows the hand of God at work in the one, it is equally at work in the other.

The acceptance of such a belief does not of itself indicate a line for the future. It would mark the end of an epoch ; it would not determine the character of their future relations, and I would not here presume even to suggest what they might be. But one thing is, I believe, mandatory upon me, speaking as I am from the Christian standpoint, and that is to urge that in the present situation the initiatives of under-standing are due from our side. Persecution and misrepre-sentation came from our side. From our side came, in our own lifetimes, the deaths of six million Jews, two-fifths of all the Jewish people in the world. Let Jewry breathe for as long as it needs the atmosphere of acceptance and equality. Only then will it be time for Jews also to examine the implications of our twin growth from a single stem.

APPENDIX: THE COVENANT IDEA IN JUDAISM AND CHRISTIANITY

IT IS MORE than seventeen years since the American tour, in the course of which I was Gilkey Lecturer at Chicago and wrote *The Concept of a Chosen People in Judaism and Christianity* at Okonomowoc, the delightful youth con-ference centre in the lake and farming country north-west of Chicago. Recently I have come to think in a somewhat similar way about the theological significance in Judaism and Chistianity of the idea of a covenant between God and man. On the surface Christianity, in claiming to be the heir to the choice of Israel, was simply claiming the inheritance of the covenant and promise made to the people of Israel. But, as I showed in my lecture, the " chosen people " in Christian thought is something fundamentally different from what it is in Jewish. In Jewish thought it covers the whole of a natural community as it is at any period of its life story. In Christian thought it is a created community, called out from the natural communities of the world, a meaning which is reinforced by the Greek word for Church—*ecclesia*, which means "that which is called out."

It would be equally profitable to examine the concept of a covenant relationship in the two religions ; for here also Christianity claims to be heir to a Jewish relationship, a relationship forfeited by Israel for its failure to accept Jesus of Nazareth as Messiah. In historical fact the Christian attitude to the covenant idea is totally different from the Jewish ; and, just as the different use of the idea " chosen people " leads to a very different pastoral theology, so here the different attitude to the covenant idea leads to a very different metaphysical theology.

The Shorter Oxford Dictionary gives as the prime meaning of the word " covenant " " a mutual agreement between two or more persons to do or refrain from doing certain acts." The word occupies three-and-a-half columns in my edition of Cruden's *Concordance to the Holy Scriptures,* and in the immense majority of cases the word refers to the relationship between God and Israel. The essence of the use of the word is that it implies responsibilities on both sides. God has His own responsibility as Creator as much as has man, his creation. Man likewise has his rights as well as God. It is at least symbolic that the first " covenant " mentioned in Genesis is an acceptance of an obligation by God, sealed by a phenomenon in the natural order. It is the promise never again to flood the whole world, confirmed by the appearance of the rainbow. (Gen. ix, 8-17.)

The essential covenant between Creator and creature is expressed in the message which Moses is instructed to take from God to the children of Israel while they are still in bondage in Egypt: " I will take you to me for a people, and I will be to you a God " (Exodus vi, 7) ; and the reply of the whole people at Sinai (" All the words which the Lord hath said will we do " [Exodus xxiv, 3]) is a human response to a Divine responsibility. All through the Pentateuch the essential mutuality of the covenant is emphasised. If the children of Israel are obedient, then the Lord is responsible for their well-being. If they call upon Him, He is responsible for listening to them.

The psalmists frequently refer to the covenant relationship, and it is a commonplace to all the major and some of the minor prophets. On the other hand, only eleven references are given in Cruden to the New Testament, and these refer primarily to an argument of Paul in his letter to the Galatians, and a somewhat similar argument of the author of the letter to the Hebrews. In both cases the argument is based on Jeremiah xxxi, 31-34.

In Galatians iv, 21-31, Paul exclaims:

" Tell me, ye that desire to be under the law, do ye not hear the law ? For it is written, that Abraham had two sons, the one by a bondmaid, the other by a freewoman. But he who was of the bondwoman was born after the flesh ; but he of the freewoman was by promise.

" Which things are an allegory ; for these are the two covenants ; the one from the Mount Sinai, which gendereth to bondage, which is Agar.

" For this Agar is Mount Sinai in Arabia, and answereth to Jerusalem, which now is, and is in bondage with her children. But Jerusalem which is above is free, which is the mother of us all. For it is written, Rejoice thou barren that bearest not ; break forth and cry, thou that travailest not ; for the desolate hath many more children than she which hath an husband.

" Now we, brethren, as Isaac was, are the children of promise.

" But as then he that was born after the flesh persecuted him that was born after the Spirit, even so it is now. Nevertheless what saith the scripture ? Cast out the bondwoman and her son: for the son of the bondwoman shall not be heir with the son of the freewoman.

" So then, brethren, we are not children of the bondwoman, but of the free."

The author of the letter to the Hebrews has a similar, but

more complicated argument in chapters viii, 6, 7 and 13, and ix, 15-18:

"But now hath (Christ) obtained a more excellent ministry, by how much also he is the mediator of a better covenant, which was established upon better promises.

"For if that first covenant had been faultless, then should no place have been sought for the second. . . .

"In that he saith, a new *covenant*, he hath made the first old. Now that which decayeth and waxeth old is ready to vanish away."

The author comes back to the new covenant in the following chapter, interpreting "covenant" this time as a Will, made valid only by a death.

From our point of view the striking difference between the Old and New Testament use of the idea is that the whole conception of *mutual* obligations is absent from the New Testament usage. In place of mutuality is set the idea of "grace" and "the free gift of God." There is a striking passage in Paul's letter to the Romans (vi, 23). Accepting that the payment of wages is a quasi-covenantal relationship, he exclaims that "the *wages* of sin is death but the *gift* of God is eternal life."

The contrasting results of the insistence on mutuality in Judaism, and of its opposite in Christianity, persist all through rabbinic and Chasidic Judaism and through Catholic and Protestant Christianity. There is in Jewish theological statements an exhilaration at a responsibility given and accepted which contrasts with the Christian note of a free grace given to a completely fallen world which the churches have inherited from St. Paul. The whole concept of a complete fall is repellent to Judaism, though it is a wrong interpretation of this rejection to argue, as some Christian theologians have done, that Judaism ignores the reality and evil nature of sin. On the other hand, traditional Christianity, with its constant emphasis on sin, emphasises likewise man's complete dependence on God and God's readiness always to answer, a substitute which, in normal times, may be an effective alternative to the covenant idea.

In contemporary theology, however, especially in those

theologies which have their origin in the German tradition
stemming from Schleiermacher and emphasised in Barth and
his followers, the absence of the covenant idea has assumed
a new importance. German Protestantism has consistently
emphasised the "otherness" of God in an extreme form
which would be quite inconceivable to any of the Jewish
traditions. All Jewish thought would endorse the statement
of God in Isaiah lv, 8 and 9:

"For my thoughts are not your thoughts, neither are your
ways my ways, saith the Lord.
For as the heavens are higher than the earth, so are my
ways higher than your ways, and my thoughts than
your thoughts."

The thoughts of God are "higher," but they are not
"other." They cannot be "other," for Jewish thought holds
closely to the original idea expressed in Genesis i, 26: "God
said, let us make man in our own image."

The "death of God" theology is a natural evolution of
the Barthian emphasis on "otherness," on the complete lack
of any common ground between Creator and Creation, or
of any responsibility inherent in the act of creation. One
might, indeed, say that it makes no difference to man that
this particular God is dead. He was never effectively alive,
and could not possibly survive the various schools of modern
analytical philosophy.

On the other side one could make out a convincing case
that the conception of Divine responsibility and human
rights had become so much a subject for the most delightful
Chasidic anecdotes or rabbinic arguments that its re-examination in the severely intellectual terms of a systematic and
thought-out metaphysic alone could save it from becoming
a mere bit of "folksiness" to an increasingly sceptical
generation, a generation which has somehow got to accept
the holocaust into its fundamental thinking.

3

THE MEANING OF TORAH

THERE IS NO subject more difficult to expound to a Christian audience than the true character of the Sinaitic revelation, the revelation, according to Jewish tradition, of the full and eternal meaning of Torah. Torah is the Hebrew word which we translate as " law " and this causes our first misunderstanding. For it has a far richer meaning. It means basically teaching, and in this context it means teaching which is revealed as the will of God. Torah is both the teaching and the content of revelation. And what is revealed is a whole way of life, in accordance with the will of God, not just a set of laws largely of a ritual character.

Our second misunderstanding comes from our habit of estimating its character by a Christian measuring rod. This is very natural, but it leads to a complete misunderstanding. For the centre of Christianity is the salvation of man as person ; and the centre of Judaism is the performance of the will of God by men in community. We cannot judge Judaism as a religion of salvation, for it is not primarily interested in salvation. It is interested in doing the will of God. One might add that Jews make just the same mistake, and judge Christianity by Jewish standards ; and by those standards it is a very inferior religion to Judaism.

Finally, the field of Judaism is the natural community, the nation or State, while the sphere of Christian activity is the Church, which is not a natural community, but a new community gathered from every nation. But it is because Judaism has its centre in the natural community that we should re-examine our attitude to it. For it is the catastrophic failure of the natural community, i.e., the State, which is

40

in danger of destroying mankind through its inability to control its own power to launch nuclear explosions against its enemies. And the moral exhortations of Christians have not proved able to turn the political leaders to a better path.

The mistaken attitude towards Judaism goes right back to the beginnings of the Church. For the apostles were not interested in the continuation of States and nations, but expected the almost immediate end of the world, and devoted their whole being to saving men from an imminent destruction. Consequently, they looked in the Scriptures (i.e., the Old Testament) only for those passages which could be interpreted as foretelling the coming of Jesus as Messiah, and which supported their view that the world was coming to an end. Jewish Biblical history was therefore the preliminary to a fulfilment of which they were themselves the witnesses and spokesmen.

This attitude appears in all the books of the New Testament. The tone is set in our earliest surviving documents, the letters of Paul. We have his explicit words that "the law was a schoolmaster to bring us to Christ" (Gal. iii, 24), so that we interpret Christ's words in the Sermon on the Mount that he came not to destroy the law but to fulfil it (Matt. v, 17) in the sense that he who fulfils the law of Christ fulfils all that the previous revelation had of permanence. In fact, Paul says so categorically to the Romans, arguing that because "love worketh no ill to his neighbour : therefore love is the fulfilling of the law" (Rom. xiii, 10).

This attitude is reinforced by our conviction that it is the prophets who are of central significance in the Old Testament ; and that they replace the curious mass of laws in the Pentateuch by a nobler and more profound morality. We are helped by the order of the books. The laws appear to come first as part of early, semi-legendary history ; the prophets come later, and in the light of established chronology. In reality the two are more or less contemporary, and prophecy is a commentary on the Law, not its replacement.

Preferring the splendid generalisations of the prophets to the minutiae of the law books, we find it easy to consider the activities of the Pharisees to be of that quality which we denigrate with the word "legalistic" and often find ridiculous. Here also we have apparent confirmation in the Gospels themselves. In the seventh chapter of Mark are a series of discussions between Jesus and the Pharisees in which he accuses them of rejecting the commandments of God to follow their own traditions. As we have it, the passage assumes that the Bible itself deals with moral issues, whereas "the traditions of men" deal with "the washing of pots and cups and many like things." This is a distinction Jesus could not have made, for he knew well that the Pentateuch had many laws dealing with the ritual cleansing of objects, and he would know also that Pharisaism dealt with many moral issues. There are equal difficulties about accepting the Marcan form of the discussion of *Corban*. But in any case the authors of the Gospels leave us in no doubt that they considered that Pharisaism had lost itself in a maze of ritual trivialities, which are summed up in the terrible denunciations of Matthew xxiii. And we must not forget that rabbinic Judaism is the heir of the Pharisees, and that the Rabbis continued a line of development which the Pharisees had begun.

The importance attached to *kashrut* and *shechita* in our own day seems to lend support to ordinary Christian opinion that post-Biblical Judaism has deviated from the true path of religion. If Christians know of rabbinical writings only from such prejudiced witnesses as the otherwise admirable William Barclay, then they are confirmed in the belief that all that was valid in Sinai had passed into the inheritance of the Christian Church.

Quite apart from the Pharisees, the whole atmosphere of the New Testament implies a distinction between the Old Dispensation and the New, which rests on the superiority of the latter. It suggests that God is no longer concerned with law but with love, that our relations with Him and with one another rest henceforward on grace and love. John implies their superiority in making the distinction: "The law was given through Moses, grace and truth came through Jesus Christ" (i, 17).

It is difficult in the face of all this evidence to assert that Christians still have something fundamental to learn from Sinai. But the present obvious human crisis calls them

urgently at least to re-examine their claim that in the present
teaching and doctrine of the churches they have all that
is needed to rescue mankind, if only men would listen to
them. To excuse themselves by calling this a "post-
Christian" age is no more convincing than it is to imply
that all the fault lies with those who relegate the Christian
message to a secondary role in human affairs. For, in fact, this
age has dismissed any claim of Christianity to play a leading
part in human affairs because no Christian leader has carried
conviction that he has the solution of the world's central
need: the discovery of how men may so order their public
lives that the danger of universal destruction by nuclear
explosions is removed from us. If there be a God who created
us, then he must be concerned with this failure, and it is no
solution for him that he can ensure the salvation of a
minority in another life. The world is full of Christian works
of deep piety and most selfless giving. But it is at best a
refuge and not leadership which the world finds in them.

The basic reason for this curious situation is the ingrained
conviction of the churches that the political sphere is at
best peripheral, and may even be quite outside the direct
interest of religion. Politics are an activity of the natural
community, whereas the Church is a supra-national community composed of "the elect from every nation." Politics
are determined by the limited perspective of this world,
whereas the Church regards this life *sub specie æternitatis*.
From this standpoint the provision of a refuge rather than
a leader is for the Church to perform its proper function. It
is interesting to note that so profound a student of human
affairs as Arnold Toynbee considers it a necessary distinguishing mark of a religion before it enters the small circle
of the "higher religions" that it finds its social expression in
independent organisations of its own, separate from natural
human ties.*

One of the reasons for this belief that politics are not a
proper concern of religion is undoubtedly the very dubious
record of past and present attempts of churches to dominate

* *A Study of History*, Vol. XII, *Reconsiderations*, p. 84. See
also Index: Religions, Higher.

their particular political situations. Malta, Ireland, Spain are not advertisements for the present political claims of Rome ; the conflict of empire and papacy did not enrich the Middle Ages ; the record of the Byzantine Church right down to the persecution of Russian Jews under the last Tsars is a disgusting one ; we look askance at the politics of Geneva under Calvin and his successors. We have certainly warnings in such events, and they exclude various identifiable forms of political activity from our consideration. But they do not provide a positive argument that success comes from ignoring the political field.

A more serious justification for abstention comes from the argument that politics are a domain of natural law, of principles common to all men, in which revelation has no special place or special insight. In fact a recent book, entitled *The Christian in Politics,* by Walter James, editor of *The Times Educational Supplement,* is based wholly on this hypothesis. James would agree that it is a good thing for Christians to take part in politics, for they have qualities of integrity, compassion and altruism which make a contribution to the world's affairs. But it is a very bad thing if they begin to think that their quality as Christians gives them an insight into, and authority in, the political field denied to those who do not share their theological outlook.

James says that :

> ". . . The conception of a Creator God, ever thoughtful for His creation, demands that He should have made it possible for men to apprehend a pattern of natural good living. If this were not part of His purpose from the first, before ever He revealed Himself, then human life would have been faced with the impossible. It must be allowed that morality was proper to man from the first, that its tenets were discoverable by reason, that some men and some societies have reached higher than others but that all possessed enough sense of its necessity to admit a moral law."*

This is only one quotation from a very lengthy and profound discussion of the necessity of Christians and non-Christians

* *Op. cit.* p. 18.

co-operating *ex-æquo* in the political field, but I believe it presents his outlook fairly. I think we can assume that James, by the words "before ever He revealed Himself" is referring to the Incarnation, to which the revelation of Sinai served only as a local preliminary. As there is no reference to the latter in the book, it is evident that he sees in it nothing permanently relevant to his thesis.

It is easy to overlook that this is a challenge which goes right to the very root of things, to our understanding of the wisdom of God and of the nature of human life ; to the basic relations of Creator and creation, and the purpose and destiny of the universe. I will not consider here the doctrine, which most people would hold to be completely unacceptable, that the purpose of the Incarnation was to ensure salvation in another world for a hundred and forty-four thousand persons (I take the figure simply as a symbol of a small fraction of humanity). I believe rather that "in the fulness of time" the true character and destiny of man as person was revealed in the life of Christ, and that the means and cost of assuring that destiny was revealed in the cross and resurrection. The very fact that Jesus was born in this world pinpoints its essential part in God's design.

But here is the challenge.

On the one hand we proclaim that the Incarnation of God Himself in a human life, and the terrible death on the cross, were the only conditions on which man could be shown his true nature and destiny. Moreover, the work was not done once and for all by the life of Christ: it needs the continuation of the work of the Incarnation in a Church, which should be eternal, universal, and present in every centre of human habitation.

That, on the one hand ; but what does James, rightly representing the Christian tradition, suggest on the other ? That the problems of man in society, his politics, economics and sociology, are so much simpler, or so much less important, that God can leave these to the workings of human reason. He has implanted in His creation the idea of natural law, which can apparently be understood as simply as the law of gravity which prevents our flying off the planet into space.

It is an inadequate defence to argue, as does James, that there were ordered human societies before the Incarnation, so that political order clearly does not rest on revelation. There were piety and saintliness before Jesus was born. But that did not make his life and death unnecessary.

I am no happier with the assumption, which seems to underlie conventional Christian thinking, that we can make a distinction between man's life in this world and his life hereafter, unless we are willing to assume that the heavenly choir consists exclusively of soloists, and that each human being's individual and unrelated destiny is " prostrate before thy throne to lie and gaze and gaze on thee." I confess that I find the prospect cramping, unattractive, self-centred and entirely unworthy of the richness and love which the earthly part of this creation manifests. So far as this world is concerned, the individual man absolutely requires both the natural community and the community of his choice to bring his gifts to their proper fruition. He can achieve nothing in isolation from both, and some aspect of his development is cramped if he is isolated from either. If, therefore, the survival of physical death involves the continuation of any life which we can recognise as human, then it involves corporate as well as individual activity. And hence man's eternal, as well as his temporal, destiny, is bound up intimately with the natural society of which he is a member, as well as of the Church which individually he joins.

But to say that natural law, governing the affairs of men in society, is as much the sphere of Divine interest as man's personal character, is not enough by itself. If we stopped there, we would be asking the world to agree to an extraordinarily unconvincing state of things. We would be asking it to accept that it is essential that the whole world should be divided into parishes, with trained clergy to look after the spiritual needs of the inhabitants. We should be asking the world to accept what this organisation involves—an immense ecclesiastical framework, innumerable theological colleges, theological faculties in countless universities, and a staggeringly vast appropriation of funds. All this for man as person.

46

But, so far as the understanding and fulfilment of God's purpose for man as social being is concerned, a few voluntary religious societies, with an occasional bishop as patron and a perpetual shortage of funds, is adequate. And man's communal, social and political problems seem so much outside the central task of the Churches *sub specie æternitatis* that many ecclesiastical leaders would judge even this superfluous. For even where it results in devoted and intense activity, one must not expect it to produce any specifically Christian contribution. So, at least, argues James; and most Church authorities, apart from pacifists, would agree.

Surely it is sufficient to pose the problem in this way for the inadequacy of conventional Christian thinking to be manifest; for Christians do not even assume, as do orthodox Marxists, that the State will wither away. They simply assume that it is not important from the standpoint of God's purposes and man's eternal destiny.

From at least the sixteenth century onwards there has been a still small voice of protest. What brings this into my subject of "The Meaning of Torah" is that this still small voice has tended to identify natural law with Judaism; and Judaism certainly does not consist of generalisations which are left to take care of themselves.

The revolutionary thinkers of the sixteenth and seventeenth centuries were, unfortunately, extremely prolix, and revelled in immense and learned digressions. Moreover, they usually wrote in a Latin of more than Ciceronian complexity. In consequence, their contribution to Christian thinking on the subject of Judaism has been wholly ignored. Here we are concerned especially with three men. The earliest was Jean Bodin (1529-1596), French political philosopher, who was a very free-thinking Catholic. Then came John Selden (1584-1654), lawyer, political thinker and Orientalist, who was an Anglican. Finally there was William Surenhuysen (Surenhuis, 1666-1729), Professor of Hebrew at the Academy of Amsterdam, who was a Calvinist.

Their point of departure was the natural law and natural religion which had been implanted in the creation from the beginning. But man's ignorance, folly and wrong-doing had

47

caused both to be forgotten, and God had then to reveal them again, and did so in a more concrete form. This revelation is to be found in the Old Testament, which thus contains man's original and "natural" religion. Now the conventional Christian tradition would have said to this proposition: "Yes, of course. That is why Christianity is the oldest and truest religion in the world." For one of the basic causes of the tragic history of the Jews within Christendom is that the Church claimed the whole of the spiritual history of the Old Testament as her own. Bodin, especially, in the *Heptaplomeres,* Selden in *De Jure Naturali et Gentium juxta Disciplinam Hebræorum,* and Surenhuis in the *Lectori Benevolo Præfatio* to his *Mischna sive totius Hebræorum Juris Systema* recognise in the first place that the Old Testament revelation was given to the Jews ; in the second that it was rightly continued and interpreted by them in their rabbinical academies and writings ; and, in the third, that Judaism was consequently still a living religion, which Christians ought to study and understand. It is owing to men such as these that our many university chairs of Hebrew exist through Europe. But instead of developing a knowledge of Judaism, their result can be described in the title of one of their successors, Gerhard Meuschen: *Novum Testamentum ex Talmude illustratum.*

Part of their failure, perhaps, was due to the absence in their lifetimes of any adequate post-biblical Jewish history. It was another seventeenth-century scholar, Jacques Basnage, a Huguenot, who produced the first such work in the opening years of the eighteenth century, and first pointed out the appalling responsibility of the Christian Church for the persecution of the Jews. Basnage has, of course, been followed by many others, and we can now approach the subject with a solid historical foundation. We can point to the extraordinary history of Jewish survival as the basic evidence for the character of the Sinaitic revelation, and justify or condemn its claim to universal significance from that solid ground.

In spite of all that Arnold Toynbee says, Jewish history for the last two thousand five hundred years has been unique. It is unique in that it is indissolubly the history at once of a coherent nation and of a universalist religion. It is unique in that people and religion were moulded into so exquisitely appropriate a form that neither geographical unity nor any political authority were necessary for their survival. Finally, and supremely, it was unique in that Jewry emerged from centuries of restriction and persecution in the ghettoes of the Christian and Islamic worlds with its basic creativity unimpaired ; and was ready to contribute, almost immediately, to the artistic, scientific, scholarly and political life of those nations in which the freedom of citizenship opened every path to the realisation of its inherent qualities.

The religion of Torah, which was evolved in the period from the return to Jerusalem of Ezra to the conclusion of the Talmuds of Babylon and Jerusalem, was tailored to a precise situation. Because that situation was very special, it required very special treatment ; and the first generalisation one should make about the power that flows from Sinai is that it does not flow in generalisations, however noble, but in concrete programmes to meet concrete situations. Ezra and his successors erected a colossal fence about the way of life in which Judaism was enshrined. We, who do not need such a fence, are apt to sneer at it. But Jews were already a series of minorities, each one of which was surrounded by a different form of paganism, was tempted to a different form of apostasy, or was offered a different seduction, sensual or intellectual, by the faiths and philosophies which pullulated in western Asia and the Mediterranean. For a few centuries there was a shadowy central authority, in the High Priest at Jerusalem, in the Patriarch in Tiberias, in the Presidents of the rabbinical Academies of Babylon ; but their advisory power was limited, and their executive power *nil*. The interpretation of Sinai had evolved in the centuries after Ezra a religious way of life which was almost completely autonomous.

The second generalisation which one can make is to emphasise that throughout the period up to emancipation in the nineteenth century the Rabbis were concerned with the whole generation of their Jewish contemporaries. Judaism never passed from being a people to being a Church. That is to say, it never passed from being the concern of a natural community to being the special discipline of a portion of the whole, however selected. It is difficult to over-emphasise the importance of the effect of this concern of the Rabbis with all their Jewish contemporaries. For it meant that Judaism, in their hands, was always concerned with the attainable ; and we Christians have it deeply implanted in us that our faith must always hold out to us a perfection which we know we cannot yet attain. A goal of the attainable seems to us pathetically limited, indeed contemptible ; and we are apt to say that it is just what one would expect from a people who turned from the majestic vision of the prophets to the narrow legalism of the Pharisees. We want our clergy to summon us to reach for the stars ; and we cheerfully sing

> " Were the whole realm of nature mine,
> It were an offering far too small."

But in plain fact we then put sixpence in the collection plate, whereas Jewish giving, with a goal of the attainable, has always been, and still is, fantastically beyond even the highest ambitions of a stewardship campaign. In the days of refugees from Hitler's Germany, it was calculated that the average contribution to Jewish refugees by the Jewish community of England amounted to about ten shillings per head per year ; whereas the average giving to Christian refugees by the churches was an astronomically small fraction of a farthing. Most of the Christian refugees were, in fact, supported from Jewish funds.

It became a fundamental principle with the Rabbis that " we do not lay upon the community burdens which they are unable to bear." They were prepared to make astonishing adjustments in previously accepted customs. They did this on the basis that God had, in giving Torah at Mount Sinai, given to men the capacity, and the whole responsibility, for its interpretation and its fulfilment. " Nothing was kept back in heaven " ; and again this emphasis on human understanding and responsibility rings strangely in Christian ears, more accustomed to set on a higher level the Tennysonian adage :

> " I cannot understand : I love."

THE MEANING OF TORAH

The doctrine of human responsibility for interpretation was so deeply rooted in rabbinic Judaism that they were prepared, under conditions, to set the oral law above the written words of Scripture. There has never been within Jewry that idolatry of the Bible which has so often reappeared in Christian reform movements and oppresses us again in the escapism of "Biblical Theology." But idolatry of the Talmud has come to play a similar part in traditional Jewish circles ; and it is, to my mind, just as regrettable and just as indefensible. But whereas Christian bibliolatry is usually an alternative to social responsibility, Jewish Talmudolatry is the almost inevitable consequence of centuries of persecution and restriction. However, I would agree that both religions need to recover from their particular form of this preference for escaping into the past to facing the present.

The third element which made possible the survival of Judaism and the Jewish people was again unique. It was the maintenance of a delicate balance between the sensitive, or creative, element in society and the executive, or practical. The Jewish nation was rescued after the fall of the kingdom by scholars. It was rescued again by scholars after the destruction of Jerusalem and the loss of all political autonomy at the end of the wars with Rome. In the succeeding millennium-and-a-half of complete dispersion there are scarcely any outstanding figures in Jewish history who are not scholars. At the same time the Presidents and councils of local communities were, within Jewry as within the other contemporary societies, men of wealth and forceful character. In view of the exclusion of Jews from landowning and citizenship, they were merchants and bankers, not landowners and soldiers. But they were essentially executives, and their relation with the scholars was not always easy.

The only Christian Church which has attempted to maintain a similar balance between the sensitive and the executive has been the Roman Catholic. It has attempted to maintain this balance as a central aspect of its life and duty. But the differences between the Jewish and the Roman Catholic methods of dealing with the problem are illuminating. In the Christian tradition, and in the present Roman

Catholic Church, the function of the sensitive is completely in the hands of the clergy. It is a clerical, especially episcopal or monastic, monopoly. The executive members of a community, on the other hand, are expected to be laymen, whether princes or parliaments. In traditional Judaism both the sensitive and the executive were expected to be drawn from the whole life of the community. The emergence in the Synagogue of a salaried Rabbinate, definitely distinct from Jewish "laymen," is a modern and regretted innovation. It is due to a multiplicity of causes, but it is basically un-Jewish. Judaism and Jewry were enabled to survive because in the critical and formative centuries it did not exist. The Jewish way of life, with all its complexities and austerities, was ordained by men who followed every occupation open to Jews. It was not ordained by a clerical caste, itself apart from the anxieties and strains of daily life, for laymen to carry out. A celibate clergy did not decide in Judaism on issues of birth control or family planning.

Moreover it was not ordained by a central body, which laid down the exact manner in which a local community should perform the action involved. Various centres of Jewish life acquired eminence because of their reputation for learning ; but the leaders of a local community had the right to decide for or against opinions or directions which came from such centres. Further, these "central bodies" of which I have just spoken were never a fixed and recognised apex to a hierarchy. Any body, or, more often, individual scholar, might be the one whom local leaders decided to consult.

Laid out schematically, as it is in the last few pages, Judaism, of course, looks a much more consistent and tidy religion than it is in practice. Every great and ancient human tradition has rightly and inevitably many paradoxes and contradictions within an overriding and identifiable unity. The responsibility of which I have spoken was often not exercised. The written Talmud and its codifications came to assume undue authority. The traditionalist became fearful of making reasonable and necessary adjustments to the manner of fulfilling the Jewish way of life. But not only does no religion exhibit all the virtues of its inheritance at any one time ; but we have to recognise, where Judaism is

concerned, that the outside world of Christendom and Islam
has so battered and crushed it for such long periods that
the traditional Judaism of today is too often most untradi-
tionally reactionary, timid and narrow-minded. For no
religion profits by a long period of oppression and humiliation. One of the penalties which we Christians have to pay,
if we wish to understand the power which flows from Sinai,
is that we have to look for it as it manifested itself in past
centuries, when it was able to mould relatively free communities. We must not judge it by the often unhappy
quarrels of modern Orthodox Jewries of Israel and the
diaspora. Their pettinesses help us to understand the effects
of our wrong-doings: they are no part of the real material
Judaism offers for the understanding of the meaning of
Torah, or of the revelation of Sinai and the continuing
dynamic which flows from it.

We should not regard the events of Sinai as a preliminary
to the greater events of the Incarnation which fulfilled and
replaced them, but as the permanent revelation of the will
of God for men in community. It preceded the Incarnation
because, as all anthropologists tell us, man, as a social being,
had to reach an advanced stage of fulfilment before man as
person could develop his separate individuality. But as
natural communities still exist, the revelation of Sinai is still
relevant. Where it appears to be in tension with the later
revelation of the Incarnation, it is because there is constant
tension between men's personal and men's public and social
responsibilities. Where it differs in content and interest from
Christianity it is because God deals in the appropriate way
with nations and with persons, and these ways are necessarily not identical. But the pattern of Judaism is as relevant
to men as citizens as is the pattern developing from the
Incarnation relevant to men as persons. But, I emphasise
again, they are different patterns ; and that is why Judaism
differs from Christianity. God has not chosen to resolve the
tension for us ; He has rather made the tension the dynamic
of our growth. Judaism is no more an imperfect Christianity
than Christianity is an imperfect Judaism. But only blindness can conceal from us that each religion has enormous
areas of common concern with the other. Of course it has,

53

C

for it is the same man who is at once person and citizen.

There are four points which merit the attention of the Christian world, points which we can see revealed in Jewish history.

God deals directly with the natural community, and the natural community is as much a sphere of His revelation and activity as the Church.

The pattern of Divine revelation to a natural community is not primarily a creed but a way of life, very concrete in its positive and negative patterns of living.

It has to be interpreted to each generation, on the basis of the actual capacities of that generation.

It has practically no generalisations which men have not the right and duty to modify, but it is consistent in its fundamental conviction about the Divine-human relationship.

Its interpretation is not the function of a clerical caste, but of the wisest representatives of the whole life which is to be directed according to the will of God. The Church will merit the attention of those who are struggling with the problems of peace between the nations only when it is seen to have given the same attention to the problem as it does, for example, to its missionary responsibilities, or as politicians do to the problem of peace. The balance of authority between the sensitive and and the executive aspects of the nation is one needing perpetual attention, just as much as the problem of liberty needs perpetual vigilance. The Church will not merit the attention of the world if it is seen to be treating political, social, or economic issues with what the world must consider frivolous superficiality. It is no good passing resolutions exhorting somebody else to do something, forming committees of men who are wholly occupied with something quite different, and can only meet for short sessions on rare occasions, or gathering conferences of experts, half of whom do not believe in Christianity. There is no short-cut. Nor is it, unfortunately, a task which we can individually set about performing. As individuals, all we can do is to keep on pressing that our leaders in the universities and the assemblies of the churches begin to consider their responsibilities in this immense field.

I would close with a fifth point. Behind the concrete and

detailed pattern of living which we find in Jewish history lies one unchanging and profound conviction: that God would in His own time bring this world to the perfection which He designed for it. We are so convinced that Jews are in error about the person of the Messiah that we overlook that the fundamental belief in Judaism is not in the Messianic person but in the Messianic Age. To recover the meaning of Sinai, and to accept its tension with the Incarnation, is impossible so long as the Church cannot make up its mind whether it sees the final destiny of the present age as destruction or fulfilment. Either is consistent with the differing Christian convictions of a life to come. But the conviction that God's purpose is attainable has played so central a part in sustaining Jewry in its distresses, that it is difficult to believe that a theological background of world pessimism will provide Christian leaders with an outlook on contemporary world affairs which men will find relevant and creative in the present distress. One does not inspire those whom one leads into battle if one starts with a conviction of defeat.

II

****

Judaism among the World's Religions

****

4

JUDAISM AND CHRISTIAN CIVILISATION

IN THIS SERIES of lectures, which trace the influence on Judaism of the civilisations through which it has passed in its millennial history, I have undoubtedly the longest, most complex and most dolorous course to pursue. For I have in some measure to traverse all the periods dealt with in greater detail by the other lecturers, and must collect data from those other civilisations—Hellenistic, Roman, Eastern and Islamic—which lead up to the modern period, with which I am also concerned. On the other hand, I am dealing with the complex of Christian societies— Roman, Byzantine and European—which have probably least influenced Judaism, and, so far as post-biblical Judaism is concerned, been least influenced by it.

The basic explanation of this paradox is to be found in the fact that Judaism had already become the religion of a dispersed people some centuries before Christianity emerged. It had already erected that fence about the Torah which had enabled it to keep its sanctuary inviolate from the allurements of Levantine sensuality, Iranian dualistic mysticism, Hellenistic philosophy and Roman tolerant indifference, before it had to meet the more difficult and penetrating challenge of Christianity.

The Christian challenge had a unique quality of intimacy because it was first preached by devout Jews in Judea and the diaspora ; because it proclaimed that the Messiah, whom all Jews longed to welcome, had appeared and had dramatically risen from the dead ; and because it flattered Jewish pride and dignity in no ignoble way as Jews witnessed the joyful acceptance which the Gospel—the Good News—

rapidly commanded among the Gentile populations where Jewish communities were most numerous and best established. Indeed, its first non-Jewish converts were drawn from those Gentiles whom they knew most intimately, Gentiles who had already been attracted to the ethical monotheism and the uplifting worship of the synagogue. It is not surprising that the Jewish reaction to these events has remained a perpetual puzzle to Gentile Christians, right down to our twentieth-century contemporaries in all the Churches. The immense majority cannot understand why Jews have rejected the claims of Jesus of Nazareth, and have refused to see in the proclamation and expansion of Christianity the fulfilment of ancient Hebrew prophecy and the culmination of Jewish history. The more learned will admit that there were genuine difficulties, and see some of the real problems which acceptance of the Christian claims involved; but, even so, they marvel that Jews were not able much more rapidly to overcome them.

Being a Christian myself, I am naturally precluded from giving the reasonable Jewish answer that Jews rejected the Christian claims because they were, in fact, false. What, then, can I offer as the explanation ?

In one way or another it would now be generally agreed that the historical answer lies somewhere in the career of the Hellenistic-Pharisaic Jew, Saul of Tarsus, known as Paul after his acceptance of Jesus of Nazareth as Messiah. For it is generally conceded that Jesus himself lived and died within the four corners of Judaism, and did not command the separation of his followers from other Jews. In the older view it would simply be assumed that Paul changed his religion from Judaism to Christianity. Modern scholars say that both terms admit of a wide variety of forms in the time of Paul, and that the truth is not so clear-cut. Extremists claim that Paul founded Christianity and turned the simple and pious Galilean preacher, Jesus, into a Hellenistic mystery god. They find confirmation of this in such things as his use of the term *Kurios*, Lord, to describe Jesus, for this was the usual term by which the saviour of a mystery religion was addressed. I cannot accept this myself, and take the more conservative position that the mission of Paul through the diaspora Synagogues to the Gentile world was the logical consequence and development of the mission of Jesus at the hands of those who believed that in him the Messiah had come. For it was a wholly Jewish idea that with the coming of the Messiah a new approach would be made to the Gentiles, and there was at that time no halachic definition of how that approach should be made.

That such a mission would produce deep and wide controversy was natural; for Jesus did not correspond to any expectation which different Jewish opinions might hold of the Messiah. That it led to such appalling bitterness was certainly not Paul's intention, if one takes seriously, as I do, his asseverations in his defences in " Acts of the Apostles." There he affirms on three separate occasions that he had never been disloyal to Judaism in a single word. What, then, happened ? One factor was certainly Paul's own temperament. The idea that all saints are calm, placid, and cautious in their utterances is not borne out by history ; and I should imagine that Paul was by no means easy to live with. Nor were all Jews averse from holding extreme opinions, whether for or against Paul's gospel. That also would be borne out by history. The activities of the early Jewish and Gentile believers in Jesus as Messiah led quickly to such a deep cleavage that separation into two religions was inevitable. This was due, I believe, not to the actions of Paul, however vehement his partisanship, but to the way in which his Gentile followers and successors interpreted certain aspects of his teaching as we can trace them in his letters.

His letters dealt with both theological and practical issues. In both sections he made constant use of the Greek word *nomos,* law ; and these Gentile Christians assumed that every time he used it he was referring to the Jewish religion. For *nomos* is the Septuagint translation of the word Torah, and Judaism is the religion of Torah. But in almost every case Paul is using the Greek word *nomos* to describe not *the Law* but laws, especially those ritual laws which mark a man externally as a Jew. For his letters deal with practical issues ; and the context of the word is usually an argument that you cannot accept Jesus as Saviour except by a change of heart. No ritual act will win God's forgiveness. In this he was being completely Jewish. No Rabbi would have said otherwise; and any diaspora Rabbi, in contact with the mystery religions and their elaborate and secret rites of initiation, would have said it just as vigorously as Paul. God's forgiveness comes only as men turn their hearts to Him. They never suggested that any ritual was an acceptable alternative.

Why, then, the calamity? Because of two things. In the arguments *nomos* is contrasted all the time with grace and faith, the marks of the Christian life, and so emphasised a contrast between Judaism and Christianity, a contrast which seemed to Gentile Christians to involve such incompatability between two different religions that a Christian, even if a Jew by birth and upbringing, had to abandon any Jewish practice or he would vitiate his Christianity. Human nature being what it is, such an attitude inevitably carried with it the implication that the practices of Judaism were wrong in themselves, and so led to the appalling travesties of Judaism which one finds already in the apologists of the second Christian century.

But there was a second reason, for which the theology of Paul himself was responsible. This was his belief in Torah as "a schoolmaster to bring us to Christ." Paul, in common with other Christians, saw the Revelation of Sinai as temporary and preliminary, a stage towards the fuller revelation in the Incarnation of the Divine *logos* in Jesus of Nazareth. John, and the author of the epistle to the Hebrews, paint in their own language the same picture. "The Law was given by Moses, but grace and truth came by Jesus Christ," says John in his Gospel (i, 17); and the epistle to the Hebrews opens with the contrast between the revelation which God gave "in sundry times and in diverse manners in time past" with the full truth "spoken unto us by His Son, whom He hath made heir of all things, by whom also He made the worlds."

This conception of Judaism as a preliminary to Christianity has remained the basic—one might say the "official"—attitude in all the churches down to the present time. Apart from rabid antisemitism, one would not expect the abuse of Judaism in a modern approach which one finds too often in the earlier centuries. But the theology is the same. With

the coming of Christianity Judaism becomes *functus officio*
in the Divine economy.

The upshot is that there never has been a genuine dialogue
between Jews and Gentile Christians on the claims of Jesus
of Nazareth, considered on their merits. From the beginning the religious Jew has been presented with an " either
—or " which he rightly found intolerable. Nor can one claim
that the situation today is very different. And it is unfortunate that the word "dialogue" is to be found in circles
where there has been no basic change of attitude. It is
merely seized upon as a new missionary technique. There
cannot, in fact, be any genuine dialogue between the two
religions until there have been real efforts of Christians
to re-examine their own past attitudes. It is they who have
raised the highest barriers by their constant misrepresentation of the nature of Judaism. Even then there are problems
to be faced in all suggested religious dialogue. All of us are
apt to have inherited the idea that if my religion be true
yours must be false, and some of us are not prepared just to
leap on the bandwagon of the alternative that all religions
are equally true, and that it does not matter which one
accepts. Religious unity poses new and difficult problems
which we have not yet solved.

One can, however, raise a preliminary question. Since the
historical fact is that, within a century of the crucifixion,
Judaism and Christianity were two separate religions, why
is it that their subsequent relations present such a tragic
picture ? To that the answer is clear. It lies in the Christian
claim to sole possession and right of interpretation of the
Jewish Scriptures. It is here that the most striking contrast
exists between the Jewish-Islamic and the Jewish-Christian
relationship. Islam was just as intolerant as Christianity, and
Moslems just as pig-headed as Christians or Jews. But it was
a matter of indifference to the Moslem that Jews should
possess their own Scriptures; for the Moslem had a complete
and superior revelation in the Quran. But Christians found
it unbearable that Jews should claim rights in the pre-incar-
nation history of the Church, or refute Christian expositions
of the meaning of Hebrew prophecy. So completely did they
assume that the Old Testament was exclusively their own.

Before each religion went on its own way there were three centuries of bitter struggle. It was not merely that Christian theologians found the Jewish insistence on the Jewish interpretation of the Jewish Scripture to be insupportable impertinence, but that the practical spokesmen of Christianity found that it seriously embarrassed Christian apologetic to the pagan world, and put unnecessary difficulties in the way of converts. When apologists claimed that Christianity was the true original religion of humanity, because Abraham and Moses long pre-dated any Greek or Oriental philosopher, when missionaries spoke of Jesus as the fulfilment of Old Testament prophecy, there were always Jews to claim that this was a distorted picture of their own Scriptures. Jewish neighbours could shrug their shoulders and remark to one contemplating conversion to Christianity that it was odd that no Jew accepted these claims about the Jew Jesus. We must remember the *mise en scène* of the period in which these attitudes became standardised. We must put away the picture of little Jewish minorities in an overwhelmingly Christian world, and think of two equal antagonists, with Jews having the slight advantage that Judaism had been a *religio licita* for centuries during which Christianity was still proscribed; that Jews were as numerous as Christians and probably better educated. In any case they could read Hebrew, which Christians—with rare exceptions —could not. There was not much exaggeration when Augustine described Jews as wolves surrounding the Christian sheep, ready always to pounce upon their victims.

Our picture of this period is inevitably incomplete, since no Jewish literature from the Western diaspora survives. We have nothing to balance the immense mass of letters, sermons, treatises, controversies, which fill the Greek, Latin and Oriental patrologies of the Christian Church. We can see only the ultimate residue of Jewish thought about Christianity in rabbinic literature or deduce it indirectly from Christian references.

The most interesting survival is the Jewish interest during the third and subsequent Christian centuries in the sacrifice of Isaac, the *Akedah*. It was the Jewish reply to the central emphasis which Christian preaching had given to the atoning death of Jesus on the cross. Rabbinic legend, which had already placed the scene of the sacrifice on the exact site of the altar before the Temple in Jerusalem, and the time of it on the Day of Atonement, put into the mouth of Abraham the words " Mayest Thou, when the children of Israel commit trespasses and because of them fall on evil times, be mindful of the offering of their father Isaac and forgive their sins and deliver them from their sufferings." (Ginzberg, *Legends of the Jews,* I, p. 284.) The sacrifice of Isaac came to be thought of as but one, if the principal one, of the *Merits of the Fathers,* to which some Jewish teachers sought to attribute the same role in popular Judaism as the merits of the Saints in popular Christianity. But the central place which Yom Kippur came to occupy in all Jewish religious tradition and observance is the ultimate rabbinic reply to the Christian doctrine of the Atonement. God's forgiveness follows only on man's repentance. Because it deals with the very foundation of the Divine-human relationship, the inadequacy of sinful man in the presence of the holiness and purity of God, the development of the Jewish and Christian doctrines of at-one-ment, each equally profound in its theology and psychology, provide the most searching field for the understanding of the character of the two religions.

It is probably in their formal teaching about human repentance and Divine forgiveness that the two religions present the greatest contrast. But it is in these two fields that each ought to view the teaching of the other with the greatest sympathy and respect. The Christian emphasis on the mediation of Christ, and the Jewish insistence on the direct access of man to God, have allowed the polemicists of each side in the past to launch bitterly untrue accusations against the other. It has allowed more peaceable men on each side to be convinced that there is a fundamental spiritual lack upon the other. There will begin to be a true dialogue between the two religions only when each can recognise and accept the integrity of the experience of the other. Both Jews and Christians have, in fact, known the joy of Divine forgiveness through the different media of the two religions. To both, such joy belongs to the most solemn realities of religion. We stand today a long way from being able to examine our common experience together.

Jewish rejection of the mediatorial and atoning role of Jesus as Messiah involved at the same time the rejection of any belief that the Messiah would be in some sense a Divine figure. Fortunately it had no impact on the more fundamental Jewish belief in a Messianic Age, though it meant that the figure of the Messiah himself, after being foolishly identified with the military adventurer, Bar Kochba, declined into being an almost anonymous travel agent, concerned with the geographical transmission of the diaspora to Eretz Israel. It is yet another reason why there has been no Jewish-Christian dialogue even down to modern times. Christians force the argument along the lines of the Christian doctrine of the personal Messiah, a doctrine very Hellenistic in form, and they show no understanding of the concern of Judaism with the ultimate coming of a Messianic Age as the very touchstone for the existence at all of a Divine-human relationship in a world visibly far from its redemption.

While firmly maintaining belief in the coming of the Messianic Age, the Rabbis refused to agree that it would involve a new Torah, such as Christians, relying on Jeremiah xxxi, 31, asserted to have come with the Incarnation. The eternal validity of the revelation of Sinai and of the Torah which flowed from it was their reply to the Christian proclamation of its temporary and preparatory role in the Divine economy. Historically it has been this teaching which has been presented on both sides as determining the absolute incompatibility of the two religions. Men had to choose between the Torah of Sinai and the Torah of Incarnation. Those who accepted the one were Jews; those who accepted the other were Christians. The recent judgement in Israel in the case of Father Daniel emphasises their irreconcilability.

An indirect consequence of the growing strength of Christianity in the Hellenistic and Roman world was the gradual rabbinic withdrawal from direct competition. Philo had few successors in his attempt to express Judaism in terms acceptable to Hellenistic philosophers, and this had the result that Jewish thinkers were not compelled, as were

Christian thinkers, to interpret their monotheism in philosophic terms, or submit it to the analysis and challenge of
Greek inquiry. Much that remained implicit in Judaism had
to become explicit in Christianity. Judaism was content to
remain without the systematic theology which Hellenism
forced on the Church. This had amusing historical consequences in the differing fates of Jewry under Christendom
and Islam. For Jews (and fortunately Moslems also) were
convinced during the vital centuries of Fatimid and
Ayyubid supremacy that the Jewish and Moslem theologies
were identical and sharply contrasted with the confused
and meaningless Christian doctrine of the Trinity. The plain
fact is that the Jewish and Christian doctrines are identical.
Both of them are infinitely richer than the Islamic. Both of
them have shown it historically in their respective abilities
to preserve and develop the dynamic of the societies in
which they are embodied. But neither of them has done
anything but despise the identical doctrine in its presentation
by the other. Christians find ludicrous, and even blasphemous, the richly pictorial Jewish doctrine of the Divine
fulness poured out in Torah, and Jews exactly reproduce
the sentiment in their absolute refusal to understand the
Trinity in Unity of the Christians.

It is strange to us that Jews thought Islamic theology to
be identical with their own, for we accept the idea that
popular and pictorial myths reflect real underlying truths.
So we are not shocked by them. But it is difficult to imagine
a Moslem believing that Allah was found crowning the
letters of the Quran in anticipation of the birth of Averroes
or al-Ghazzali. Would Allah spend so many hours a day
instructing children who had died too young to have learned
the Quran from their parents ? Does He observe a daily
period for the study of the Sura allotted to that day's reading
in the mosque ? Does He laugh when His children have
defeated Him ? All such stories reflect a much more complex
attitude to, and belief in, God than Islam knows.

This is not really surprising, for the Christian doctrine
of the Trinity is no more than the Jewish conception of God
put through the mill of Hellenistic analytical thought. It is
designed to combine the facts that the nature of God is

67

beyond any human calculation or definition, with the conviction that His creation has a real and concrete experience of His presence. It leaves men therefore, quite deliberately, with a paradox ; and it should be remembered that, just as in Judaism there are no *mitzvot* defining how one is to love God or one's neighbour, so in Christianity there is no definition of how one is to reconcile the different truths of human experience and human definition about God. Each has seen that the supreme mystery of its religion, whether an orthodoxy or an orthopraxy, cannot be reduced to a logically coherent definition.

The Trinity asserts that God is complete in Himself apart from His creation ; that He is omniscient, omnipotent and incomprehensible (a theological word meaning "unlimitable"). It asserts likewise, as a fact of human experience, that He, the infinite, can be expressed in the finite, and not in a static finite, but in a revelation that grows and develops, and has a real existence in human history. Christianity asserts this truth in terms of Jesus of Nazareth who "increased in wisdom and stature and in favour with God and man" (Luke ii, 52) and in the Church which is his body; and Judaism asserts it in terms of Torah, claiming that men have the right to amend, develop, or even abandon, its precepts as the time shall demand or human life compel. Nor is this all. Both religions assert, with the minimum of definition, because nobody thought of challenging the assertion, that God is Himself the motive force within His creation by which it evolves to the perfection designed for it. For both religions accept the doctrine of the Holy Spirit, which is fundamentally different from Islamic fatalism.

I am not claiming that none of these ideas is present in Islam. But Moslem theologians have so ironed out the paradoxes and uncertainties which Jews and Christians have held to be essential when finite man approaches the Divine infinity, that the result is an impoverished Deity, left with little but omnipotence and a mercifulness which is but the arbitrary condescension of omnipotence. By this process of logical elimination man also loses his stature. Jews and Christians feel themselves to be sons in a father's house. I well remember Herbert Loewe, who had spent several years in India, telling me that he once wrote to a Moslem friend a letter of commiseration on the death of his only son. Thinking to comfort the father, he wrote of men as sons in a father's house, whether here or in the world beyond. His Moslem friend was deeply grieved that he should ask him to be comforted by such blasphemies; for man was not the son, but the slave of Allah. Indeed, the word Islam implies the slavish quality of complete submission. He would be a rash Jew who proposed to call Judaism an Islamic religion.

So there it is: two religions with an identical theology of God, though neither will acknowledge the authenticity of the other. In this case the Christian blindness is indeed the more parlous, because of the Christian missionary imperative. Judaism can sit back and say that the righteous of all nations shall inherit the world to come. Christianity, by insisting on a Christo-centric, instead of a theo-centric approach to the other religion, sees Judaism as something outside the fold instead of a full member of the ecumenical body, but with different emphases within its theology of the Godhead. But this is the only basis on which a real dialogue between the two religions is tolerable, or even possible— a statement which, I believe, I can make as a traditional and orthodox Christian without stepping an inch outside the proper bounds of a fully trinitarian theology.

The Church not only approached Jews from a Christo-centric standpoint, but it ensured that any self-respecting Jew would reject its approach by the insolent manner in which it carried it out. Compulsory disputations and compulsory sermons delivered in the ghetto synagogues by converted Jews have to be added to mob violence and legal persecution if one is to get the picture of Christianity which was presented to generation after generation of Jews, a picture which, for the majority of the Jewish people in the ghettoes of Tsarism, lasted into the twentieth century. It is no wonder that the influence of Christianity on Judaism has been nugatory.

Over the greater part of Christendom, and over most of the time during which Jews and Christians have confronted each other, the disparity of power has been such that

Judaism has survived only because the influence of the Church affected Jewish lives only in the most trifling and external details. As far as they possibly could, Jews withdrew from any public or private argument on the fundamentals of their faith ; and kept their apologetic and polemic literature concealed in the depth of their ghettoes. They certainly did not wish to challenge the inquisitors or the doctors of theology with it.

Some modifications of Babylonian prescriptions there had to be, because conditions in Europe and Babylon were completely different. They are admirably described by Professor Jacob Katz in *Exclusiveness and Tolerance.* I find the most amusing to be the reasons why at last Christianity was adjudged by the medieval Rabbis not to be idolatry. This involved no theological rapprochement, but was an urgent consequence of the economic organisation of the Middle Ages. The great centres of economic exchange were the annual fairs ; these were always held at important religious festivals, usually at the patronal festival of the local church, abbey or cathedral. Jews, as merchants, did a very large part of their business at such fairs ; and it was there that the leaders of different Jewish communities met to transact non-commercial matters concerning the welfare of their Jewries. But *Abodah Zarah* I.i. is quite categoric that " on the three days preceding the festivities of idolators it is forbidden to transact business with them." There was only one possible solution. Christianity was solemnly declared not to be an idolatrous religion, whereby Jewish money-lenders were enabled to collect their debts, and Jewish merchants to carry on their trade. As a son of Oxford, brought up in the belief that the Warden of Wadham is allowed to marry by the provisions of the Great Western Railway Act, I find the decision admirable.

Doubtless many similar trifles could be extracted from a study of medieval *Responsa,* but they would all show that it was only in such matters that Judaism admitted of modification as a result of its Christian environment. Moreover, these modifications were normally made in such a way that the original principle involved was deemed to remain valid. I am not sure when Gershom's limitation of Jewish matrimonial ambitions to a single wife will expire, but I believe that it is valid only for a thousand years.

This immunity of Judaism from the influence of its Christian environment is the more striking in that quite a number of Jews passed substantial periods in the bosom of the Christian Church. Spasmodic compulsory baptisms are recorded from the fifth century onwards in various countries of Western Europe, and it must have been relatively easy for a Jew who had been thus baptised to return to the Jewish fold. There were many such baptisms at the time of the First Crusade in 1096, and a considerable proportion returned to Judaism. But the main group which obtained an intimate knowledge of Christian doctrine and practice was that in the Iberian peninsula. The Marranos in some cases remained nominal Catholics for several centuries before the occasion arose which allowed them to revert to Judaism. That is to say that generations of children were baptised and brought up in the Christian faith, and yet retained a belief in Judaism as the true religion.

In *The History of the Marranos,* that early masterpiece of Cecil Roth, there is no suggestion that their Catholic experience made any permanent contribution to their Judaism. Of course, those who found complete spiritual satisfaction in Catholic faith and practice remained Christians. The very fact of returning to Judaism implied that a man or woman had not obtained that satisfaction. But for a generation or two at least after return some of the aura of their Spanish Christian past still clung about them. In subtle ways Catholic manners of thinking survived, and those aspects of Judaism which they had been able to retain assumed for a while an undue importance in their new religious life.

The Marranos were, of course, quite ignorant of rabbinic literature. They based their Jewish faith on the Bible itself, which they read in the Vulgate. From their Catholic practice they included the Apocrypha, and this collection, less familiar to Jews, includes the moving " Prayer of Esther " which came to be one of the most popular Scriptural passages in the Marrano repertory. For they found in the position of Queen Esther so many parallels to their own unhappy

71

fate. Hence the Fast of Esther took the place of the joyous Festival of Purim. In Latin also they had the Psalms, and were able to share this unique book of devotion with their fellow-Jews in freedom in other countries.

More subtle still was the conviction that remained with them after they had returned to Judaism that this religion was, like Christianity, a religion of salvation, and one demanding the strictest theological conformity. The salvation, of course, was acquired only through Moses, and not through the Christian Redeemer; and the orthodoxy, embodied in Talmudic or Maimonidean form, required the authority of communal discipline for its enforcement. I suspect that this Spanish background played a considerable part in the tragedy of the relations of Spinoza with the Amsterdam community and in the unhappy suicide of Uriel Acosta. Of the attitude of the *Parnasim* in the former case Roth significantly remarks that "it seemed almost as though they endeavoured to set up a miniature Inquisitional tribunal of their own" (p. 247). And, indeed, was it not as Spanish Catholics rather than as Dutch Jews that they set up a tribunal at all to try a theological offence on the basis of a Catholic conception of monotheistic orthodoxy?

The horrifying history of spiritual and physical cruelty which gave rise to Marranism, and which has made the word "Inquisition" synonymous with everything which is detestable in religion, explains more than anything else why Christianity has had so little influence on Judaism. Centuries of experience of ordinary life and teaching within the embrace of the Christian Church have not been able to wipe out the appalling memory of the massacres, tortures and legalised cruelty by which Jews had been made to pass forcibly into the arms of the Church. And until the nineteenth century the activities of the Inquisition in Spain itself, though not in Portugal, continued to exhibit its revolting travesty of religious authority.

In the thirteenth century a new approach was made in the Christian attempt to influence Jews to accept the Gospel. It was made possible by the foundation of the Dominican order, and by its encouragement of Hebrew studies largely, but not entirely, carried on by converted Jews. This shifted the scene of controversy from the interpretation of Scriptural texts to an examination of rabbinic literature, and opened the interesting chapter of the Christian Hebraists. One effect of the opening of this new field was that it gave fresh impetus to the perpetual Christian questions: why did not Jews accept the Christian interpretation of the Scriptures, and why did they not accept Jesus as Messiah ? And it found an unexpected answer to the questions.

In some of the more irresponsible apocryphal gospels of the Eastern Church it had already been alleged that the high priest Caiaphas had found the tomb of Jesus empty, and had recognised that he was the Messiah. But the idea was not, as far as we know, current in the intellectually more responsible Western Church until it was rumoured that Christian Hebrew scholars, penetrating the mystery of the Talmud, had discovered that in actual fact the Jewish leaders secretly did admit that Jesus was the Messiah. Not only that, but it also contained proof that Jews acknowledged the Holy Trinity. Not, of course, in the sense in which I have suggested the identity of the basic Jewish and Christian metaphysic, but as Christian creeds defined it. All these things were concealed from the ordinary Jewish public under various guises, anagrams, obscure allusions and so on. As the field of rabbinic writings is vast, the quarry opened to this kind of discovery was inexhaustible.

The medieval Hebraist confined his interest in these discoveries to the denunciation of Jewish hypocrisy and blindness. I suppose that by the laws of probability some conversions must have been achieved, especially in Spain, by the argument that, as they already acknowledged secretly that Christianity was true, they might as well do it openly and so avoid the Inquisition. For, of course, this discovery laid bare all Jewish belief to inquisitorial inspection. With the Renaissance and the Reformation the interest widened and became more objective. Some Christians became genuinely interested in what Jews believed ; but in the main the spread of rabbinic works by printing only introduced more Christian scholars—Catholic, Lutheran, Calvinist and Anglican—to the game of discovering Christian beliefs hidden in rabbinic writings. As the great sixteenth-century

Catholic student of the Cabala, Petrus Galatinus, expressed it: *Revera innumerabilia arcana ad Messiam et ad veritatem catholicam spectantia in ipsis latent. (De Arcanis Catholicæ Veritatis,* i, 7.) In the next century Johannes Buxtorf said the same. The most interesting aspect of these otherwise somewhat barren studies has nothing to do with Judaism; it is that Christian Hebraists formed a kind of close corporation which overcame denominational barriers. They quoted each other extensively; they approved or disapproved without reference to the Catholicism or Protestantism of the author; they tended to admit a limited number of Jewish scholars to their club; and not one in a hundred gained the slightest real understanding of Judaism from their studies.

Needless to say, their influence on Judaism was nonexistent. They brought into existence a few Jewish scholars of a novel kind—polite apologists and commentators like Leone Modena, Elias Levita and Menasseh ben Israel, who were perfectly at home in Christian circles. But they had no contact with the ordinary ghetto Jew and his religion. Their Hebrew knowledge was a polite form of escapism, akin to the passion of contemporary New Testament scholars for the absurdities of the Dead Sea Scrolls. Only a very few gained a genuine spiritual insight into their subject and sought to bring a fresh knowledge of Judaism to their Christian contemporaries. William Surenhuis, or Surenhuysen, and John Selden are the greatest. Profound Talmudists like John Lightfoot or the Buxtorfs added nothing to our understanding of the continuing spiritual validity of rabbinic religion.

The writings of the Christian Hebraists became fewer as the eighteenth century passed its meridian. But as the Hebraists dwindled, Christians directly concerned with the conversion of Jews increased. It was, of course, nothing new in Christian history, but it began to change in tone. Traditionally the language of disputation and of conversionist literature was rude, contemptuous and abusive. How the authors expected Jews to be attracted remains a mystery. Let me take one seventeenth-century title page as typical of the whole; it has the additional point that, like so much of this stuff, it is written by a convert:

Detectum Velum Mosaicum Judaeorum nostri Temporis
Das ist

Jüdischer Deckmantel des Mosaischen Gesetzes under welchem die Juden jetziger Zeit allerley Bubenstück, Laster, Schand und Finantzerey etc. üben und Treiben, auffgehoben und entdecket durch Dietherischen Schwaben, auss einem Juden einen Christen zu Paderborn 1666.

or one of the following century :

Gründliche und Wahrhaffte Abbildung des verstockten und durch ihre eigene Bosheit

VERBLENDETEN JUDENTHUMS

Alles zur Ehre Gottes und denen verstockten und verblendeten Juden ihrer wahren Bekehrung in 17 Capiteln getreulichst dargestellt von einem aus dem Judenthum zur seeligmachen den Evangelischen Lehre Jesu Christi übergetretenen Proselyten.
1749.

Judaism is commonly described as *insania*, ridiculous, laughable, or offensive. Jewish converts were expected to be dishonest, insincere and avaricious, and humiliating regulations were imposed upon them. And, of course, the churches so effectively barred the way to the entrance of any decent Jew that it was mostly knaves who sought conversion. Where the situation was different, as in Renaissance Italy, genuine understanding and genuine conversions were possible, and Jewish converts to Christianity were honest exponents of their late faith. Paulus Riccius was a faithful translator of the 613 commandments, and Biagio Ugolini spent his whole life in collecting, and publishing in thirty-four vast folio volumes, the work of Christian Hebraists on every kind of rabbinic contribution to Biblical interpretation.

In the Protestant world a new missionary interest began to exhibit itself towards the end of the eighteenth century. That it should have any direct influence on Judaism was not to be expected ; but in its early days one or two of its leaders made contributions of a certain interest. Lewis Way, one of the earliest leaders of the Church of England mission to the Jews, was a protagonist of Jewish emancipation, and presented a memorandum to the conference of Aix la Chapelle in 1818 asking for political equality to be given to the Jews of Europe. He was also interested in the restoration of Jews to Palestine. A generation later, his successor, Alexander McCaul, collected, for the first time, an impressive group of signatures from Jewish converts denying the authenticity of the accusation of ritual murder. In this he was followed by the Russian Jewish convert, Daniel Chwolson. When it is remembered that the whole accusation was launched by a converted Jew, Theobald of Cambridge, in the twelfth century, one can only lament that it took so long to make amends.

When one realises that the Roman Church was still implicated in the Inquisition just over a hundred years ago ; that Mr. Khruschev was brought up, and passed the impressionable years of his adolescence, under the aegis of the antisemitism of the Orthodox Church in the Ukraine ; that political antisemitism in Germany and Austria in the nineteenth and early twentieth centuries had the blessing of some leaders of both the Catholic and the Lutheran churches ; while the New Testament travesty of the nature of Pharisaism is still met far more frequently than sober studies based on George Foot Moore or Travers Herford ; it is not surprising that nearly two thousand years of close association between the two religions have shown the Christian influence on Judaism only in the inevitable excessive conservatism and caution which all religions reveal under prolonged stress and persecution.

It is a sorry record ; and there is no sign that an essential difference is on the way. It is not enough to talk of "dialogue." For any true dialogue about the Messianic claims of Jesus of Nazareth must also be a dialogue about the eternal validity of the revelation of Sinai and the authority of its rabbinic interpretation. It may be that Rome, under the influence of the paternal spirit of the late Pope John, is nearer understanding than the other churches. In Anglican and other non-Roman bodies our academic and popular New Testament scholars are still under the influence of a school of continental Biblical study known as " Biblical Theology." As one aspect of this is based on the idea that only through the New Testament can one understand the Old, and that all the events of the Old Testament are Divinely designed to be understood only through the New, it is an effective barrier to any genuine Jewish-Christian understanding. For such understanding must be based on the recognition that it is Jewish history with which the Old Testament deals and that it is out of Jewish religious experience that its interpretation arises.

5

VERDICT ON FATHER DANIEL

In December, 1962, an Israeli court ruled that Oswald Rufeisen, an undoubted hero of the Polish Jewish Resistance to whom many other Jews owed their lives, had ceased to be a Jew because he had become a Christian. He had become a Carmelite monk and is better known as Father Daniel, and he had applied to be accepted as an Israeli citizen, not by naturalisation but under the Law of Return which was applicable to all Jews.

Because the man in question was so worthy, because the court was so obviously reluctant to decide as it did, because the judges were clearly unaffected by any kind of religious intolerance, the verdict (from which one of the five dissented) came as a painful shock to those who hoped that time and tolerance were smoothing over the historic hostility between Jews and Christians, the gulf between Judaism and Christianity.

Then in February, 1963, there took place in Berlin the first performance of *Der Stellvertreter*, an epic drama by a young German, Rolf Hochhuth, in which Pope Pius XII (*Stellvertreter* means equally " vicar," i.e., Vicar of Christ, or Deputy, i.e., representative of all Christians) is presented as a cold and inhuman diplomat who, in order to preserve the institution of the Church, refused to protest effectively against Nazi policy towards the Jews, and thereby became guilty of the blood of six million of Hitler's victims.

It is inevitable that these two events should be inexpressibly painful to many deeply sincere Jews and Christians. They bring us starkly up against an aspect of reality which we would much rather forget. There are sincere converts from Christianity to Judaism and from Judaism to Christianity who would deny from their own experience so unbridgeable a gulf between Sinai and Calvary; and there is truth in the statement of one heroic survivor of Hitler's policy towards the Jews: "Remember that for each of us who had been under the eyes of the Gestapo and escaped, ten Germans risked their lives."

But the verdict of the court, and the play of Hochhuth, are not directed at these admittedly special cases. They are directed at the total situation in its historical perspective and its present actuality. As such they may be painful, but they are right recalls to reality, recalls especially to the conscience of each and every Christian to face without equivocation Christian responsibility in the presence of Jews, of Judaism and of Israel.

For the few who are all the time concerned with the relations between the two religions and their adherents, it may seem a wearisome repetition to say once again that the verdict on Father Daniel is the reply to nearly two thousand years of Christian denigration and persecution directed against both Jews and Judaism. But it is a truth which many millions of Christians are still reluctant to face. It is well to remember that it was based on the conclusion which men, trained in judicial examination and the weighing of evidence, reached unemotionally and objectively about the effect which past Christian conduct had had on Jewish feelings and consequently on the natural Jewish attitude to one who claimed to be a Jew of the Christian religion. The judges emphasised that their verdict was a political and not a religious one. The religious verdict would have been that an apostate remained a Jew, since, so long as he was alive, there was always the possibility of his returning to the Jewish fold. But the practical effect would have been no better; for, so long as he remained a Christian, he would have been excommunicate and refused entry to the Jewish community, whether in Israel or any other land.

It is not because Christianity is a separate religion from Judaism that this situation, political and religious, exists. A Jew can become a Moslem or an atheist without stirring up any similar feelings. But if he become a Christian then, said

79

the court, he is rejected politically as well as religiously from the Jewish people—or, as a Jew would express it, he rejects himself, he casts himself out of the community.

We who are Christians of Gentile stock are responsible for this grievous hurt to our fellow-Christians of Jewish origin. It is our Christian ancestors who have made the word "Christian" stink in Jewish nostrils. The Christian Church through the centuries has loaded the Synagogue with denigration and abuse, and, as long as it had the power, has done everything to humiliate, oppress and ostracise such Jewish communities as lived wthin Christendom. Even if we say that in Western countries Jews have enjoyed a century of emancipation, we have to remember that Germany was also a "Western country"; but in Eastern Europe, under Russian or Rumanian rule, Jews suffered the bitterest persecution right into modern times, and in both countries the Orthodox Church took the lead in stirring up anti-Jewish feeling and sometimes even in urging its members to murder and physical violence.

With such an inheritance, lasting over so many centuries and as wide as Christendom itself, we have to face a second evil, still more loathsome, which we Gentile Christians have created. Jews who genuinely accepted Christianity, and the opprobrium from their Jewish contemporaries which that acceptance earned, have too often found that they were not particularly welcome members of their churches. For we have so shut off decent Christendom from decent Jews that a sad proportion of those of Jewish birth who sought baptism did so from every evil and unworthy motive which a diseased brain might suggest. These are strong words, but they are supported by the abominable fact that every false accusation, which has cost the lives of tens of thousands of Jews, originated with a Jewish "convert" accepted as genuine and truthful by the Church authorities.

It was a converted Jew, Theobald of Cambridge, who in the twelfth century invented the accusation that the Jewish community officially committed ritual murder on a Christian child in preparation for Passover. It was another convert who, later in the Middle Ages, invented the lie that Jews were in league with the lepers to destroy Christendom, and

by their poisoning of the wells of Europe in the middle of
the fourteenth century had prepared the Black Death in
which a third of Europe perished. And in the nineteenth
century it was yet another convert, a Russian Jew named
Jacob Brafman, who invented the lie of a Jewish world plot,
controlled by a secret Jewish world government, masquera-
ding in the guise of the immense charitable activity of the
Alliance Israélite Universelle and similar Jewish bodies in
Western Europe or America.

That is why, traditionally, Jews regard a Christian of
Jewish birth with hostile feelings. There is nothing in the
millennial relations of Judaism with Islam to stir up a similar
emotion, much though Jews have suffered from the
stagnation of Moslem society and the arrogance and intolerance of Moslem majorities. Father Daniel, an individual man
worthy of all honour from the Jewish community of Israel,
suffered from the slur which the Gentile Church had put
upon him from the moment when he first turned his
thoughts towards the Christian religion.

In the same way Pope Pius XII, in the play of Hochhuth,
is made to play a role which was, in fact, the role of
Christendom as a whole. Christians are tempted to evade
the challenge to their own consciences by proclaiming
loudly that Hochhuth has been unjust to a man who was as
noble as he was powerless. Maybe he has. But it is much
more important to reflect that he has not been unjust to
Christendom. The reparation which Christendom owes to
Jewry is infinite. It is a debt which can never be paid, but
which can only be acknowledged.

❈   ❈   ❈

*Oswald Rufeisen, now Father Daniel, a Carmelite monk,
was born in Poland of Jewish parents. He was brought up a
Jew, and belonged to a Zionist Youth Movement. During the
Nazi occupation he rescued hundreds of his fellow-Jews
from the Gestapo in legendary feats of daring. While hiding
from the Nazis in a Catholic convent he was converted to
Catholicism. In 1945, when the war had ended, he joined*

*the Carmelite Order in the hope that he would be transferred
to one of their monasteries in Palestine. In 1958 he was
finally permitted by the Order to go to Israel. In his
application to the authorities to be allowed to leave Poland
he gave as his reason for wishing to go to Israel the fact that
he was a Jew, albeit of the Catholic religion, and had always
wanted to live in his ancestral homeland.*

*His application to leave was granted only after he had
renounced his Polish nationality. He was given a travel document similar to those given to all Jews emigrating from
Poland to Israel.*

*When Father Daniel arrived in Israel he applied for an
immigrant's certificate and declared himself a Jew for
purposes of registration in the Register of inhabitants. He
was not registered as a Jew and his application for a certificate was refused by the then Minister of the Interior, Mr.
Bar Yehuda, who wrote to him saying that in his own
personal opinion he was fully entitled to be recognised as a
Jew but that he was powerless to grant him the certificate
he sought in view of a decision of the Government that only
a person who in good faith declares himself to be a Jew and
has no other religion should be registered as a Jew. Mr. Bar
Yehuda concluded his letter to Father Daniel with the
apologetic explanation that a Minister may not act according
to his own lights and concepts but must act within the
existing lawful limitations, while continuing to press for their
amendment.*

*Father Daniel eventually petitioned the High Court for an
order* nisi *which was granted him.*

*Section 2 of the Law of Return provides that every Jew
has the right to come to Israel as an immigrant, while section
3(a) lays down that " a Jew who has come to Israel and
subsequent to his arrival has expressed his desire to settle
in Israel may, while still in Israel, receive an immigrant's
certificate."*

*The English text of the verdict, and the summary of the
case, are taken by permission from* The Jerusalem Post,
weekly edition, of December 21, 1962.

VERDICT ON FATHER DANIEL

In the Supreme Court sitting as High Court of Justice before Justices Silberg, Landau, Berinson, Cohn and Many, Oswald Rufeisen was the petitioner *v.* the Minister of the Interior. The High Court, by majority decision, discharged an order *nisi* calling on the Minister of the Interior to show cause why he should not grant the petitioner an immigrant's visa under the Law of Return, 1950.

Verdict delivered by Justice Silberg

We were confronted at the outset, in this most unusual of cases, with the psychological paradox that we felt that we, as Jews, owed the petitioner, an apostate, all our admiration and thanks. For this man risked his own life times beyond number during the dark days of the Holocaust in Europe, to rescue his brother Jews from the very jaws of the Nazi beasts. It was difficult to envisage how such a man could be deprived of his life's aspiration to identify himself completely with the people whom he loves and to become a citizen of the country of his dreams as of right, as a Jew, and not as an accepted stranger.

But we dared not allow our appreciation and gratitude to betray us into desecrating the name and content of the concept "Jew." For the petitioner has asked no less of us than to ignore the historical and sanctified meaning of the designation "Jew" and to forget about those spiritual values for which we were massacred at various times during our long exile. If we were to accede to his request, the aura of glory and splendour surrounding our martyrs of the Middle Ages would pale and vanish without trace and our history would lose its continuity and begin to count its days from the beginning of the Emancipation, after the French Revolution. No man is entitled to demand such a sacrifice from us, even though he have as much to his credit as the petitioner.

The concrete question before us is: what is the meaning of the term "Jew" in the Law of Return and can it be so interpreted as to include an apostate who regards and feels himself to be a Jew despite his religious conversion? The answer to this question depends on whether the "Jew" of the Law of Return must be given a secular or a religious

83

meaning. The ruling opinion in Jewish law is that an apostate remains a Jew for all purposes save (perhaps) in certain marginal cases which do not affect the general principle. This may be seen from the writings and opinions of leading Talmudic commentators and scholars (from whom Justice Silberg quoted extensively). In other words, according to Jewish religious law, a Jew remains a Jew, for all practical purposes, even though he may deliberately change his religion.

But here comes the rub—if rub there be. The term " Jew " in the Law of Return does not refer to the " Jew " of Jewish religious law, but to the " Jew " of secular law. For the Law of Return, with all its historical importance, is a secular law which must be interpreted in the light of the legislative purpose behind it. And as this law is an original Israeli law, drafted in Hebrew and not translated, its terminology must be given the ordinary everyday meaning which the ordinary Israeli man in the street would attach to it. And the ordinary everyday meaning of the designation " Jew," in my opinion, undoubtedly precludes the inclusion of an apostate.

It is not my intention to preach any religious philosophy or to take up the cudgels for any specific view on what path the future development of the Jewish people should follow. I am well aware of the fact that opinions on this score are divided into all the shades of the spiritual rainbow. There is, however, one thing which all Israel has in common: we do not wish to sever ourselves from our historical past or deny our heritage. Only the very naïve could possibly believe or think that we are creating a new culture in Israel. It is too late for that. A nation which is practically the same age as the human race cannot start *ab ovo,* and any new culture which we may introduce cannot, even in the most extreme cases, be anything more than a new edition of our past culture.

Whatever the theological outlook of a Jew in Israel may be—whether he be religious, irreligious or anti-religious— he is inextricably bound by an umbilical cord to historical Jewry, from which he draws his language and his festivals and whose spiritual and religious martyrs have nourished his national pride. An apostate cannot possibly identify himself completely with a people which has suffered so much from religious persecution, and his sincere affection for Israel and its people cannot possibly take the place of such identification.

[At this stage Justice Silberg went on to emphasise, in order to obviate any misunderstanding, that he had no quarrel with the modern Catholic Church nor did he intend, for one moment, to compare the petitioner with some of the notorious apostates of the Middle Ages. But he felt that the petitioner's personal decency and humanity did not affect the question of whether he was entitled to arrogate to himself the designation of " Jew."]

As to the petitioner's counsel's argument that only a theocratic State could refuse to recognise the petitioner as a Jew, it is completely unfounded. Israel is not a theocratic State as it is not religion which regulates the daily life of its citizens but the law, as witness the very case under consideration. For if religious doctrine were to be applied to the petitioner, he would be regarded as a Jew. On the other hand, the fundamental conception that " Jew " and " Christian " are a contradiction in terms is something which is unreservedly accepted by all, as can be seen from the quotations submitted by the State Attorney. Furthermore, the healthy instinct and urge for survival of the Jewish people also contribute towards this conception, as experience has shown that apostates are eventually lost completely to the national family tree for the simple reason that their children inter-marry. As for the petitioner's counsel's frivolous remark that there is no fear that the petitioner's children would inter-marry as he is a monk sworn to celibacy, it was, to put it euphemistically, not in the best of taste.

Justice Landau

I concur unhesitatingly with the opinion of Justice Silberg and wish only to add a few observations.

The fact that we are denying the petitioner the title of " Jew " only because he changed his religion, whereas Jewish religious law itself continues to regard an apostate as a Jew, is not really as surprising and paradoxical as it would appear to be on the surface. For it must be remembered that Jewish

85

D

religious law does not recognise the possibility of a Jew's removing himself from the faith even if he fervently wishes to do so. This stand on the part of Jewish religious law does not arise from an attitude of forgiveness and tolerance towards the apostate but from a complete and contemptuous disregard of any desire on the part of a Jew to turn to Christianity. The petitioner, as a man of conscience and pride, should not have sought succour from Jewish religious law, in the light of its disdainful attitude towards a Jew who has changed his religion.

However, as Justice Silberg has already explained and to whose opinion I subscribe absolutely—the fate of the petitioner's prayer must be decided according to the Law of Return which is a secular law, and the only question which arises is what the legislator intended by the appellation " Jew " in that law.

This law gives expression to the realisation of one of the aspirations of Zionism, and in order to seek its meaning recourse may be had to the opinions and writing of the fathers of Zion (here Justice Landau quoted from Herzl and Ahad Ha'am and Ruppin). From these we learn that a Jew who cuts himself off from the national past of his people, by changing his religion, ceases to be a Jew in that national sense which finds expression in the Law of Return. Furthermore, in addition to cutting himself off from his past, a Jew who changes his religion also erects a barrier against any future identification with the Jewish people—and this all the more so when the change of religion takes so extreme a form as entering a monastery.

That the petitioner, by his own volition, no longer shares a common fate with the Jewish people, but has joined forces with other powers whose commands he obeys implicitly, would be the general feeling of the decisive majority of Jews—a feeling based on positive, national sentiments and not on any desire to pay back the Catholic Church in its own book for its treatment of the Jews in the past.

The respondent has, quite correctly, drawn a line of distinction between a non-believing Jew and a non-Jew, insofar as the Law of Return is concerned. For our State is based on freedom of conscience, and no Jew should be prevented from declaring himself, for registration purposes, as non-religious. But a person who sets so great a store on religious faith as to convert voluntarily from one religion to another—and how much more so would this apply to the petitioner who has made religion the central point of his life—thereby creates so complete a contradiction as to preclude him from being regarded as a Jew, within the meaning of the Law of Return, even though he remains a Jew by race.

One final remark: Zionism emphasises the national aspect of Judaism in contrast to those who regard Jews as a religious entity only. But it is a fact that even in our day religious identification continues to be the principal link between State and the Jews of the diaspora. For the diaspora Jew, conversion is the first step towards complete assimilation. This, plus the fact that the Law of Return was enacted for those Jews emigrating to the State from the diaspora, brings all the more prominently to the fore the basic weakness of the petitioner's suggested interpretation of "Jew" in this law.

Justice Berinson

I do not think it possible to justify the argument of Mr. Bar Yehuda, when he was Minister of the Interior, although on the merits of the petitioner's case I am in complete agreement with his opinion. I, too, feel that if I could follow the dictates of my heart I would allow the petitioner's prayer. But, to my regret, I am not at liberty to do so, as I am in duty bound to interpret the term "Jew" in the Law of Return as it is understood in our day in the parlance of the people and not according to my own wishes.

It would appear that Mr. Bar Yehuda thought at the time that he was bound by the decision of the Government as to who should be considered a Jew, and for this reason gave precedence to this opinion above his own. In doing so, however, he had undoubtedly erred. For the power to grant an immigrant's certificate under the Law of Return belongs exclusively to the Minister of the Interior and not to the Government. The Minister is the one to decide who is a Jew, and he is not compelled to accept the opinion of the Government. The Knesset did not elect to define "Jew" for purposes of the Law of Return, leaving this question to the discretion of the Minister of the Interior and, in the last instance, to the decision of the courts. The opinion of the Government on this point is of importance only insofar as it reflects the sentiments prevailing among the leaders of the State. The courts, however, must interpret the law according to its letter and in keeping with the aims of the legislature.

There is no longer any practical importance to be attached to the reasons for Mr. Bar Yehuda's refusal to grant the petitioner an immigrant's certificate as, in the meantime, a new Minister of the Interior has taken his place in the Cabinet and he has no qualms about the Government's definition, which, apparently reflects his own personal opinion on the subject.

As I have already said, if I were permitted to decide the question of whether the petitioner is a Jew or not according to my own personal sentiments, I would unhesitatingly reply in the affirmative. For the petitioner has, during the twenty years since his conversion, consistently, at every opportunity and in the best of faith, proclaimed that he is a Jew by race, taking pride in his Jewishness, which was forged by such suffering and courage as cannot be easily exampled even in this generation of suffering and courage. This should have been reason enough to open the gates of Israel to him as an immigrant and to register him in the Register of Inhabitants as a member of the Jewish race. He has renounced his Polish nationality and never regarded himself as Polish by race. Now that he has been refused registration as a Jew he is a man bereft of a nation—and only because he changed his religion. It is strange that a Jew who is irreligious, and even actively anti-religious, yet remains a Jew ; whereas the petitioner, who became converted to another religion, but has remained devotedly attached to his people, is not regarded as a Jew. If only he had declared himself a Buddhist —a faith which does not require any conversion—and had become a Buddhist monk, he would, apparently, have still been recognised as a Jew.

Howsoever anomalous the position may be, the fact remains that the Jewish people as such have always regarded a fellow Jew who became an apostate as having abandoned not only his religion but also his race. This was put into so many words by Mr. Sharett in his testimony before the special Palestine Committee of the United Nations, and it is in this spirit that the Law of Return was framed.

My final conclusion is, therefore, that an apostate cannot be regarded as a Jew within the meaning of the Law of Return and the order *nisi* must be discharged.

Justice Many concurred with Justices Silberg, Berinson and Landau.

Justice Cohn

I agree with Justice Silberg that according to Jewish law an apostate remains a Jew. I agree also that the Law of Return should be construed according to the rules and principles of interpretation generally applied by the courts of Israel to enactments of the Knesset. I wish to add that, in my opinion, all the traditional religious tests applicable to the question of who is a Jew are irrelevant to the interpretation of the Law of Return. For the law of Israel is that religious laws are applicable to matters of marriage and divorce only. It is the demarcation line between obligatory law and non-obligatory religion which symbolises the rule of law and ensures the citizen of his fundamental rights.

I agree also with Justice Silberg that we cannot cut ourselves off from our historical past or deny our heritage. I would add that a basic law such as the Lew of Return which translates from theory into practice the " I believe " of the State, demands an interpretation in keeping with the background to, and the idea behind, the establishment of the State of Israel. But I cannot agree that such an interpretation of the Law of Return demands that the petitioner be denied the right to be called a Jew.

It is true that throughout our history, tens of thousands of our people have been tortured, slaughtered and burnt at the hands of the Catholic Church. Not even the latest catastrophe of the Nazi Holocaust can wipe out the memory of those murdered in the Crusades, in the Inquisition and in pogroms, ostensibly in the name of God.

If I have correctly understood my honourable colleague,

PRELUDE TO DIALOGUE

he cannot, for historical reasons, ever envisage the possibility of regarding as a Jew a person who has allied himself
to the Catholic Church, even though this Church is no
longer, either in theory or in practice, an enemy of the
Jewish people. I for my part, however, feel that change and
progress are the very breath of historical continuity. The
establishment of the State was a revolutionary event in the
history of the dispersed Israel. If in the diaspora we have
been either a tolerated or persecuted minority, in our own
State we have become a nation like all other nations, standing on our own feet. This revolution demands a change in
values and in attitude, a revision in our diaspora thinking.

The petitioner is knocking on the gates of the homeland
which, in the words of the Declaration of the Establishment
of the State, were to be " opened wide to every Jew " and
the Minister of the Interior refuses him entry because he is
wearing the robes of a Catholic priest, because a cross hangs
from his neck, and because he declares that he believes in
the faith of the Gentiles. If, however, he had packed away
his robes, hidden his cross and concealed his faith, the gates
would have been opened wide to him and no one would
have barred his way. One cannot but recall, in this context
those Jews [Marranos] who only by concealing their Jewishness had found the gates open to them.

Times have changed and the wheel has come round full
circle. Should a man who regards Israel as his homeland,
who is passionately imbued with the desire to live here, but
who is a Christian by religion, be denied entrance through
the portals of the country for that reason only ? Should the
State of Israel which is " based on freedom, justice and peace
as envisaged by the prophets of Israel " behave towards
those returning to her shores as the Catholic monarchies
behaved ? And did not the prophets of Israel envisage that
the gates will be opened so that " the righteous Gentile who
keepeth the truth may enter in " ?

If it had not been for the petitioner's faith, no one would
have denied that he is a Jew. But only because he is of
another religion does the edict of the Government make
him a non-Jew. I, for my part, am willing to accept only
the first part of the Government's definition of a Jew: a

person who in good faith declares himself to be Jewish. I am not prepared to accept their proviso that he must not have any other religion. In the absence of any objective yardstick in the Law of Return itself, there is no alternative but to assume that the legislators wished to make do with a subjective yardstick: that is that the right to return to Israel is reserved to every person who declares he is a Jew returning to his homeland and wishing to settle there. The addition of the demand that that person should have no other religion goes beyond the powers of the Government and is therefore invalid and not binding. For all the above reasons, the Order *nisi* should be made absolute.*

By majority decision the Order *nisi* discharged without costs.

Decision given on December 6, 1962.

---

* These are technical legal terms. If the Order *nisi* had been made absolute, it would have meant that Father Daniel would have been accepted as a Jew. The majority decision confirmed the decision of the Minister of the Interior that he was no longer one.

6

TOYNBEE AND THE UNIQUENESS OF JEWRY

I HAVE A very great admiration for the work of Arnold Toynbee. Even if all the criticisms of detail launched by professional historians were true (though I doubt if they are), *The Study of History* is a masterpiece in which the imaginative genius of the author provides even the critic with constant flashes of insight into the nature and balance of human experience. What is more important is that its range and comprehensiveness provide a standard and a basis by which any subsequent attempt to portray even a part of his vast structure can see a whole scaffolding in place, so that it can judge what to strengthen, to omit or to change. All writing of history will for the foreseeable future be influenced by what Toynbee tried to do and by what he did. Moreover, to know him is to know someone who is incapable of insincerity or deliberate prejudice ; wherefor I have long been troubled by the apparent exception to everything which I have said when I read his writings or hear his speeches on the subjects of Jews, Judaism and Israel.

It is not that I am still open to be converted to his views on these three topics. I know enough about the subject to make that impossible, and I think I know enough about Toynbee to realise that whenever he reaches this point in his progress, something extraneous comes in and distorts his vision. That majestic tricycle (whose wheels are knowledge, intuition and integrity) on which he moves confidently through the mazes of the whole human story and the geography of all continents, meets some stone in its path which causes it to wobble wildly, and ultimately throw its rider, once Jews, Judaism and Israel rise over the horizon.

If I have any complaint, it is that it is not until page 620 of volume 12 (*Reconsiderations*, 1961) that he tells us what that stone is ; and this is a little late to confess and expound so important a limitation. We reach it at last in the heading of the first section of the fourth chapter (" Effects of being what one is "), of the annex (" Ad Hominem "), to main chapter two (" The Relativity of a Human Observer's Approach to Human Affairs ") of main section A (" Philosophical Considerations "). The heading is: " Irreverence Towards Pretensions to Uniqueness." So there is the nub of the Jewish offence.

But that is not all. Toynbee speaks very sincerely and wisely of the inevitable bias of a personal background and of the tradition in which a man is brought up. He is himself by birth a Protestant middle-class Londoner. Although a traditional Christian he reacts as vigorously against the claim of the Church that Jesus of Nazareth is " unique " as he does against the claim that the Jews are " the chosen people." But his definition of what a " higher religion " is, and his choice of the characteristics which it should show, are, quite unconsciously, those precisely of a Protestant middle-class Englishman. He omits the principal characteristic of Judaism by defining the purpose of all higher religions as being to bring the *individual* into contact with Absolute Reality. When further he defines the corporate expression of religion as being by its nature separate from the natural community, he extrudes Judaism still more firmly from any balanced consideration.

He first aroused a storm of criticism from Jewish quarters by his description of Judaism as a " fossil " of the Syriac civilisation, and the footnotes and references in his twelfth volume show that he has since done a great deal of reading, and of reading the right books. George Foot Moore and Travers Herford are quoted extensively, as well as the American scholar and Conservative rabbi, Jacob B. Agus, with whom he has evidently carried on quite a correspondence. Yet the two fundamental matters of debate still remain untouched. Is a society or system to be thrown out of court without further consideration the moment it declares itself, or is declared, unique ? and : Is the fact that the natural community is fundamental to Jewish thinking about the purpose of God automatically a blemish ? These are the two issues which Toynbee still leaves untouched ; and they give rise to the further question: Is Toynbee's substitute for the traditional values of Judaism, that it is a universally significant means of preserving cultural autonomies in diaspora, meaningful and valid ?

There is obviously a sense in which we must rightly say that no man or society can claim to be unique in the universe. The extent of human ignorance about the universe makes any such claim inherently absurd. But is there no resting point between that extreme and the casual application of the word "unique" to anything that is either excellent or unusual ? There is a second question: Must we rule in advance that Reality (in which Toynbee avows his belief) is prohibited by its universal responsibility from any action which is not immediately universally apprehended or apprehensible ?

I would reject as fiercely as Toynbee that whole section of the traditional doctrines of the "Judaic monotheisms" which condemns to a hell the majority of created beings because they do not accept a particular—let me use the word at the moment without explaining it—"revelation." I would equally condemn the belief that there is a "unique" way from man to God. But it is loose thinking to identify a demand for the inevitable variety of universality with a refusal to accept to the full (Toynbee does somewhere give it a grudging admission) the idea that a Divine intention may be best communicated first in a single "unique" event, provided that the event is universally communicable. That is the rock of stumbling. *Historically* the event of Sinai received an immensely complex interpretation through the very peculiar tenets evolved to meet the very peculiar situation of the Jewish community in the worlds of paganism, Christendom and Islam. *Historically* the event of the Incarnation was interpreted through the medium of the Hellenistic philosophy (with Western and Oriental variations) of the Church of the first four centuries. If there is no other possible and right interpretation of these two events, so that the experience of Reality in other parts of the world

94

is permanently excluded from understanding or accepting them, then they are not universal or universally significant.

If, however, each event (though not its historic interpretation) can be mediated through the diverse channels of the whole world's search for ultimate truth, then there is nothing derogatory, or meriting contempt, in the event being first mediated in a unique manner.

It is true that such an idea is a novelty to most Christian thinkers, and has not yet come into the purview of corresponding scholars among Jews. This has a very simple contemporary explanation. Christian thinkers are at last being compelled to translate into ecclesiastical and doctrinal terms the sudden collapse of the political hegemony of the West. All through Asia and Africa there are coming to be Churches, Roman, Anglican or Protestant, which have become autonomous or completely independent, whose hierarchy arises from the soil and is not imported from abroad, and whose faith is judged and defined by synods of believers who are looking at religious truths and doctrines directly from their own standpoints, and not from the Hellenistic expressions of the West. It will take some time before the consequent transformations of accepted dogmas become stabilised, but I have no doubt that they will present the older Christian churches with many difficult and heart-searching problems. The Synagogue has not yet had to face this situation for obvious historical reasons.

I must define more closely what I mean by the universal communicability of any Divine communication (revelation) which was claimed to be unique. And inevitably I must define it from the standpoint of one who believes in the existence of Toynbee's Absolute Reality, and of that " personal aspect of It which we call God." It is a reasonable assumption of those who believe in a Creator that this Creator is interested in his creation, that he communicates with it, and that the purpose of that communication is to give to the creature both insight into how to live conformably to the Divine plan, and power to help him to do so. This communication I call " revelation." The Jew believes that such a revelation took place at Sinai ; the Christian in the Incarnation.

The Jew has interpreted that revelation in all that he calls Torah, both written and spoken ; those who have accepted Jesus as Messiah first put together a group of biographies, letters and history, which they accepted as inspired, and then built on them the doctrines and dogmas of the Christian Church. In both cases this is a description of what the particular people who received the revelation made of it in their particular times and circumstances. Now if the revelations themselves are both unique and universal, then they must be potentially the source of both insight and power to those who are brought into contact with them, even if they knew nothing of the events when they happened, and do not understand or accept the original historic interpretations of them. In other words, to put it rather crudely, they must be able to accept Sinai without interpreting it as involving the non-eating of pork ; and they must be able to accept the Incarnation without interpreting it in terms of " Three persons in one God." If one asks " why should one accept them ? " then the answer would lie in the realm of a discussion of their influence on human life, not on their expression in a particular orthodoxy or orthopraxis. For undoubtedly Sinai did create a remarkable human society, and Christianity has shown equally remarkable power to transform the life of individuals.

There remains the question : If this be so, then why did not the same Divine Being repeat this essential revelation to all parts of His creation ? Why both in Judea ? By these *unique* incursions into human affairs was He not unnecessarily allowing a lot of other systems foolishly to emerge, and was He not depriving most of His creation of the means of knowing His purpose ? (I apologise for this intrusion of theology, but it is only out of Toynbee's suppositions that one can produce a counter-argument to Toynbee's conclusions. There is no sociological need of, or interest in, uniqueness.) There is a reasonable answer to the question, based on the suppositions of one who accepts the existence of a Reality " which in Its personal aspect we call God," and who believes that this Being communicates with the creatures for whose existence It is responsible. The answer is that we believe God to be inevitably of such power that, if events such as Sinai and the Incarnation were constantly repeated, there would be a complete end to human free will and human responsibility. They would overwhelm the world. There is a phrase in Christian systematic theology which speaks of *Deus absconditus*, of a Divine self-veiling ; and the idea is common to all the monotheisms, though with different expression. It is an inevitable recognition that " as the heavens are above the earth so are my ways above your ways."

It would not be by their only happening once that the revelations of the monotheisms would stand condemned, but by their happening so carelessly that they were, in fact, incommunicable. And this the thinkers of Judaism, Christianity and Islam would all claim to be a distortion of the historical—and geographical—facts. They happened, each would claim, in a " fulness of time " ; and they happened geographically where all the land-masses of the world meet (except for the Americas, and to the issue involved in that I do not know the answer), and so in a place where the communication to others could be prevented only by deliberate human action. The two religions which spread, Christianity and Islam, have reached global communication. That Judaism has not done so is the result of such human action (primarily Christian and Moslem, but Jewish as well), and cannot be blamed on God.

For the believer, then, there is no justification for " irreverence towards pretensions to uniqueness." Any such claim is justified rather in asking for serious and scholarly examination. After its credentials have been studied its claim may be dismissed as untenable ; but it is not scholarly to dismiss any such claim in advance as impossible. Among the credentials to be examined Toynbee would rightly ask that the first place be given to the universal implications of the claim. Was it a claim to privilege for a few or to service to the rest of the world ? Was there any basic exclusiveness which vitiated its claim to universal significance ? There would be many matters worthy of study. They would automatically exclude claims to be a *Herrenvolk* ; they would reveal in a historic religion all the cross-currents and contributing streams of an all too human history. But at bottom Jews have a right to submit their claim to think of themselves as a " chosen people," and Christians to consider themselves "the elect of every nation," because in their very souls, in spite of all the cross-currents of history, the beliefs they profess, and the standard of conduct they have desired to reach, both recognise a universal responsibility and accept a universal right of entry into the fellowship of their spiritual resources.

It would be a new and rather frightening idea to most theologians from any of the monotheisms that their theology, once it claimed to be universal, must be willing to be subjected to a searching examination by every religion. But it is the necessity for facing such a scrutiny that Toynbee in his universalism could legitimately demand, and not the rather perky (he himself compares his attitude in this matter to a London sparrow or bus conductor), frivolous and unworthy denial of any possibility of uniqueness. I am sure that the effects of such a survey would be enormously salutary. A lot of most offensive and odious doctrines would find themselves quite untenable, and would need a Geniza whence not even a Schechter could possibly resurrect them.

All that being said, what was the power or pattern communicated which explains and asks justification for the Jewish claim to be a " chosen people ? "

It was certainly not the merit of being a fossil survival of the Syriac civilisation. The Syriac civilisation was undoubtedly great fun, for it existed in such a nice dry climate that it can constantly be dug up ; but it was not of universal significance, either in time or space. Toynbee's comparisons, when he is trying to deny the uniqueness of Jewish history and Jewish religion, ought (had not all his attention been concentrated on his desperately wobbling tricycle) to have told him that something was wrong in his method. Did he really want a comparison with the Samaritans, then Lady Drower could have supplied him with any amount of parallels from the debris of the Middle East. But there was no real parallel in the Samaritans to a people who, during the present century, had produced a substantial proportion of the world's Nobel prizemen in quite a number of different subjects.

If the first Jewish offence in the eyes of Toynbee was that

they were seen as a chosen people, the second was that they would not abandon the paradox of particularism and universalism. As I said at the beginning, he has on various occasions demanded firmly that religions, to enter the category of higher religions, must "find their social expression in organisations of their own" (p. 84, and compare p. 218 that such a religion must not be an "integral part of the structure of some civilisation," but must be "an independent society of a new kind"). Coming from the general to the particular, he insists (p. 488, compare pp. 496 and 515) that the Jews must choose between "two incompatible alternatives," and abandon either their concern with the preservation of a natural community, or their pretension that their vision of Absolute Reality is of a God who is of universal significance.

This is another perilous wobble of the tricycle. For it amounts to the statement that the natural community is, as it were, an oversight, or matter of supreme unimportance, in the relations between Creator and creation ; and that a religion which gives it a central place forfeits thereby the right to claim to be one of the higher religions of mankind. This is a most extraordinary insistence that the sphere in which Christianity has been a conspicuous failure (witness two world wars arising within the area coloured on the map as Christendom, not to mention a possible third) must not be touched by any other higher religion! O Westerner! Westerner! What a fall is there, *my* countryman!

The strength of Judaism, yes, its uniqueness, consists just in the paradox of its universalism and its particularism. And its particularism does *not* rest on a Jewish Church as an "independent society," but on the Jewish people as a whole. In considering this in the present context I do not want to get involved in counter-argument based on the historic fact that Judaism, hemmed in on both sides by Christendom and Islam, *naturally* sought to preserve the people who practised it. That is of the accidents, not the essence, of its history. It is the preservation of the natural community *as an essential* that should be emphasised. There are all kinds of curious and otherwise inexplicable contrasts between Judaism and its daughter faith in the West which arise from this Jewish insistence. Christianity has stressed the unattainable, the vision beyond man's grasp, the city not of this world ; and Christians have been tempted to look down on the Rabbis as propagating an inferior religion in their insistence on the attainable, on the great words in Deuteronomy xxx, 11-14:

> For this commandment which I command you this day is not too hard for you, neither is it far off. It is not in heaven, that you should say, " Who will go up for us to heaven, and bring it to us, that we may hear it and do it ? " Neither is it beyond the sea that you should say, " Who will go over the sea for us, and bring it to us, that we may hear it and do it ? " But the word is very near you ; it is in your mouth and in your heart, so that you can do it.

Jews have always to think of their weaker brethren, of the men who are neither pious nor intelligent nor given to good works, and remember that they also are bound within the *lulav* of Israel. " We do not lay on the community burdens too heavy for them to bear," said the Rabbis. And by this very tolerance of human weakness they did build up a community which resisted for fifteen hundred years the temptations to apostasy of all the world's higher religions, all its most seductive cultures and (for those same weaker brethren) all the comfort of living unpersecuted and untrammelled.

Toynbee seems to believe that it is enough that the great prophets proclaimed the need for national righteousness, for the supremacy of justice, for the sanctification of mercy, in immortal generalisations. But though it be rash to contradict an expert in his own field, the study of history does not confirm this belief. The Christian churches had all these great generalisations in their Scriptures. Actually one could say that they read and preached upon them more continuously than the Rabbis. But natural communities are not changed by the noblest generalisations. European history has shown this to be true throughout ; and the men of the Great Synagogue, those anonymous leaders who turned " the religion of Israel " into " Judaism " not only realised that this was so, but found means to act upon it. It is they who for the first time made religion a discipline of the whole community by their insistence on religious education, on knowledge of the Scriptures, and on weekly congregational worship in every place where Jews lived. It is the action which they initiated, and which generations of scholar-leaders developed, that preserved the Jews, not as a church but as a people, through the many centuries between the wars with Rome and partial emancipation in the Western world.

The Christian world shares to a large extent the universalism of the prophets of Judaism. But surely for a historian the most interesting and profitable field of study in Judaism is its combination of prophetic universalism with a particularism essential to its survival, manifested in the *unique* power by which it maintained a national community without any means of enforcing membership. Rabbis had not even the threat of the pains of Hell to quell the wicked and bring back the wanderers into the fold, for their emphasis on individual life beyond death is slight.

The Parsees, interesting though they are, are no parallel ; but it is an absurd reflection on the Toynbean comparative method that if somewhere, in some forgotten century or corner of the world, something really parallel had existed, then the Jews would not have incurred Toynbee's wrath and contempt. For their contribution to the total human amalgam would have had exactly the same intellectual and moral content, but would not have incurred the indelible stigma of uniqueness, and Toynbee could have appraised it at its real interest and worth.

But I fear that we have not yet come to the end of Jewish uniqueness. We are concerned not only with the fact that Jews survived as a people but with the moral and cultural content of that survival. For it is the content, not the fact, of their survival which produced the qualities which Toynbee admires, and which produced the stream of Nobel prize winners already mentioned. And, *horribile dictu*, Jewry survived not because of the nobility of the prophets, a nobility which all men can perceive for themselves, but because of the Talmud, that strange, incomprehensible, and (I believe) unique amalgam of laws, pithy sayings, tedious lecture notes, half-finished reports of discussions, and what not, which formed the moral, recreational and intellectual pabulum of Jews for a millennium. It is no good the non-Jew digging out its absurdities, blushing at its indelicacies, raging at its exclusiveness ; for all that apparently justified contempt is shipwrecked on the plain but mysterious fact that Jewry came into the nineteenth century not a fossil but a ferment, not a solid phalanx of rigid and unadaptable fundamentalists, but a lively and attractive section of the world's life and leadership, and a willing body of followers of every reform and good cause.

The fact which merits the study of psychologist, sociologist and theologian is that the Talmud did all this. Why it did it is certainly not apparent on the surface. We can see that the Rabbis left the mind free where the other monotheisms bound it by the line between orthodoxy and heresy ; we can see that they preserved the separation of the Jews without enforcing their isolation ; we can see, in fact, that somehow their Talmud gave those services which Toynbee believes the Jewish diaspora could give to the increasingly rootless non-Jewish world. *But* the diaspora was preserved by the Talmud because within its voluminous and confused pages was a root, a unity, an identity, which made it a " portable *homeland.*" There was no central authority, there was no hierarchy of control, but Jews were identifiable as Jews from China to the Atlantic. For their Jewishness had a common root.

Here is another rock of offence from the Toynbean point of view, though I do not believe that he would treat it with " irreverence." It is indeed puzzling, but it is in no wise contemptible or superficial, for one cannot despise that which comforts a fellow-creature in persecution and distress. That common root of Jewishness was acceptance that they had only one homeland, and that was the Land of Israel, and only one centre therein—Jerusalem. There is no trace of any thought of another land or another city as a permanent home. The head of the great Babylonian community, richer and more extensive than anything the Land of Israel could offer from c.e. 70 onwards, was the Exilarch, the *Resh Galutha.* Every land save one was *exile.* Though the Passover greeting was, doubtless, often a mere formality, yet " Next

Year in Jerusalem " reflected a perfectly genuine root. The choice of words is deliberate, Jews, wherever they lived, felt that they were *rooted* in Jerusalem, and it would be quite inadequate to say that they " felt a longing for it " at some future date. Toynbee quotes with great approval the universalism of Deutero-Isaiah. There are more than a score of references to him listed in the index. But the prophecies of Deutero-Isaiah begin:

> Comfort ye, comfort ye, my people, saith your God,
> Speak ye comfortably to Jerusalem. . . .
> O thou that tellest good tidings to Jerusalem,
> Lift up thy voice with strength, lift it up, be not afraid;
> Say unto the cities of Judah, Behold your God!

Deutero-Isaiah reflects the paradox of Judaism in just the same way as other Jewish prophets.

Rabbinic Judaism turned away entirely from the welter of apocalyptic eschatology which was much beloved by the Eastern Christian Churches. In place of it was this insistence on roots in the Land of Israel, and Jerusalem as a centre for the whole world. If I am right in my conviction on this subject, then I do not think that the ability of Jews to remain a cultural unity in diaspora really provides a key to modern urban needs. They cannot provide for others this sense of belonging which is rooted in their corporate memory.

Without this clue to Jewish survival during the long centuries before emancipation, it is impossible to understand the meaning of Zionism; and it is in Toynbee's misrepresentation of Zionism, and of the significance of the State of Israel, that the wobbles become such that he is finally unseated. For it is completely misleading to explain Zionism simply by the nationalisms of the nineteenth century, although those nationalisms largely dictated the form it took for Jews, and in which it was understood by others.

While Jews still lived in the world's ghettoes, one form of Judaism prevailed with but the smallest modifications— though Sephardim thought themselves superior to Ashkenazim, and both looked down on the Jews in Moslem lands, while Mithnagedim and Chasidim quarrelled and banned each other within the same dimensions of the Pale. But with emancipation and citizenship, each Jew was free to decide in what form he would practise or neglect to practise his Judaism. He could remain a Jew and reject the contemporary expressions of his traditional orthopraxis. The vivid reality of the old centre ceased to be compelling; but the need which was supplied by the traditional centre remained the same. So long as all Jews thought — broadly — alike, the Promised Land existed, as it were, in each ghetto. When all Jews began to think differently, the Promised Land had to be an actual centre to exercise the same attraction.

It does not matter whether this attraction to an actual area of territory which has motivated two returns at an interval of over two thousand years is unique or not. The essential point is that it is real, and that it is ineradicable. In the intervening centuries there had never been an abandonment of the relationship. There were times when perhaps not more than ten thousand Jews actually lived in Palestine; but that was never because only ten thousand Jews could be found who desired to live there; it was because the land could not support more than ten thousand, or because not more than ten thousand could penetrate through all the barriers that had to be overcome to reach it. The new form of return which grew up under Zionism was merely a new form, it was not a new return.

The tragedy of Palestine since 1917 is that it is the fault neither of the Jews nor of the Arabs that a romantic vision turned into a reality resting on naked force. It was not because Zionism can be identified with fascism, as Toynbee asserts, but because of much more deep-seated and complex causes. The two groups were subjected to such different pressures, they were aware of such different areas of tension —Jews in East Europe, Palestinian Arabs in the Middle East—that it was only too easy to overlook a basic compatibility of their ideals and desires. Historically there has been no past in which the area of Palestine was exclusively inhabited by Jews; and there is no *panache* in the Arab past save in the periods when they had lived in tolerant symbiosis with other inhabitants of the Middle East, Jewish as well as Christian. Perhaps the British ought to have tried

104

to explain more why they had issued the Balfour Declaration; perhaps it would have been different if the Arabs of Palestine had not been subjected to pressures of a pathetically sterile nationalism elsewhere in the Arab world; surely it would have been different if the Jewish return had been adjusted to the Arab capacity to understand and absorb it, instead of to the growing terror of life in Europe. But the point is that it is as totally unscholarly to lay all the blame for the result on the Jews as it is to lay it all on the Arabs. Jews have as much right to be in the country as Arabs. The question of majority and minority is not in this case determinant on either side. The rights are equal. In all his treatment of Israel as a modern State Toynbee shows a lack of historical perspective which only the wobbling can explain, and which it certainly cannot excuse.

But there is, alas, for people like myself who hold him in good esteem and affection, worse to come. There is the point at which he is totally unseated, the point at which he identifies the living Arab refugees with the dead millions in the anonymous graves of Hitler's Europe—identifies those who year by year live on the world's charity amounting annually to millions of pounds with those who died without the world lifting a finger to save them. Of course it is absurd for Israel to pretend that she has no responsibility for any refugees; but it is equally absurd to lay on her the whole blame. At a point of bitter contemporary tension, at a point where the outsider has a particular responsibility for seeing the whole field, Toynbee, our greatest philosopher of history, allows his great reputation to be exploited by partisans, whether Arab or anti-Zionist Jew, in a manner which contradicts and defies the whole conception of reality on which his vast structure is reared. Oh! the pity of it, the pity of it. He might have done so much to bring together two sides, each with a just right to maintain to which only a historian could do justice; and the whole weight of his learning has been thrown on the side of division, of misrepresentation, and of falsehood.

III

****
Israel
****

7

JEWS, CHRISTIANS AND MOSLEMS IN THE HISTORY OF PALESTINE

THERE IS NO conflict before the world today in which the actual historical facts are less understood and more necessary to any conclusive solution. The Arab propagandist cries that "Palestine is an Arab country." Lately some Orthodox Jews have been demanding that Israel retain the frontiers which its armies reached in June, 1967, on the grounds that God had promised the whole land to the children of Israel, so that it would be blasphemous to pay any attention to the actual history of the last two thousand years.

In such a situation it is worth remembering one of the wisest and boldest statements made in 1947 by the Anglo-American Committee which the British Government had entrusted with the task of advising it on the future of the Mandate. It proclaimed:

> We emphatically declare that Palestine is a Holy Land, sacred to Christian, to Jew and to Moslem alike: and because it is a Holy Land, Palestine is not, and can never become, a land which any race or religion can justly claim as its very own. We further, in the same emphatic way, affirm that the fact that it is the Holy Land sets Palestine completely apart from other lands, and dedicates it to the precepts and practices of the Brotherhood of Man, not those of narrow nationalism.

It would have been well if the Committee had added that, all the same, it was a land which ordinary men and women, with passions like ourselves, had to inhabit. Yet no solution of the problem which ignores the truth of this statement is likely to be satisfactory or permanent; but it is equally important to understand the relationship with Palestine which the particular genius and history of each of the three religions has involved and developed if a right solution is to be found. For Judaism, Christianity and Islam are three different kinds of religion, united in their monotheism but differing in many other fundamentals; and in consequence the place which Palestine occupies in the thought of Jews, Christians and Moslems is peculiar to the adherents of each faith. Further, while the interest of Christianity and Islam is autonomous and evolved out of the history of each, yet the original impetus in each case comes from the prior association of the land with Judaism. For Christians its sanctity derives from its being the scene of the earthly life of Jesus Christ; but it is because Jesus was born a Jew that Palestine was the scene of that earthly life. For Moslems it derives from the respect in which Mohammed held the older faiths and which led him to venerate Jerusalem, and particularly the site of the Jewish Temple, as the place on earth nearest to heaven. While, thus, the interest of each derives from the previous Jewish association, it is also important to notice that it derives, not from an acceptance of the Jewish association as a totality, but from some special incident or aspect connected with that association—in one case the physical descent of Jesus, in the other the location of the Jewish Temple. It is this fact which makes possible the very different ways in which each religion claims a special veneration for the same land.

Though the Hebrew phrase describes the land of Israel as the "Holy Land," we shall better appreciate its significance in Jewish thought if we use the traditional alternative English phrase of the "Promised Land," for it is in the promises incorporated in the Bible that its holiness lies. To understand the significance of the promises we need to understand that aspect of Judaism in which it most deeply differs from Christianity. Judaism is, by the nature of the Sinaitic revelation, the religion of a people, of a community. While Jewish thought, especially in the Pharisaic and rabbinic period, continually emphasises the responsibility and the opportunity of the individual, and the concern of

God with the life of the individual, yet throughout there is
an insistence on the individual as a member of a community,
and of the Divine call to, and responsibilities of, the holy
community, which only superficially could be considered
identical with the Christian conception of the individual as
member of the Body of Christ which is the Church. The
history of the Jewish community in space and time is, therefore, far more intimately interwoven into the religious history
of the individual Jew than is the history of the institutional
Church interwoven into the life of the individual Christian.
The history of a community cannot be divorced from its
geographical and historical setting, and it is the historical
fact that this setting was Palestine during the whole formative period of Judaism which gives to the actual soil of
Palestine its unique place in Jewish thought and life, a place
which remains unique even among those Jews who have
followed the secularist tendencies of the age in their attitude
to religious tradition and revelation. We can see a parallel
in the respect which the secularised Christian not only
professes but actually feels for the Sermon on the Mount
or the parables, and for the person of Jesus Christ.

For the Jew the intimate geographical link is, however,
not concerned only with the past. The "promises" concern
the future also. Messianic doctrine in historic Judaism differs
profoundly from Christian Messianism. It is concerned not
primarily with the eternal redemption of the individual, but
with the future of the whole nation, and that future lies in
Palestine. Almost the most essential function of the Messiah
was that he should lead the people back to the Promised
Land.

With such a background the primary association of
Palestine in Jewish thought has always been the idea of
settlement, but settlement in the present as well as in the
past or future. For though the general gathering of the
people of Israel into the land of Israel was not expected by
the Rabbis to take place before the coming of the Messiah,
it was held always to be a meritorious act to settle in the
Holy Land ; and, in fact, at every period of history since
the dispersion Jews individually and in groups have settled
there. That their numbers have usually been relatively small

has been due to the difficulties of travel and the inability of the land to support a larger population, not to a dwindling of Jewish ardour or a change in Jewish attitude.

When we turn from the Jewish to the Christian picture, we at once observe an important difference. Nowhere in Christian history (with the exception of certain relatively modern extreme fundamentalist groups) has the idea of the Holy Land been associated with that of Christian settlement. The primary association is with pilgrimage, pilgrimage to the sites made sacred in the historic past by the presence of the Incarnate Lord. During the earliest centuries of Christianity there is little evidence that even this association played any great part in Christian thinking. The ecclesiastical centre of the country was the Roman capital of Caesarea, a city which Jesus had never visited, and the bishopric of Jerusalem was subordinate to that of Caesarea, which in turn formed a province of the patriarchate of Antioch. The sites most intimately connected with the life of Christ were largely forgotten, and had to be rediscovered when in the fourth century the initiative of Constantine himself, and the piety of his mother, Helena, led to a new demand that special veneration should be paid to all places associated with the events of the Incarnation. But from that period onwards Palestine became unique as a land of pilgrimage for the whole Christian world, and the records of pilgrimage show the same enthusiasm among the most distant churches of the British Isles and Gaul as among the nearer communities of the eastern Mediterranean world. Throughout the centuries during which Palestine was ruled by Islam, therefore, the main concern of Christendom was to safeguard the right of residence of a limited number of clergy for the maintenace of the Holy Places, and the right of access of pilgrims from all countries to the sites venerated by the Church. These sites were not confined to Jerusalem. In the north were Nazareth, Cana and the Sea of Galilee ; in the Jordan valley were the Mount of Temptation and the scene of the Baptism on the river itself ; in the south were Bethlehem, Ain Karim (the home of John the Baptist), Bethany and other lesser sites.

When we turn to Islam, the picture changes again ; and

there are certain initial difficulties which do not exist in relation to the two other religions. In the first place, even those who deny any Divine purpose or control in the history of Jewry cannot deny the historical fact that it was in Palestine that the formative period of the Jewish people took place; similarly those who do not accept the Christian theological interpretation of the person of Jesus of Nazareth must recognise that it was in Palestine that he lived and died. But the direct association of Mohammed with the land depends on our willingness to accept in its literal interpretation the Moslem belief in the flight of Mohammed on a winged horse, al-Burak, from Arabia to Jerusalem and back in a single night, in order that he might mount to the heavens from the sacred site of the Jewish Temple. In the second place, the holiness of the land to Jews and Christians arises out of associations proper to those religions themselves. But the sacredness to Islam of nearly all the sites which Moslems venerate in Palestine arises out of their associations with the story of Judaism and Christianity. This is true even of the miraculous journey of Mohammed, since it was the Jewish Temple which gave the site its holiness. It is still more true of such sites as the Haram at Hebron, which contains the tombs of the Jewish patriarchs, the mosque on the Mount of Olives which marks the spot of the Ascension of Jesus Christ, the shrine on the Jericho road which marks the reputed grave (according to Moslem tradition) of Moses, as well as hundreds of lesser sites throughout the country celebrated by the erection of village shrines (*mukams*).

It is true that Christianity had already, to some extent, set a precedent by adopting into the Christian hierarchy the heroic figures of the Old Testament. Among the saints, particularly of the Eastern churches, are to be found the patriarchs, kings and prophets of Jewry. But Christianity had also retained the text of the Scriptures in which these men's works and lives were recorded. Islam did not. It regarded the " book " of the Jews and Christians as holy, for its time, but superseded by the Koran; and it is in general true that Moslems had no idea of the actual lives of such men as Abraham, David, or others, when they claimed their shrines from the Jews or Christians who occupied them.

It is therefore untrue to say of Palestine that it is unique in Moslem eyes, as it is, though for different reasons, in the eyes of Jews and Christians. Insofar as there is a land unique for Islam it is Arabia ; and the holiest shrine of Palestine for Moslems, the Haram ash-Sharif of Jerusalem (embodying the Dome of the Rock and the mosque of Aksa as well as lesser sites) is the third and not the first of the holy shrines of Islam. But, lest this should appear to imply that Moslem interests in the land are so inferior to those of the two older religions that they could be ignored, we must remember that this lesser position in religious history is offset by the fact that Islam has been the religion of the majority of the population—if not, as is sometimes assumed, from the Arab conquest, certainly for many centuries.

A further point, which stands on the borderline of a genuine religious tradition and that nationalist sentiment possessed by all peoples, lies in the close association between Mohammed and the Arab lands, peoples and language. While it is alien to the spirit of Islam to accept grades of equality among Moslems, and the lack of racial or national feeling has been a matter of pride among them, there is no doubt but that the Arab peoples regard it as a special privilege that Mohammed was an Arab and Arabic the sacred language of Islam, and that the Moslem world for this reason regards the lands conquered by the early Arab caliphs as peculiarly a patrimony given by Allah to Islam. This does not involve any sentiment about Palestine differing from that, for example, about Syria, and it has not prevented the toleration of Jewish and Christian minorities (except in the peninsula itself), but it explains the vehemence with which Arabs, and Moslems elsewhere, regard Palestine as part of their peculiar heritage.

II

IF WE SURVEY the history of Palestine during the last nineteen hundred years we find, as we might expect, that the different meanings which it possesses for the adherents of the three religions have worked themselves out in different ways.

Since for more than half the period involved Islam has been the religion of the majority of the inhabitants, this time it will be proper to consider the Islamic relationship first. Palestine did not become a Moslem land through the entry of new inhabitants professing Islam, for the Arab conquest involved practically no change in the population. Insofar as the peasantry are concerned, the Moslems of today are in large measure descendants of the Jews, Christians and pagans of earlier centuries. As in most countries, it is the urban population and the landowners who represent more recent immigrations. Among the latter in particular are some ancient Arab families, but in general the word Arab, before its modern nationalist use came into fashion, applied only to the Beduin, and it would have been no compliment to a fellah to call him an " Arab."

In the first years of Mohammed's mission it looked as though Jerusalem was going to be the central shrine of the new religion. The still pagan city of Mecca was hostile to him, and it was towards Jerusalem that he directed his followers to pray. But once Mecca had fallen, it was the obvious central shrine, since Jerusalem possessed no special interest for Arabs in the peninsula ; and, indeed, later Mohammed transferred to Mecca not only the direction of prayer, but the promises made to Abraham, so that the " promised land " became the district around Mecca and not Palestine. Jerusalem, however, remained the seat of the final judgement, and was allotted in subsequent Islamic thought the position of third shrine. Pilgrimage to Jerusalem ranked after pilgrimage to Mecca. During two brief periods it occupied the premier place, when Mecca was rendered inaccessible. It is probable that the Umayyad Caliphs, with their capital at Damascus, would have liked to raise its rank, and it was an Umayyad who built the exquisite shrine of the Dome of the Rock and the original mosque (on the site of the "mosque of Aksa "). It would have been politically useful, financially profitable, and it would have provided an impressive counterpart to the Christian pilgrimage to the Church of the Holy Sepulchre. But Moslem opinion was too strong, and Jerusalem became only a venerable sanctuary, receiving the gifts of princes and the visits of mystics and scholars.

Though it always attracted pilgrims, it is interesting to find that when the Crusaders were approaching it, and the local ruler applied for help to Baghdad, none was forthcoming. In its recapture by Saladin, religion as well as politics certainly played a part ; but in the following century Saladin's successors of his own family were twice prepared to barter it for Damietta, and his nephew on the throne of Egypt actually did exchange it with Frederick II (though the Haram area was left in Moslem hands) in return for an alliance against his cousin on the throne of Damascus. Nor is there any record that these transactions particularly shocked Moslem opinion.

Its subsequent history was untroubled by political events, though there were occasionally local disturbances, and riots against the Christians or Jews in the city. Its schools were not outstanding, and though one or two prominent Moslem scholars and writers were born within the territories of Palestine, their careers lay in the more populous centres of the Moslem world. Some time during the Middle Ages a second attempt was made to provide an Islamic counterpart to the Christian pilgrimages. This was the festival of Nebi Mussa. Moslem legend recounted that Moses, feeling lonely on Mount Nebo, had been transferred by angels to a tomb near the road from Jerusalem to Jericho, and an elaborate shrine was built there in the thirteenth century. A pilgrimage from Jerusalem to the shrine was one of the main events of the religious year, and drew a certain number of pilgrims from other parts of the Moslem world. The purpose of the innovation is shown by the dating of the pilgrimage, which follows the Greek and not the Moslem calendar, so that it always falls at the time when the city is filled with Easter pilgrims to the sacred shrines of Christianity.

Much has been said recently of the toleration which Jews and Christians enjoyed under Islam, and Palestine offers an excellent field for the study of the subject. Mohammed extended his protection to the two " peoples of the Book," and forbad his followers to kill them, provided they accepted the Moslem rule and paid the special taxes

116

imposed on them. Their status was definitely inferior to that of the Moslem ; they might on no account lift a hand against one (even up to 1914 all Christian consuls had to be accompained by a Moslem *kavass,* since the consul, officially, could not have defended himself if attacked by a Moslem), or copy their dress. But on these conditions they were guaranteed life, liberty and the control of their own affairs. These conditions the Moslem religious authorities upheld, even against their rulers. There was one occasion when a Turkish sultan proposed to massacre his Christian subjects ; but the Moslem judges forbad him to do so. On another occasion the governor of Nablus proposed to exterminate the relics of the Samaritans, but the Jewish Rabbi of Jerusalem produced evidence that they accepted " the Book," and were therefore protected by Mohammed's ruling, and the Samaritans were saved. It would, in fact, be difficult to find evidence that Moslem judges had ever attempted to overthrow the right Mohammed had conceded them. But, unfortunately, the Christian and Jewish populations had to deal with the political authorities and live among the ordinary population, and with both it is a very different story.

On the borderline of religion and politics comes the question of the actual ownership of a shrine. According to Moslem practice the ownership lay with the Moslem ruler, and it was by his grace that Christians or Jews enjoyed possession of it. At all periods of the story they felt free to take possession of any building they decided to be of religious significance to Islam. The most outstanding example of this is the fifteenth-century seizure of the Franciscan convent on Mount Zion, on the ground that it contained the tomb of the Moslem prophet King David ; but other examples are to be found all over the country. The marble panelling of the Church of the Nativity is to be found in the Dome of the Rock. Churches were pulled down without scruple if a ruler wished for its columns or decorations to adorn his own monuments. In most cases, when a building had been seized, its previous owners, or worshippers, were totally excluded from it. This is the case with the tombs of the patriarchs of Hebron, and the tomb of David, but there are examples where Moslems shared a building with Christians. They were satisfied with the right to worship in the south transept of the Church of the Nativity, in the Church of the tomb of the Virgin, and in the convent of St. Catherine at Sinai.

Insofar as the rulers are concerned, to speak of toleration is, except with a small minority, a misnomer. The Christian shrines, and Jewish privileges, were a continual source of profit, and this source was exploited to the uttermost. Lesser shrines, out of which money could not be made, were seized or destroyed without compunction. But the pilgrimages, and the maintenance of the hostels and churches for the pilgrims, formed a very important element in the incomes of the governors of the country.

The avarice of the rulers was balanced by the arrogance of the Moslem townsfolk and peasantry. Moslem practice certainly did not conform to the teaching of the Quran, and the sufferings which were endured both by visiting pilgrims and by the resident clergy made the maintenance of a Christian foothold in the country an act of continuous heroism, or at least endurance. What was true of the Christians was still truer of the Jews ; for they had to bear the contempt and ill-usage not only of the majority but of the Christian minority also.

Only in two periods of Islamic rule is it true to say that life was pleasant for the minorities : during the early days of the Arab Caliphate, i.e., from the conquest to the middle of the ninth century, and during the great period of the Osmanli Turks—i.e., from the end of the fifteenth to the end of the sixteenth centuries. In the former period the greater toleration was, perhaps, enjoyed by Christians, in the latter by Jews.

The Christian story presents certain parallels to the Islamic. The land never became of central significance in the development either of the institutions or the theology of Christianity. Apart from a certain—not always desirable— prominence in eastern monasticism, it was always as a centre of pilgrimage that it was considered. As such it was more comparable to Mecca, but pilgrimage in Christian thought never had quite the same place as in Islamic, since it is not enjoined in the Christian, as it is in the Islamic, scriptures. The story of the Christian devotion to the Holy Places is a story of strong lights and shadows. On the one hand is the devotion of the pilgrims themselves in all centuries. From the Western Europeans of the early Middle Ages to the Russians of the early nineteenth century, a high proportion sacrificed their lives to accomplish their purposes ; and in all periods it was a long and dangerous journey for those who took it. To the credit balance must also be set the amount of fellowship between the different churches which was engendered by their common devotion to the scenes marking the life, death and resurrection of their Master. While our records before the Crusades are scanty, it seems that even then orthodox and monophysite, bitterly divided in their homelands and in ecclesiastical synods, managed to worship together in Jerusalem. During the Crusades, when the patriarchate and the higher clergy were all Latins, the Greeks and Syrians (monophysites) were not excluded from the shrines. But it is this problem which provides the darkest side also. With the restoration of the Greek patriarchate after the loss of Jerusalem, the step was taken by the Latins of buying from the Moslem rulers rights in the Christian Holy Places at the expense of the Greeks ; and from then onwards an increasing bitterness between the Eastern and Western Churches marks every incident in the story. Bribery and bloodshed took the place of brotherhood, and even during the British mandatory period little change can be recorded.

A new chapter opens at the beginning of the nineteenth century with the coming of the Anglican and the Protestant churches to the Holy Land, a chapter in which we can take a modest pride. The Western missionaries came to make no counter-claims to Holy Places, and even sought, by a self-denying ordinance, not even to win adherents to their own denominations. Their purpose was to spread the knowledge of the Bible, whose complete Arabic translation was made by the American Presbyterians at Beirut, and to set up schools. In 1840 a curious Anglo-Prussian bishopric was established in Jerusalem, with friendly relations with the Greek patriarch. It lasted for forty years, and was responsible for a considerable spread of education. But it also created many problems, and lapsed in 1880. One of its most famous—if least expected—consequences, was to drive Newman to the final step of adhesion to the Roman Church. In 1886 a purely Anglican bishopric was established in its place ; and it is interesting to record that Anglican and American episcopalian clergy may celebrate in the chapel of Abraham in the Church of the Holy Sepulchre, at the express invitation of the Greek patriarch. That, and similar relations with the Armenian Patriarchate, provide examples of a fellowship between the churches which has been unhappily absent in the main conflict between East and West.

Finally we come to the Jewish relationship, and at once we find two striking differences. Pilgrimage plays but little part, save in the form that elderly people came to Palestine in all centuries in order that they might die and be buried in the sacred soil ; but settlement plays a predominant role in all centuries ; and at recurrent intervals in Jewish life dispersed throughout the world, Palestine has played an essential and central role such as it has never played in the life of Christianity or Islam.

The story of settlement is one of heroism, tragedy and pathos. Though at no time, before the nineteenth century, were the numbers very considerable, it can be said that in every century they amounted to hundreds, and in some to thousands. But not only was the voyage both expensive and dangerous, for the Jewish traveller was at the mercy of both Christian and Moslem princes and pirates, but there were the most meagre possibilities of an economically independent existence once the object of the journey was achieved. For under Moslem rule the land was perennially insecure, and increasingly barren. It could not support any extensive increase of population. Even when in the sixteenth century opportunities for settlement were offered on a most generous scale by the sultan, only a few thousand could take advantage of the offer. In some cases the travellers were seized by the knights of Rhodes ; in others their lands were constantly raided by Beduin. Yet, as long as it was possible, Jewish life was self-supporting ; but for nearly five hundred

years before the beginning of Zionist settlement, Jews of
the Holy Land mainly had to be supported by the communities of Europe, in order that there might be continual
study and prayer in the Holy Land itself. The life led by
these Jews supported by *Halukkah* was miserable in the
extreme, but there are relatively few instances of men
abandoning Palestine to return to life in the diaspora. It is
worth noting that, while Christian pilgrims were only
allowed a limited stay until the middle of the nineteenth
century, it was not until the beginning of Zionist colonisa-
tion that any action was taken against settlement by Jews.

The second peculiar feature of the Jewish association is
the recurrent emergence of the Holy Land into the very
centre of Jewish life. After the second, disastrous, war with
Rome, when the Jews of the dispersion enormously out-
numbered the relics in Palestine, it was yet from Galilee that
the whole ordering of the newly scattered Jewish life issued.
The creation of the patriarchate, the codification of law into
the Mishna, the development of the rabbinic school and
court, all came from Galilee. Thereafter for half a millennium
the centre passed to Babylon. But when Babylonian Jewry
collapsed before the onslaught of the Seljuk Turks, for a
brief moment Jerusalem, miserable and impoverished as its
community was, held the gaonate (the central religious
authority) before the stream of Jewish life was ready to
pass to Egypt and thence to the Spain of the Western
caliphate. When medieval Jewry suffered the last tragedy
of expulsion from Christian Spain, it was in Safed, the hill
town of Galilee, that Jewish Orthodoxy was renewed in the
Shulchan Aruch, and Jewish mysticism reborn. When, after
the assassination of Alexander II in 1881, Jewish life in
Russia again faced tragedy, it was but continuing an ancient
tradition that some returned to Palestine; and it was
actually young Jews of Jerusalem who began the first agricultural settlement in Petach Tikva.

It is not possible, in the period under review, to speak
of the attitude of Jewry to the other two faiths, for at all
times it was the Jews who were the underdogs. It was a
community which, as far as it possibly could, kept itself

apart; for close relations with either Moslems or Christians were almost impossible to them.

In the phrases quoted from the Anglo-American Committee at the beginning it was said that Palestine should be a land in which the keynote was brotherhood. Up to modern times that keynote has been but too rarely heard. That the picture is not all black the previous pages will have shown; but they show also how many changes, on the part of all communities, are needed before the words of the Committee can represent the facts of the situation.

To hope that any part of this vision may possess negotiating governments may be utopian; but there remains the question of the future of the Old City of Jerusalem, with its Jewish, Christian and Moslem Holy Places. Surrounded as it is with walls, it would not be difficult to turn it into a kind of Vatican City, with outlying possessions such as the Church of the Nativity at Bethlehem—just as the Vatican City has possessions outside its own boundaries.

But, if that were done, would the three religions be likely to turn it veritably into a City of Peace, or would it be the centre of the kind of intrigue, brutality and hatred which has too often marred the relations between the guardians or possessors of Holy Places? I doubt if the right way to achieve anything of value would be to entrust the government to those representatives of the three religions who have historically fought for the rights of their own faithful. But Judaism, Christianity and Islam are world religions. There is in all of them a sense of responsibility for brotherhood and peace, however much there has also been narrowness and intolerance. Jerusalem is the only city in the world where all are present of their own right, and none is in a relationship of host and guest to the others. There is an opportunity here which is unique, and potentially of relevance to the whole world. But who is going to seize it?

8

THE NEW FACE OF ISRAEL

IT IS APPROPRIATE to begin this lecture, established in
memory of one who was both a distinguished scholar and a
distinguished Jewish patriot, with a quotation which reflects
that period in the history of Jewry and of Israel in which
Selig Brodetsky was a leading figure. In a lecture published
by Chatham House in *International Affairs* for April, 1964,
Brigadier Allon, then the Israel Minister of Labour, said:
" The Jewish people have returned not only to the land
which was theirs in history but also to the continent from
which they once sprang and to the nations among whom
they once dwelt."*

In this sentence Yigal Allon reflects perfectly the outlook,
and the situation, of Brodetsky's Zionist activity. That, in
fact, it is dated to that period, and is no longer appropriate
to tomorrow or accurate for today, is not a blemish, but a
tribute to the breadth and determination which charac-
terised the builders of Israel. It requires courage to build
for a foreseeable future. It requires vision so to build that
your labour may successfully meet demands which are
unknown to you.

That which is out of date in the statement of the Minister
of Labour is the double implication that the people of Israel
have returned " to the continent from which they once
sprang, and to the nations among whom they dwelt." For
the fact is that the majority of the Jewish inhabitants of
Israel have never, in the more than three thousand years of
their recorded history, lived in any other continent or among

* *International Affairs*, Vol. xl, No. 2, p. 207.

any other nations. Israel is today a Middle Eastern country, the majority of whose inhabitants are descendants of the oldest identifiable group of Semitic-speaking peoples in the Middle East, a group which left the Semitic heartlands in the Arabian peninsula two millennia before most of their cousins who are now identified as Arabs, but which went no further afield than the Mesopotamian empires in the East and the North African peoples in the West. The only part of the statement which is still accurate is that which refers to the recent concentration in a single part of the area of those who were previously scattered in all parts of it.

A more interesting estimate of the actual situation today is given by Manfred Halpern in his brilliant study, *The Politics of Social Change in the Middle East and North Africa.** In an aside in his foreword he writes:

> Since nearly 95 per cent of the population in the region from Morocco to Pakistan is Moslem in its religion and way of life,§ it seemed unfruitful to interrupt the flow of thought about the consequences of social change in Islamic society with the phrase " except in Israel."
>
> Yet as the book progressed, it became apparent that Islam shared many problems with Israel. Like Islam, Israel presents a society whose modern, Westernised élite will have to learn how to assimilate an Oriental majority. Both are intent upon creating secular States despite the presence of important religious political parties. One society faces the problem of converting Zionism, as the other must transform anti-colonialism, into a nationalism appropriate to a generation that has known neither exile

---

* A study made for the Rand Corporation (a private American Foundation which undertakes research into matters of political interest) and published by The Princeton University Press (1963), pp. xiv f.

§ The principal religious minorities among the 230,000,000 people who live in this region are: 10,000,000 Hindus, 7,000,000 Christians and 2,500,000 Jews. However, about 30,000,000 Moslems belong to various heretical sects, while in Iran the heretical Shia form of Islam is the State religion.

nor foreign rule. Israel is challenged by the task of making
Judaism relevant to a modern environment quite different
from the one that has nourished it, either in Europe or in
Oriental countries, for the past two thousand years, and
thus finding new sources for moral judgement. Moslems
face the same challenge in Islam. Israel must renovate
Hebrew, as other countries must Arabic, so that it can
deal clearly with modern science, politics and philosophy.
Israel has the special opportunity of demonstrating
whether large infusions of capital into an under-
developed economy can succeed in raising both the
political and economic standard of living. Its experiments
with trade unions, co-operatives and collectives are
immediately relevant to the general social and economic
problems of the area.

The discovery that "except in Israel" is increasingly
inapplicable to any general assessment of the Middle East
reinforces the obsolescence of the attitude illustrated by
Brigadier Allon. Halpern's shrewd description of the present
position rests primarily, though not exclusively, on the concentration of Jews from Middle Eastern countries in Israel.
They have not ceased to be Middle Easterners because Arab
countries, in their emergent nationalism and their hostility
to Zionism and its flowering in the State of Israel, have
expelled them. Everywhere in Israel one will meet recent
immigrants from North Africa, Iraq, Yemen, Egypt or from
some other part of the area, and it is these, with their high
birth-rate, who have effected the statistical transformation.
But we shall still have only an imperfect perspective if
this present and future fact does not make us also re-examine
the past, and relate it to this present condition. For we shall
then see Jewish history in its true balance between East and
West, between Europe and America on the one side, and
the Middle Eastern countries on the other.

Up to the present the whole tradition of Jewish historio-
graphy has been to present the Jew of Europe, and later of
America, as the heir to an earlier Jew of the Middle East.
He has indeed provided the central figure of Jewish history
since about the thirteenth century. At that time Puritan

reactionaries destroyed in Fatimid Egypt and the Western Caliphate the happy symbiosis of Jews and Christians with their Moslem rulers and their Moslem neighbours. Because of the long stagnation of the area, the Jewish historian tended to forget that substantial Jewish communities went on living there, except when there was a European Jewish irruption such as populated sixteenth - century Safed. European Jewish history was more exciting in its continuous incidents, whether tragic or inspiring. The general traveller also, though visiting a vast area inhabited by many different peoples and religions, thought of it as Moslem and Arab, because all peoples alike spoke Arabic, and because Moslem intolerance had pushed the religious minorities into the background, where, in any case, prudence imposed silence in the presence of a foreigner.

A truer picture of Jewish history must balance the essential contributions of both West and East, and expound why the Western appeared of exclusive significance during the formative years of the modern age. For the fact that Israel has become statistically a Middle Eastern country was quite unforeseen by its Zionist founders, but at the same time it does not divorce it from the links which bind it to Western Jewish history.

While the only true origin of Zionism lies deep in the qualities and hopes of Judaism itself, its manifestation in the second half of the nineteenth century was a purely European affair. It was the natural, if unconscious, reaction to the destruction by emancipation of the unity of the ghetto and the sufficiency of rabbinic orthodoxy ; and it expressed itself equally naturally in nineteenth-century secularist and political forms. The Zionist settlement of Palestine was a European settlement. The settlers came from Rumania and from the Russian Pale. But the economic and technical know-how came from Western Europe. It was men of German education like Ruppin and Bodenheimer, or Frenchmen like the agents of the Baron, who directed the beginnings of Zionist organisation, agriculture and finance, whether in the land itself or in the European headquarters.

It is not merely this historical background which emphasises the European end of Zionism, but the fact that it was European pressures which brought about the Balfour Declaration and the immigration of the inter-war years. The period from 1917 to 1939 witnessed both the building of the National Home and provided the evidence on which present Arab propaganda accuses Israel of being a stooge of European imperialism set in the heart of the Arab world. It is therefore of considerable importance to examine this particular period and its justification.

I doubt whether one can find any important—or even unimportant—contribution to the upbuilding of Zionist ideology from the Oriental Jewish communities. Pioneers and pioneer philosophers were all from Europe. Their general background was emancipation into European democracy and industrial society, and their background within the communities was the European Jewish *Haskalah*. When American Jews came into the picture they were indistinguishable from their European brethren. But it was not merely the background which was European. More important was the fact that the pressures and the urgency were also European. When my wife and I spent three months in the country in 1946 I found myself again and again explaining to British officials what the ghettoes of Eastern Europe had been like between the wars, how completely the Minority Treaties had failed, and how endemic was anti-semitism. They were almost wholly ignorant of the impossibility of the solution envisaged in the Minority Treaties, of the hopelessness of outlook of the Jewish intelligentsia in countries like Poland and Rumania, or of the power of Nazi propaganda among the Fascist parties and governments of Eastern Europe.

I am not blaming them for their ignorance, for Palestine was part of the Colonial Service. In particular it was closely linked to the larger career area of the countries in which Arabic was useful and an understanding of the Arab mentality profitable. So far as I know nobody in Whitehall had had the imagination to add to the Secretariat a sprinkling of men who knew the Jewish world as intimately as their colleagues knew the Arab, men who would have had to be drawn from the consular and diplomatic service in countries from which the immigrants, or would-be immigrants, also came. Had this knowledge been always a part of the equipment of the British administration, there might well have been a different attitude in many officials whom the Jews felt to be hostile and unsympathetic. I say this with the more confidence because we found the British officials in Palestine to be an exceptionally intelligent and honourable group of men. But they were completely bewildered by Zionism, and any open Zionist sympathy isolated them from the large British community in the commercial and political life of the area as a whole. They administered their Arab areas directly, but their Jewish only indirectly. Hence they never responded with an automatic understanding to pressures, the reasons for whose overwhelming insistence were quite unfamiliar to them. They had not themselves witnessed the Jewish life from which the immigrants came ; they saw only the hostility with which the Arab spokesmen received them.

The wall of misunderstanding was heightened by the lack of sympathy of the Zionist immigrants from Europe, or the leaders of the Jewish Agency, with the Jews whom they encountered who were themselves Middle Easterners, whether resident in the Holy cities of Palestine, or elsewhere in the area. There is an interesting reflection of this lack recounted in *Orientations,** the memoirs of Sir Ronald Storrs. Storrs came to Jerusalem from Cairo, where he had become friendly with cultured and distinguished Jewish families. He sincerely felt—it is a subject I discussed with him a number of times—that this friendship could well enable him to secure the help of Egyptian Jews in establishing contact between Arab notables in Jerusalem and the leaders of Zionism. But he found the Zionist personalities too impatient, too insistent that things must be done at once, for them to tolerate the leisurely courtesies, the slow deliberations, by which Sephardi Jews were seeking to reassure their Arab neighbours as to the intentions of the Balfour Declaration and the lack of danger involved in Zionist immigration. But Storrs himself was as unfamiliar with the pressure of Eastern Europe as were his Egyptian

* Pp. 426 ff.

Jewish friends. It is fascinating, but, alas, useless, to specu-
late what would have happened had any of the parties
involved realised that they were laying the foundations for
Israel to become a normal Middle Eastern country in less
than half a century! But one must hasten to add that it is a
Middle Eastern country of 1964, not of 1924. The scientific
institutes of Rehovot may constitute the Israeli version of
a modern scientific revolution which has equally made
possible the evil activities of German and Russian scientists
in the Egypt of 1964. They correspond to nothing which was
foreseen in the Egypt of 1924.

If there were walls of misunderstanding and division
between the Zionists of this period and both Eastern Jews
and British officials, the walls were even higher between
the Zionist leaders and the Arabs. The Zionists did not
intend that this should be so. Dr. Weizmann took what steps
were open to him to negotiate with the Emir Feisal, but
Feisal was the leader of the Arabs only from the point of
view of European negotiators. He had no authority to commit the Arabs of Palestine to any decision about the future
of the country. There was, in fact, nobody who was com-
petent to take such a decision, not merely because there
was no representative organisation of the Arabs concerned,
but because the decision demanded was on a unique
proposal, and required unique understanding.

By all the international precedents available at that time,
when the Wilsonian proclamation of the rights of self-
determination was paramount, it was an Arab country in
which certain minorities had ancient prescriptive rights.
European Christians had settled since the time of Mehemet
Ali early in the nineteenth century; but those who were
already Turkish subjects, Jews or Christians, had rights
going back to the original Arab conquest in the seventh
century. Mehemet Ali permitted European Christian foundations to be established, and Jewish enterprises in favour
of the Jewish population to be undertaken; but the Quranic
definition of Dhimmis protected, though with a status of
inferiority, Jews and Christians who were regarded as
indigenous subjects. Actually Jews could come from abroad
and settle in the country until Abdul Hamid became afraid

of the Zionists towards the end of the nineteenth century. But such rights were far from adequate to the demands and the needs of the Zionists. They would have allowed some thousands to enter the country gradually, but still as Dhimmis, a prospect which fell far short of the needs of Eastern Europe or of the demand for a National Home to which any Jew could come as of right and not on sufferance.

I do not think it is possible to read any of the English or American literature of the time and fail to realise that there was no common ground between the minimum Jewish demand and the maximum Arab concession. A serious study has recently been made of the American King-Crane Commission,* and it seems to me to reveal, not that the Commissioners were biased, but that those they interviewed had no basis for any answer except that they wanted independence. What else were they expected to want? They added that, if there was to be a Mandate, they wished the U.S.A. to be the Mandatory. What else were they likely to say to two American Commissioners? It was quite futile to ask them whether they approved of the Balfour Declaration. Of course they did not. To understand and accept it involved a knowledge of history, especially of Jewish history, of international standards and of contemporary needs, all of which were completely outside the vision of an Arab of what was then Syria.

There was no alternative but to impose the Balfour Declaration by European, and primarily British, authority; and because this was so, it encountered also the difficulty that the British had become by 1920 the last people to impose a solution on an unwilling people, and maintain it day in and day out in the routine of local administration. Now that all that is past, we lose nothing by admitting that this is so. Nor does the historic justification for the establishment of the National Home and the subsequent State of Israel, suffer by the recognition. As I have expressed in *End of an Exile*, and republished in a revised form in *Five Roots of Israel*,

* "An American Enquiry in the Middle East: The King-Crane Commission," by Harry N. Howard, Beirut, 1963 (distributed by Constable in England).

the Balfour Declaration and Mandate are unique, not because Jews wanted privileges denied to other peoples, but because Jewish history and the Jewish contemporary situation were unique. To this it is important to add that the emptiness of the area and the fluidity of its total situation made the project realisable without inflicting any wrong on any one else. Factually, the Jewish and Arab peoples could have grown to prosperity with mutual advantage, and without either suffering damage. There was ample room in the Middle East for both peoples. It was not facts, but human psychological prejudices and limitations on both sides which made so idyllic a result unattainable.

Hence it was a period in which people did come from outside into an area to which they had long been strangers. They did settle among nations which did not desire their presence. It was not their fault. Nor was any alternative open except national suicide, by assimilation, by conversion to one of the dominant religions, and by reduced birth-rate. But even during that period it was realised that some, at least, of the Jewish population had an absolute right to be there.

I have not, however, been able to find any evidence that Jews settling in Israel from Europe thought of themselves as increasing an already existing indigenous population. They thought as Brigadier Allon thinks. Partly this was because it became increasingly dangerous for a Jew in any Moslem or Arab country to identify himself with Zionism. But partly also it arose because to most traditionalist Jews —and there was no modernism among the Jews of the Middle East—the return to the Land of Israel should be the work of the Messiah, not of a human and political agency. European and Eastern Jews felt extremely little fellowship with each other.

Storrs remarks that it was not until 1931 that Weizmann saw in Jews who lived throughout the Middle East possible interpreters of Zionist aspirations to their Arab neighbours.* By that time it was too late. Not only were the Jews settled in Syria or Iraq unable to help, but the same was true for

* *Op. cit.* p. 430, n. 2.

the ancient eastern communities in Palestine itself. Some of these supported Zionism but many kept completely aloof, and waited for the action of the Messiah, an attitude they shared with the older pre-Zionist settlers from Eastern Europe who had come to study and to die in the Holy Land.

The transformation from a unique European experiment to a normal Middle Eastern country was not in any way due to the action either of the European or of the Middle Eastern Jews. It was due entirely to Arab hostility which, factually or officially, made it intolerable for Jews to remain in the countries of which they had been millennial inhabitants. From Morocco to the Yemen or to Kurdistan, Jews moved to Israel, usually with no more property than they could carry, because they could not stay and had no other place to go. In the 1930s it was said that in Haifa a Zionist immigration officer stood at the gangplank of ships coming from Europe, asking each immigrant: " *Kommen sie aus Deutschland oder aus Ueberzeugung?* " Many of these new immigrants have not come out of *Ueberzeugung*. Nevertheless, they have worked a complete transformation in the nature and destiny of the State of Israel.

I have called it, as it is today, a " normal " Middle Eastern country. I do not by that mean that it is just like every other Middle Eastern country, for it is normal that countries in that region should present as many features which are unique to themselves as features which they share with their neighbours. I would emphasise also that it is normalcy of the decade of the 1960s of which I am speaking. As I said earlier, this differs completely from the situation in the 1920s.

This is the position in Israel today. And this is its final paradox. The position was created by the Arabs! They would not accept the establishment of a Jewish State on the basis of its having a unique claim. They insisted that the claims of the natural majority were paramount. And then they create in Israel a State where the natural majority demands a Jewish State. It has never lived anywhere in the world save in the Middle East, and now lives in that part of the Middle East which the Arabs themselves have determined.

It is not surprising that Arabs have not yet recognised the

consequences of their own action. But it would help if the European and American pro-Arab would be more realistic in his—or her—continual emotional propaganda. But we do well to recognise that the situation has been a very considerable surprise to the Israelis themselves, and that they are still somewhat confused about it.

So then let us turn to the picture presented today by the situation of the Jews in Israel. I am not going here to discuss the Arab minority, but I would not leave them without mention as a normal part of a Middle Eastern State. They are an embarrassed minority, because, as long as Israel is surrounded by hostile Arab States, so long do her Arab citizens know that a peculiarly beastly fate would await them were there a sudden attack on Israel, and did they fall prisoners to their brother Arabs. Many dare not show excessive Israeli patriotism, and the Israelis are realists enough not to expect them to. Much of the propaganda alleging that they are treated as second-class citizens ignores these obvious facts. It is part of the paradox of Israel that only the surrounding Arab States can make the Arabs of Israel into first-class Israeli citizens. But, within Israel, their difficult and isolated situation is well understood but little talked of. A high Israeli official once told me: "My chief assistant is an Arab. He often tells me he wants to take the week-end off, and I know he wants to visit relatives in Lebanon, Syria and Jordan. It is quite illegal, but I would do exactly the same in his shoes, and I never raise any objection."

I mentioned that, as a minority, they were normal to a Middle Eastern State. They are, as a matter of fact, rather better off than most such minorities. Christian Copts in Egypt, Kurds in Iraq might well envy the lot of Arabs in Israel.

In considering the effect of the immigration which has created the New Face of Israel, there are four points to bear in mind. At this stage it is easiest to use the names of Ashkenazim to describe Jews from Europe and America, and Sephardim for Jews from the Middle East. The latter are called "Spanish" or "Sephardi" because they include the descendants of Spanish Jews who emigrated to North

Africa and other parts of the Turkish empire after the
expulsion from the Iberian peninsula at the end of the
fifteenth century, and became prominent in communities
which they found already established in countries we now
call Arab. It also distinguishes them from the small communities of Oriental Jews from India and elsewhere.

The first point is that, even among those of Ashkenazi
origin, it is a dwindling number which has any direct European experience. For their own children, even if they were
not born in Israel, Europe is already a remote experience,
and, for the majority who are sabras, it very likely seems
more remote than the time of the Bible and the Maccabees.
One of the main reasons for the form which the Eichmann
trial took in Israel was the conviction of Ben-Gurion and his
generation that they must make their successors understand
what life in an antisemitic Gentile environment had been
like. It is this which explains why so much of the evidence
seemed to bear little on the personal guilt or innocence of
the defendant.

The break between the generations is a common human
phenomenon. It has a peculiar poignancy in this case because
the older generation feel that they have so much to transmit
from their experience and their inheritance, so much that,
forgotten, will bring their descendants into unnecessary
dangers. One senses this anxiety running all through the
public life of Israel as the generation of Weizmann and
Ben-Gurion passes away. Its reluctance to surrender power,
whether in politics, in the Histadrut, or in other realms,
is neither personal ambition nor a contempt for the younger
generation. It is linked with this feeling that changes have
been so rapid and so fundamental that there is danger that
much will be forgotten which ought to be remembered.

Of course, this nobler sentiment has many human frailties
as well. Storrs, whom I have already quoted, remarks of
contacts with the generation of 1900 to 1920 that " their
Kultur was exclusively and arrogantly Russian. Your
smatterings of early Latin and Greek, your little English or
other classics that might survive twenty years marooning
out of Europe, were sounding brass and tinkling cymbals if
you had not also Turgenev, Gogol and, above all,

Dostoevsky—of whom you were reminded that no transla-
tions conveyed the faintest reflection."* When refugees came
from Germany after 1933 they were looked down on by
Jews of Russian origin as *Jäckers*; and Russian Jews
found the moderation of loyal English Jews like Norman
Bentwich or Albert Hyamson to be indistinguishable from
anti-Zionism. They were quite incapable of sympathising
with the difficulties of the British administration, which had,
after all, to remember both that the majority of those it
governed were Arabs, and that it was itself merely part of
a world-wide British civil service, and responsible also to
the League of Nations. It was never easy to be a British
official in the days of Ussishkin or Berl Locker!

For them the integral execution of their interpretation of
the Balfour Declaration and the Mandate was perfectly easy,
and they coupled it with a conviction that they had the
right and duty to create a future Jewish State in the image
of their Eastern European Zionism. A legacy from which
Israel has not yet escaped is the Eastern European democracy based on the party list instead of the identifiable
constituency, a system which proliferates parties, makes
every government a coalition, and allows minorities inexhaustible powers of political blackmail—difficulties all of
which Israel has encountered, and which it needs a giant
like Ben-Gurion to surmount.

The second point to remember is that this whole European—or Eastern European—background and temperament
represents an experience and an history absolutely unknown
to the present majority in Israel. The sabra of European
background may have a vestigial affection for Dostoevsky
—rather like a human appendix, a survival from an earlier
biological condition. But to the Jew from Morocco or Iraq
the whole set of ideas mean absolutely nothing. But this
ignorance is not merely cultural. He has never experienced
emancipation and its subsequent frustrations. He has had
no contact with political responsibility, he has no acquaint-
ance with scientific methods of thought, he did not partake
in the movement for the emancipation of women ; and much

* *Op. cit.* pp. 431, 432.

135

that is commonplace to a European, of whatever species, has no part in his consciousness.

The third point is that his ignorance of European Jewish history is almost as complete as his ignorance of European cultural and political development. Of course, if this began as a book and not a lecture, these generalisations could be supplemented with many qualifications and exceptions ; but as generalisations I believe them to be fair and accurate.

Probably the most important aspect of his ignorance of European Jewish history arises from the very different experience of Jews under Islam and under Christianity. It is a myth, at any rate since the arrival on the Islamic scene of the al-Muwahhid and the al-Murabit by the twelfth century, that Jews have enjoyed their lives as minorities under Islam. That is true of a small minority of rich merchants, though these paid for their wealth with increased insecurity ; but for the immense majority it was a life of dull oppression and humiliation, even though many were skilled craftsmen, like the Yemeni silversmiths. There were never the abominable false accusations, the massacres, the sudden and bitterly unjust expulsions, which were the shame of Christendom ; but a status of grinding poverty and permanent inferiority, exposed to insults and assaults which they dared not reply to, was not the blissful existence propagandists sometimes describe.

The fourth point concerns their position as immigrants in Israel. They were mostly extremely poor, with a high proportion that were quite unskilled by Israeli standards ; and from certain countries they had a high incidence of various diseases. Coupled with these disadvantages was the undoubted fact, over which much ink has been spilled, that some of them tended to be considerably darker than European Jews. The words " colour prejudice " rise easily to the lips in controversy, but the truth is probably akin to the famous remark of that remarkable Yorkshireman, W. R. Maltby, when he was asked whether Methodists could dance. He replied: " Some can and some can't." So, I have no doubt, some European Jews exhibit colour prejudice and some don't. But I am sure it has no public or communal endorsement, and I doubt its being a serious aspect of the problem of the large Sephardi immigration of recent years.

There are two other statements which seem to be commonly made and to need examination. One is that all that the present holders of power in Israel think of is turning these Sephardim into imitation Ashkenazim ; and the other is the opposite, that there are two definite cultures in Israel, a Western and an Eastern one, and that this Eastern one is distinct and must be preserved. I recognise that the inevitable complexity of any educational or social problem in Israel is capable of causing the maximum degree of personal and communal infuriation ; but I doubt whether either of these statements covers a real problem.

The real issue is best seen by examining Israel as a normal Middle Eastern country, while remembering that there are not two cultures in Israel but a multiplicity of backgrounds, each with its cultural attachments. A recent group of South American immigrants, for example, created new diversity ; the possible arrival of Jews from the Soviet Union, who have known nothing but the Marxist interpretation of history, would create another set of problems, and so on. But all this can be seen within the general Middle Eastern pattern, which has nothing to do with West or East.

A secular scientific outlook on life is no longer a *Western* outlook. It is the universal outlook of those who have received even the beginnings of some form of public education. It is inescapable. It poses the same problem to Nasser's Minister of Education as it does Eshkol's, because it is an educational discipline quite foreign to the majority in both countries. But it has to be pressed upon the general population because both countries need a sufficiency of workers who can be trusted with a modern plant, whether in field or factory, army or merchant marine. And from the secondary stage such an education creates the cadres of power which are replacing all forms of hereditary dignity.

The other side of the medal is also universal. Such an education creates of itself no roots, and so makes no contribution to national stability. Here the achievement of Nasser appears to be in striking contrast to those of his political contemporaries in Syria or Iraq, who are still witnessing the confusion of continuous seizures of power by successive leaders from the new educated class. But Nasser's government appears stable only by contrast. It is still dangerously fragile, because it is as true of Egypt as it is of all other countries of the Middle East that the leading products of such an education are opportunists when it comes to the prizes which personal ambition can win in the gambles of politics or the search for wealth.

The situation is cushioned in Europe, or in such countries as the United States, by the gradual modernisation and adaptation of once universally accepted roots whether in religion, in social status, or in hereditary monarchies and aristocracies. In the Middle East Israel, in common with its Arab neighbours, has a completely unreformed and unadapted religion in stark contrast and opposition to the contemporary secularism. The only difference is that in Israel's case it is Judaism, in that of Egypt, Syria or Iraq, Islam. And there at once is a most penetrating difference.

It is rightly called " penetrating," because for both Israel and its Arab neighbours the traditional pattern of religion provides, at present, a lonely element of stability and common mutual loyalty. The theological dogmas of the religion in question may have become completely unreal for most of the educated population, but they still see in it a valued social cohesive force to which is offered more than purely formal acceptance. The statement made of the Marxist Mapam during the war with the Arab States that, though they had abolished God *de jure,* they recognised Him *de facto* is more than an amiable witticism.

In Israel it is this lonely eminence of religion which provides the final answer to those who speak of the danger of two cultures, one Ashkenazi, one Sephardi. From one point of view Israel is, and always will be, a land of many cultures; but from another Israel is basically a land of only one culture, because there is only one Judaism, only one Bible, one Talmud, one historic tradition, even if it has widened out in modern times like the estuary of a great river with many channels and islands.

This is not perhaps the age in which the theological issues involved, fundamental as they are, will be resolved for

either Judaism or Islam. It is an age which thinks theologically with difficulty; and if this makes the majority
unusually sceptical and self-assertive, it naturally makes
the devout minority exceptionally determined to surrender
no iota of their traditional inheritance. The Moslem
Brotherhood is as much a thorn in the flesh of Nasser as the
Neturei Karta in the flesh of Eshkol.

What, on the surface, is more tragic is the lack of creative
leadership on the part of the spokesmen of either religion,
the *Ulema* on one side, the Chief Rabbinates on the other.
They have, so far as I have seen, never stepped beyond the
benign platitude in the contemplation of any actual twentieth-
century issue—an attitude which I must say with regret is
completely shared by the Archbishops of the Anglican
Church or the deliberations of the World Council of
Churches. But if we study the contemporary secular societies
which have their roots in Judaism and in Islam, we find
that, in fact, religion has been and is still a very potent
influence, both on the positive and on the negative sides.

At the very foundation of our study we have the contrast
that Islam is a religion of the city and the desert. It has a
historical contempt for the agriculturist. Judaism, in spite
of the long separation of the majority of the people from the
Promised Land or land ownership elsewhere, has never lost
its basic attachment to the actual physical reality of land
and soil. That modern practical Zionism began with the
agricultural pioneer is no accident; and it is only by the
Jewish attachment to the soil that Israeli politics can undertake such projects as the cultivation of the Negev, or the
creation in the desert of cities such as Arad. Under Islam
the individual cultivator is, of course, as much attached to
his own lot as any smallholder, but the state of physical
desolation of all Arab countries at the beginning of modern
reclamation is sufficient evidence of the contempt for the
soil of a Moslem State. Some among you will probably
remember the drive from Jerusalem to Jenin by Nablus in
Mandatory days, and the single great pine tree which was
the only tree (apart from olives and fruit trees) which one
saw on the whole journey. The Moslem Turks rivalled the
Beduin as destroyers of trees, and the fertility which goes

with them. Manfred Halpern, in the book already quoted, says that " Orthodox Islam is an urban religion with an urban way of life, and hardly any Moslem in literature or song, by word or deed, admires the peasant's style of life ; not even the peasant does so."*

On the other hand, a Moslem country can rely on the extraordinary patience of its peasants, a patience often indistinguishable from complete fatalism, but with a deep realism within it. Nasser is given time for his projects which would be vociferously denied to any Israeli government. The whole section of Halpern which deals with the peasant in the contemporary Islamic world is well worth reading.

The peasant has need of this patience because of another characteristic which brings Islam into sharp contrast with Judaism. I quote again from Halpern : " Solicitude for the welfare of his subjects as a whole was required neither by the *Shari'a* nor by sultanic tradition."§ It has been the perpetual misfortune of Islam, a misfortune which weighs heavily on a modern Moslem ruler with his need to create a decentralised welfare State, that many of his predecessors built magnificent works of piety and charity, hospitals, schools, schemes of irrigation, and so on ; but he can fall back on no tradition of honest administration by which these benefactions have been preserved after their creator has died. This is in equally sharp contrast with the perpetual rabbinic insistence on social responsibility, an insistence which has flowered equally in the great Jewish charities, such as the " Joint," or in the immense funds which are contributed to the upbuilding of Israel by the communities of the diaspora.

In this field we have, in fact, an absorbing paradox of likeness and unlikeness. Israel is typically Middle Eastern in the fact that all great projects have to rely on State capital, and that the State capital has to come from outside. In Egypt it comes by the immense loans by which the U.S.A. and the U.S.S.R. do battle for predominance of influence. Without them Nasser could do little. In other countries it comes from equally large foreign payments for oil. In Israel

* *Op. cit.* p. 89.

§ *Op. cit.* p. 13.

the proportion which comes from international loans is undoubtedly considerable; but the immense sums contributed as gifts by Jews living elsewhere have no parallel in any Moslem country. Even the Arab refugees have to be supported by international charity. Had I time I would draw the parallels and contrasts involved also in the upbuilding of the Middle East by Western expertise— foreign experts in Egypt or Iraq, European settlers in Israel.

Striking as these differences are, they are still variants of a single monotheistic tradition which has its roots in the Middle East, roots which Christianity also shares. In the past there have been times of borrowing between all the Monotheisms. Each still bears marks of the influences of the others during some century or other of their common existence. There is also a certain basic pattern reflected in the adjective " ethical " which characterises the three Monotheisms. The differences which have been illustrated between Judaism and Islam do not cancel out the similarities, though they make mutual influence almost impossible when there is such political hostility as there is at present. That hostility also brings those who ought to be the ministers of reconciliation into the forefront of hostility. The Arabic-speaking Israelis are often the bitterest enemies of the Arab, because in so many cases their coming to Israel was involuntary, and they came stripped of most or all of their material possessions.

We should, however, remember that the Arab, though he is capable of keeping up a quarrel for centuries, is also capable of accepting an act of reconciliation. What one may call the European phase of the rebuilding of Israel was carried out against continuous Arab protest and opposition, which were as justified from the Arab standpoint as were the Declaration and the National Home from the Jewish. It would do no harm to acknowledge that fact, now that Israel is, by Arab action, a truly Middle Eastern country. The War of Independence was a war in which all the right and all the heroism, like all the suffering, were not on one side only. There were Arabs who fled in panic; there were Arabs who were induced by their leaders to flee; but there were Arabs who were driven out by the Israeli army. Such differences are a universal fact of war which it is foolish for Israelis to deny. At present violent hostility to Israel is a useful paste with which to cover the cracks of Arab division. The opposite would be equally true. Friendship with Israel, and mutual service between Israel and her neighbours, would remove many of the causes of friction. The act of reconciliation, well established in Arab tradition, would be an act from which all alike would profit.

The whole Middle East has suffered enough from the obscurantism of its traditionalists. It is a pity if *amour propre* prevents it from also taking advantage of a tradition which is both realist and effective—the act of reconciliation based on recognition that one's own past is not impeccable.

9

ISRAEL AND THE DIASPORA

THERE IS A verse in the nineteenth chapter of Exodus which expresses in a nutshell the two ideas which have determined the whole of Jewish history and given it its peculiar character. As the Israelites approached Mount Sinai they received from the lips of Moses this message which had been delivered to him on the Mount: "If ye will obey My voice indeed and keep My covenant, then ye shall be a peculiar treasure to Me above all people: for all the earth is Mine. And ye shall be unto Me a kingdom of priests and a holy nation." In these few sentences are asserted both the universalism which is inherent in any monotheistic religion, and the particularism, the conviction of a special function, which lies at the root of the will of any people to separate survival. "All the earth is Mine" is a clear declaration that the God of Israel is likewise God of all other nations. "Ye shall be a peculiar treasure . . . a nation of priests" becomes, indeed, within that framework a responsibility more than a privilege, but it is also the assertion of a Divine justification for separate survival. It is on the tension between this universalism and this separatism that Jewish history is built: and both are essential for its development, its health and, indeed, its continued existence.

Again and again the Hebrew prophets insist that the God of Israel is the God of the whole earth. And with them this is no philosophic abstraction but the basis of ethical judgements and of political actions. Within a few centuries of the time of Eli, when the ark of God was taken into battle in order to force the Almighty to preserve His people from final defeat by the enemies who had already proved too

143

strong for them, Amos is challenging them with a question:
" Are ye not as children of the Ethiopians unto me, O
children of Israel ? saith the Lord. Have not I brought up
Israel out of the land of Egypt, and the Philistines from
Caphtor, and the Syrians from Kir ? " (Amos ix, 7). He makes
it equally clear that the call to be a nation of priests is in
sober reality a responsibility and no automatically valid
privilege when he utters the searing denunciation:
" You only have I known of all the families on the earth:
therefore I will punish you for all your iniquities."
(Amos ix, 2).

Even if we reject religious orthodoxy, it makes no difference to the statement that the history of the Jews rests
on the tension between universalism and separatism. The
most complete secularist can find no other foundations on
which that history is built. He may speak of universalism in
philosophic rather than theistic terms ; he may speak of
" folk-ways " instead of Torah. But the foundations remain
the same ; and the explanation of subsequent Jewish
history is unchanged.

It is the presence of these two ideas which explains how
the Jews came to think of all history as a process, working
from a creation to a culmination. Their universalism made
them see one moral order and one purpose embracing all
peoples and the whole of history. Their own reverses and
distresses forced them to expect a development within
history to a culmination in which the righteousness of God
would be vindicated, and history achieve a Divinely fore-
ordained climax. This long view enabled them to adjust
their conception of themselves as a chosen people to a
realistic estimate of their place among the nations, and to
view the world outside their frontiers with a singular lack
of imperialism or condescension. Of course they had their
chauvinists, but no other people treasured as a Divinely
inspired record such candid judgements on themselves and
their rulers. Their history books—and they regarded them
as sacred books—dismissed the greatest conquerors among
their rulers with the cold verdict that " they did evil in the
sight of the Lord." So, for example, is Jeroboam II condemned (II Kings xiv, 24), and it needed the research of

modern Christian historians to discover the greatness of the realm which he conquered and administered. Equally no other people accepted as sacred writ such estimates of their place in the world as that, probably from an unknown post-exilic prophet, in the nineteenth chapter of Isaiah:

" In that day shall there be a highway out of Egypt to Assyria, and the Assyrian shall come into Egypt, and the Egyptian into Assyria, and the Egyptians shall serve with the Assyrians. .In that day shall Israel be the third with Egypt and with Assyria, even a blessing in the midst of the land: whom the Lord of hosts shall bless, saying, Blessed be Egypt My people, and Assyria the work of My hands, and Israel Mine inheritance" (Isaiah xix, 23, 24, 25).

Even more striking, perhaps, are the words of the great exilic prophet, the Deutero-Isaiah himself, when he speaks of Cyrus as the shepherd, an anointed of God (Isaiah xliv, 28 ; xlv, 1).

From the date of the Babylonian exile onwards, the story of the Jewish people becomes the story of an Israel and a diaspora ; and this tension between universalism and separatism becomes the key by which their mutual relationships can be interpreted, and the relations between the Jewish story and the story of the nations and peoples among whom they lived, illuminated. On the one hand we have the nostalgia of Psalm 137, recalling the sorrows of exile and proclaiming that:

" If I forget thee, O Jerusalem,
Let my right hand forget her cunning,"

and we are reminded that at no time, from then onwards, did any Jewish community contemplate any alternative permanent home to that originally established in the Promised Land. But, on the other hand, life in Babylon was not merely a pale replica of life in the Holy Land. It was autonomous and creative ; and it is from the religious initiative of the exiles that came the foundations on which rabbinic Judaism itself was subsequently reared. For the institution of the Synagogue, with its ideal of congregational worship and an educated laity, probably dates from the

145

Babylonian exile ; and the unique use of the written history and law of the nation as the medium of religious activity has the same origin.

That it is the Babylonian, and not the earlier exile, which occupies this important place in the story is confirmed by the strange history of the Jews of Kai-feng Fu in China. Inscriptions which have been deciphered in their temple show that they knew nothing of the Mediterranean origin of the Jewish people, of a Promised Land to which they should return, or of the synagogue as a centre of congregational worship. But their ancestry has been traced to the northern exile of the eighth century, whatever later strains may have subsequently joined them.*

It is from the Babylonian exile that Jewish history begins to manifest characteristics which compel us to call it unique ; and at the centre of this uniqueness is the complicated interplay between the homeland and the dispersed communities, and between these two together and the non-Jewish world surrounding them. But the full picture is not revealed at once. What we see from this chapter of the story is, first, the real autonomy of diaspora life, exposed to the influences of its situation and its environment ; and, secondly, the ability of diaspora experience to modify and develop growth in the homeland.

The Jewish community in Babylon developed religious forms which were appropriate to itself, and which were unknown in the Holy Land. It settled down, and, indeed, founded a community which has lasted more than two thousand years ; yet it never thought of severing its ties with the Promised Land, to which many of its members returned when they had the opportunity. But it felt free to develop in its own manner its religious inheritance ; and those Jews who returned in the days of Ezra and Nehemiah brought with them religious forms which they had evolved in exile. Though they rebuilt the Temple, they retained the synagogue. The Babylonian community was also open to influences from its Gentile environment ; and those who returned brought into Jewish religious development certain

* See A. H. Godbey, *The Lost Tribes a Myth*, pp. 391ff.

elements which had been culled from their Mesopotamian and Persian neighbours, an angelology, and a gnosticism which appear in later biblical writings, in apocalyptic literature and in Cabalism.

Here, then, is the first example of the main lines of the pattern we shall be able to trace in all subsequent history. A diaspora community shows itself, on the one hand, conscious of its " exile " and its need to " return " to the homeland. But, on the other, it regards itself as autonomous, it creates its own religious forms ; and it accepts influences from its non-Jewish environment. To what extent the Babylonian Jews also influenced their environment we do not know. For that part of the pattern we must wait for later periods where our knowledge is more extensive.

From the return we see another part of the pattern. The new community of Jerusalem does not discard its exilic experience, but incorporates it into the total experience of the people, and makes it a permanent part of the Jewish inheritance.

The creative interdependence between the Holy Land and the diaspora reached its full stature, and the full complexity of the tension between universalism and separatism was revealed, in the period which begins with Greek influence some centuries after the return and continues until the ghetto walls close in on the Jewish people, first within Christendom, then within Islam. This period of more than a thousand years was the most continuously brilliant and dynamic in Jewish history, and was constantly productive of new experience.

The two books of the Bible most intimately connected with the returned community are the Psalter and the Book of Proverbs, the first example of the Wisdom Literature. Both are intensely Jewish. The Psalter, in spite of the presence of many earlier psalms, has been called the hymn book of the Second Temple ; and the collection of Proverbs in the book of that name stems directly from the moral teaching of the prophets, and the concern of the Law with all aspects of everyday life. But both are of universal significance. The psalms have been taken as a unique book of devotion by Christians of all centuries and denominations,

147

and Jewish proverbs have passed into the sayings of all peoples. The Book of Proverbs also, by its elevation of wisdom as the supreme objective of man, opened the door to the influence of Greek philosophic thought, most fully exploited in Alexandria.

Welcoming without reserve the challenge of the Hellenistic world which surrounded it, the Jewry of Alexandria sought to express the essence and experience of Judaism in the language and dress of Hellenistic philosophy. The Bible itself was translated into Greek. The largely unformulated theology which satisfied the Semitic mind was tailored and systematised to fit into the precise categories of Greek thought. Wisdom was exalted as the Divine agent in creation, and thus was found a theistic basis for philosophical speculation. The Jewish way of life, expressed in Torah, was rationalised and allegorised to smooth away its harsh imperatives and so make it comprehensible and attractive to the eclectic and often superficial culture of later Hellenism. But the men who did these things did not think of themselves as divorced from their brethren of the Holy Land. They were still part of Israel. The wisdom of which they spoke demanded of them " the fear of the Lord." They still attended the feasts at Jerusalem. They had their synagogues and communities within the Holy City. This time, however, the result was not what it had been when the exiles from Babylon brought back their religious forms to Jerusalem. For the religious leaders of the Holy Land decisively rejected this Judaism in Hellenic dress, condemning it as an invitation to desert the essentials needed for Jewish survival. From one standpoint they were undoubtedly right. For the work of Alexandrian Jewry immensely facilitated the first instance of what recurs throughout Jewish history: the final hiving off of a substantial number of individual Jews from the mother community. The Greek translation of the Bible, and the theology of Alexandria, provided essential elements out of which the Christian Church grew to be a world community.

Such events are with difficulty accepted by Jewish historians and thinkers as being inescapable and authentic productions of the basic universalism which is fundamental to Jewish history. The tendency has been to denigrate, to belittle and to condemn those trends within Jewry which have led to such results. But my purpose is not to pass judgements of value, but to record the facts ; and in the totality of the Jewish story such things have happened too often for them to be dismissed as either peripheral or accidental. Christianity, Islam, Marxian and European Socialism, all, in their origins at least, have their place within, not outside, the story of the Jewish contribution to world society ; and the part played by Jews in the development of Humanism merits also special consideration. In each case we find the inescapable consequences of an element in Jewish experience which cannot be excised without destroying the whole, and — even more — without destroying the moral foundations for the continuation of that other pillar on which the story rests, the separate survival of Jewry. Moreover, the universalism of Jewish monotheism should invite Jews themselves to examine these successive developments of the human spirit from the standpoint, not of their effect on the Jews, but of their effect on the pilgrimage of humanity. And from that standpoint they can with difficulty be condemned.

Gentile Christianity took to itself basic elements which were authentically and honourably Jewish. It is now recognised, even by conservative Christian theologians, that Jesus of Nazareth lived and died within the fold of Judaism. It has been shown by scholars such as W. D. Davies that Paul's roots were deep within rabbinic Judaism. With the subsequent story I am not here concerned. It is enough to claim that the universal religion of Christianity has its roots in the healthy heart, not in some diseased extremity, of Jewish experience.

This feature also will recur. It is a healthy, not a weak or diseased Judaism which is productive of such an outflow into the non-Jewish world. In this case, the period which witnessed the rise and separation of Christianity witnessed also the intensive spiritual and intellectual activity which ensured the continuance of Jewish history and the Jewish religion into that long period when heart and diaspora were geographically to be found in the same scattered Jewish

F

communities, and when the Holy Land itself contained an ever-diminishing community, increasingly dependent on the diaspora for its physical and spiritual survival.

Rabbinic Judaism is too often judged by the evidence offered by contemporary orthodoxy. This is unfair: for the orthodoxy of the last few centuries, whether it be accepted or condemned, is something which is the product of centuries of persecution, humiliation and restriction, and is both more narrow and more rigid than the Judaism which emerged in the first centuries of the common era from the furnaces of national defeat and the attractions of an environing paganism. The Judaism which was then developed was well defined, coherent and unified. The fence which was created around Jewish life was high, and the openings in it were narrow. But no force maintained its structure. There was no attempt to create a central authority which could condemn or control any community which opened itself too sympathetically to influences from without. And the religious urge and discipline which had the task of maintaining the fence was positive, not negative. Only in times of stress was the attitude to the outside world unrelievedly hostile and contemptuous. The law of the land wherever Jews lived was law for Jews. The righteous of all nations would inherit the world to come. The God of Israel was still God of all the earth. The only compelling force which retained Jewish separate existence was that, in spite of hostility or persecution from without, it was good to be a Jew.

In estimating the courage and psychological penetration of those who created so intimate a basis for survival, we have to remember that Jews were exposed, from China to the Atlantic, to the seductions of all the great civilisations of the ancient and medieval world. They could measure their Jewish values against the ideas of Lao Tse and Confucius; against the philosophy of Buddhism, and the religious literature of Hinduism; against Zoroastrianism and the admirable ethics of the Parsees; against all forms of Islam, and the profound philosophical, scientific and cultural schools of the Islamic East, or of the western caliphate in Spain; against Eastern and Byzantine Christian theology and mysticism, as well as against the new civilisation of Europe, with the intellectual vigour of scholastic theology, with the ethical codes of its commercial gilds, and with the spirit of adventure which brought it gradually into the fore-front of the culture and civilisation of the world. All these temptations surrounded the Jewish community, scattered, without any central authority, through all the continents ; and everywhere and at all times the path was open for a Jew, or a Jewish community, to enter into the fold of the majority. Many individual Jews did so, and their passage must sometimes have entailed the dying out of a Jewish community, for example in Islamic Palestine. But there is no record, I believe, of any Jewish community, by a deliber-ate act, quitting the Jewish fold during these long centuries of trial.

There is, however, a second "hiving off" of individual Jews with the emergence of Islam. Judaism was not so exclusively the parent of this new monotheism as it had been when Christianity was born ; for Eastern Christians had influenced Mohammed as well as Eastern Jews ; and men of Christian as well as of Jewish origin were among the earliest thinkers and administrators within the Arab empire. More-over, the Judaism of the seventh century was more compact and unified than that of the first. Nevertheless there must have been many voluntary conversions to the new religion before the period in which economic and political motives led to a desertion of their ancient faith among the adherents of both the older monotheisms. The Moslem inhabitants of those portions of the Islamic world which lie within the Roman borders must, in the majority of cases, be descended from Jewish or Christian ancestors.

The passage of Jews to Islam differs from the previous passage of Jews to Christianity in this important respect, that the Judaism of the first century contained many varieties, of which the Judeo-Christian sect or " denomina-tion " could remain one for more than half a century without being ejected from the Jewish fold. This was not possible in the seventh century. Here was a clear " either—or," even though in later days Jews were sometimes able to combine a formal recognition of Islam which satisfied the Moslem authorities with continued loyalty to the Jewish religion. But this was not a conversion or "hiving off," but merely an early form of Marranism. Nevertheless, this passage of Jews to Islam, like the earlier passage to Christianity, is, to the historian, but another example of the consequences of the universalism inherent in Judaism ; and, on this occasion, it allows of an interesting, if unexpected, conclusion about the Jewish story. On the surface it might be thought that it was the separatism, the fence about the law, which prevented more such conversions. But this is not true. It is its universalism which, as has already been said, preserved Judaism against the temptations, social as well as religious, which the new monotheism offered. For what neither Islam nor Christianity had been able to prove to the overwhelming majority of Jews was that their religion was visibly inferior in its ethics and way of life to the new rival. Jewish moral values were just as universal in their significance and validity. It is likewise true that the complex pattern involved in the separatism operated not merely to preserve the community, but also to facilitate and justify the desertion of the Jewish fold.

The Christian Peter was not the only Jew who ever complained that the prescriptions of the Law were "a yoke upon the neck which neither our fathers nor we were able to bear." (Acts xv, 10.) And this complaint might be heard from the philosopher or mystic as well as from the *Am-haaretz*. As always, universalism and separatism are inextricably interwoven into every page of Jewish history.

From the time of the defeat of Bar Kochba, the diaspora was entrusted with the heart of Israel. Each community lived both in exile and within the homeland, now become portable. And the Judaism which was the basis and justification of their survival was handed to them, not as a precious inheritance to be maintained intact, but as a living plant, full of sap, for whose further growth they were responsible. We are apt to overlook the remarkable nature of this transmission. Elsewhere religious minorities, exposed to the temptations of a foreign environment indifferent or hostile to the faith which they profess, have shown their main qualities in a rigid conservatism and an intolerance of that environment. We justify the harshness of the covenanting Scot of the seventeenth and eighteenth centuries on such a basis. We justify the fossilisation of Christian forms in the Eastern churches by pointing to the hostile environment of Islam. Indeed, it is on this same basis that we explain the Pharisaic opposition to Jesus of Nazareth. But rabbinic Judaism *grew* in exile ; it developed new forms under these unfavourable conditions ; and it showed itself willing both to accept foreign influences and to enter into intimate relations with members of the majority. It was not until it had passed through a millennium of restriction, denigration and persecution that it began to become rigid, reactionary and unwilling to change.

It often seems that Jews themselves believe that Judaism has never been a missionary religion, and that Jews have neither sought to influence their neighbours, nor been willing to receive influences from them. There is lttle historical evidence for this belief. It is true that direct conversion became so dangerous as to be practically impossible within both Christendom and Islam. But the mutual influences went on. The most horrible and violent denunciations of Judaism to be found in the writings of a Christian theologian are contained in eight sermons delivered by John Chrysostom in Antioch in the fourth century. The reason for his venom lay in the friendly relations the Christian congregation maintained with the Jews, and the influences which the Jews exercised on their thinking and actions. When in Carolingian France we have similar denunciations from Agobard, Archbishop of Lyons, the reason is the same. And, indeed, these Gallic Jews seem to have gone further, and to have enjoyed poking fun at the superstitions and theological complications of Christian belief. Even during the Middle Ages, in that epoch of hatred, fear and persecution, there were innumerable examples of the fearlessness with which Jews would explain their beliefs to any Christian who would listen, and would indulge in theological argument with any Christian rash enough to give them an opening. They freely translated Greek and Moslem works for medieval Christian scholars, and made their own theologians available to them. Thomas Aquinas, for example,

153

was familiar with the works of Maimonides, and other Christians were familiar with Rashi. When asked to explain their Hebrew Bible to commentators who had discovered the weaknesses in the Latin Vulgate used by the Church, they freely did so ; and there was even a project for making a new translation from the Hebrew, which could only have been done with their help. In controversies they went as far as prudence permitted, or even further, as Nachmanides discovered when he retired hastily to Jerusalem after winning a public argument in Barcelona.

Many centuries of relationship with Christendom show Jews willing to influence Christians. But they show few examples of successful influences in the opposite direction, for Christianity sought, not to influence, but to convert by denigrating the faith the Jews already held. But that Judaism was willing to be influenced as well as to influence, is shown by the parallel history of relations with Islam. It is in relations with the Fatimite society in Egypt and the western caliphate in Spain that Judaism showed its greatest fearlessness. The Hellenism which had been rejected in the days of Alexandria was freely accepted in the centuries between Saadia Gaon and Gersonides. Maimonides was at once a commentator on the Talmud and a guide to the perplexed orthodox, and a bold adventurer into the realms of Aristotelian-Arabic philosophy. The science and medicine of Greece, the romantic poetry of the Arabs, their mathematics and astronomy, were all accepted with enthusiasm, and incorporated into Jewish life.

It is time to return to the land of Israel. It is not merely of importance that throughout the period under discussion there remained always the Messianic hope of a return at some distant date to the land promised to their fathers. The contemporary Jewish population which had remained, or had returned, to the land plays a special role in the story. Physically the Jewry of Israel was of little importance in the total picture from, say, the third century of the common era to the nineteenth. Intellectually it could not raise up men to compare with the giants of Fustat, the western caliphate or the Europe of Gershom of Mainz, Rashi, or his successors. The role which the land plays in the story is more curious ;

and gives an unexpectedly solid historical basis to the claim, made often by modern Zionists who are in no sense themselves religious, that there is a mystical and regenerative value in the land itself and that contact with it brings new strength to Jewish life.

It is in the land of Israel, defeated, half depopulated, robbed of almost every measure of self-government and infinitely less secure or prosperous than, for example, the Jewry of Alexandria, that the whole fascinating structure of rabbinic Judaism, whose operations we have been discussing in the previous pages, was first brought to birth. Humanly speaking it is impossible to believe that the Galilean Rabbis who elaborated its complex pattern of social and individual discipline could have dreamed of the stresses which it would have to meet, or the dangers which it would have to overcome if Jewry was to survive. Of many creative periods in history the verdict is uttered that " they builded better than they knew." Of none could it be truer than of those Galileans who, for a century before Judah the Prince, produced the material of the Mishna and laid the foundations for its further development in the great schools and academies of Babylon.

When those schools began to decline, and almost all the basic work of commenting on the Mishna had been completed in the Babylonian Talmud, it was again in obscure corners of Galilee that a task which had been forgotten or ignored in Babylon was undertaken. The whole work of preserving and fixing the actual text of Torah was undertaken by the Massoretes of Tiberias. Without them the work of Rashi and his school could, with difficulty, have been undertaken ; and without the work of Rashi and his successors the Christian development of study of the Hebrew original behind the Latin Vulgate would have been practically impossible. And that study, in its turn, played an important part in the biblical emphasis of the Christian Reformers of the sixteenth century. From Rashi through the scholars of the Victorine order to Nicholas of Lyra, and from Nicholas of Lyra to Martin Luther, the line is direct.

But that is not the only significance of the Land during

this period. For an obscure century, when the sceptre was falling from Babylon and Jews of Spain and Egypt were only beginning to assume their prominence, the last heirs of the Babylonian academies lived a shadowy life, first in Jerusalem then in Galilee, till they disappear at the beginning of the Crusades in Damascus. It was but a formal holding of the sceptre which fell to the Land in a period of no great scholars. But it has its place in the total picture.

At the end of the period which has been reviewed its significance and uniqueness become much more evident. When Islam had sunk into stagnation, and its Jewries with it, and when medieval life in Europe had suffered the final expulsion from the Iberian peninsula at the end of the fifteenth century, it was in Safed that almost simultaneously Joseph Caro gave new coherence to orthodoxy in his *Shulchan Aruch,* and Isaac Luria a new popularity to mysticism in his cabbalistic studies. The Mithnaggedim and the Chasidim from Eastern Europe who were to dominate Jewish life during the succeeding centuries both owe an incalculable debt to that Galilean hilltown.

Up to this point the story has been mainly concerned with religion, and with mutual influences in the field of religion and culture. But the Jews are not merely members of a religious denomination. They are a people ; and the same pattern is repeated whenever conditions made it possible, in the economic and, finally, in the political sphere, though the latter became realistic only with emancipation. Such influences on the political life of the nations as could be called Jewish in previous centuries came from the Christian use of the Old Testament without the mediation of contemporary Jewish thought.

In the ancient world there was no particular economic activity which could be called Jewish. Jews were not conspicuous as financiers, though there were rich Jews who, like other rich men, lent money. They were not the most prominent traders, but shared the caravan routes with Syrians, Byzantines, and others. They cultivated the soil, where they had access to it, but most of them were artisans dispersed in many different trades.

Any specialised experience in the economic field began

in the Middle Ages; and it follows closely the religious pattern traced in previous pages. It shows Jewish communities readily adventuring into new fields opened to them by their relations with their Gentile environment, and absorbing the consequent experience into their Jewish heritage. In the Middle Ages Jews were the private property of princes; and they were employed by them as sponges, to feed money into the princely treasuries by making loans to the prince's subjects. Now the interesting points about the medieval Jewish money-lenders are these: first that the conditions of their money-lending were worked out by their Rabbis, and moneylending was made an honest business, a fact which medieval man was quick to recognise in his preference for Jewish over Christian lenders; and secondly, that they left a permanent mark on European economic history by their innovations, especially the mortgage on property. There is little evidence of their trying to live apart from their Christian neighbours, or unaffected by contemporary conditions and opportunities, except in those religious matters where separation was inevitable. They lent money to churches, farmers and merchants indifferently; and, though their basic status was imposed on them by their fundamental rightlessness, they were quick to adapt it to make a tolerable life for themselves. As their activities diminished in Western Europe, through the increasing severity of princely persecution and popular hostility, they are found busily creating an appropriate economy for the emerging kingdom of Poland, both in the field of public revenues, and of commercial enterprise.

In the post-medieval period the pattern is repeated. In the new markets opened to European commerce by the discoveries of the sixteenth century, and by improvements in the art of navigation, Jews took a full part, and again provided valuable assets both for themselves and for their non-Jewish neighbours. They evolved nautical instruments, which all sailors came to use; they created conditions for the Levant trade from which others also profited; they crossed the Atlantic, and they brought new prosperity to the Atlantic ports of Europe, whether in Germany, Holland, England or France. In the eighteenth century the famous

Court Jews who were to be found in almost every petty
court of the innumerable principalities which made up the
Germany of that day played an even more striking role.
They laid many of the foundations of the nineteenth-century
German economy by their rescue of revenues and productive
monopolies from a morass of medieval futility and aristo-
cratic corruption or incompetence.

In the general development of modern capitalism,
whether in the highly productive countries of Western
Europe, or in the primitive economies of Eastern Europe
and the Balkans, they continuously played a role which
demanded initiative, imagination and audacity, and which
left a profound mark on the economy of the countries in
which they worked. Railways, shipping and mines owed as
much to them as manufacturing or retail trade. Towards the
end of the nineteenth century they carried the experience
which they had thus gained across the Atlantic, and played
an equally interesting part in the unfolding economies of
the United States and Canada. There are, of course, several
standpoints from which this fascinating story can be
assessed. To a Jewish student the extraordinary ingratitude
of the nations whom his people had benefited — Russia,
Germany, Austria-Hungary, Poland and Rumania in particular—will be in the forefront of the picture. To a socialist,
the exploitations of the capitalist entrepreneur will loom
larger than the benefits that, at that stage of economic
development, capitalism secured. And so on. But to the
historian it is an essential part of Jewish history ; and here
I am only concerned with one thing : the consistency of
this part of the story with the record already discussed.
It is moreover in accordance with that attitude to note that
these diaspora developments were of great importance to
the Jews themselves. Had it not been for the wealth which
this intense economic activity brought to the Jewry of the
twentieth century, the tragedies of modern Jewish history
would have been even greater. For it has been only by
Jewish money, collected and poured out by such organisations as the Joint Distribution Committee, the Central
British Fund, the Keren Kayemeth and many others, that
tens, indeed hundreds of thousands, of Jews were saved

from the effects of modern antisemitism even before the coming of the Nazis.

In other words, in economics as well as in religion, the diaspora was an essential part of Jewry, was continually exercising an influence on its non-Jewish environment, and was continually drawing from its contacts with that environment experiences which developed and enriched Jewish life.

The final section of the whole picture concerns the Jews as citizens. It is but a small section; for Jews were only admitted to citizenship in modern times and, even then, it was only a minority within Jewry which was ever able to profit from genuine citizenship. The majority, living before the Nazi massacres in Eastern Europe, never knew what real citizenship was. Yet though the story concerns only a small section of the Jewish people, and that for scarcely a century, it is an extremely important part of the whole picture. For the Jewish citizens of the Western democracies had stepped straight out of almost medieval conditions into modern life; and since many of them, especially after 1881, were actually born in the ghettoes of eastern Europe, they did not even pass the formative years of childhood in the environment on which they were to leave so great a mark. They stepped into the modern atmosphere of free thought and widespread agnosticism from an orthodoxy which almost entirely ignored the modern world.

Yet these men and women provide a fascinating example of the pattern which has already been established. They brought into the Western world traditions and ways of thinking which were authentic expressions of the universalism which is inherent in all Jewish history, while they shed, with astonishing rapidity, the forms which separatism had assumed after centuries of oppression and narrow opportunities. They were passionately concerned with justice, with intellectual initiative, and with mutual responsibility—and these were all values which they had learned and discerned through the veil of an orthodoxy most of them discarded.

At the time when modern antisemitism made such a literature desirable, there was almost a plethora of books

159

dealing with the contributions to civilisation which these
Jews made in every walk of life. For there were few fields
in which the nations who granted their Jewish subjects full
citizenship did not profit from the gift. The number of
political leaders, social reformers, scientists, scholars, patrons
of art and music who were drawn from the ranks of Jewry
is astounding ; their names form an inevitable part of any
modern history. It is likewise true that they drew from their
new experience much advantage for their own people. The
work of individual philanthropists was supplemented by
such great organisations as the Alliance Israélite Universelle,
the Anglo-Jewish Association, the American Jewish Committee and Congress, the World Jewish Congress,
the Joint Distribution Committee, as well as what
came to be the most far-reaching of them all, the World
Zionist Organisation. All of them drew on the experience
of emancipation ; all of them poured knowledge gained in
the Gentile environment into the Jewish pool.

The modern world has seen also a repetition of what had
happened previously with Christianity and Islam. There was
a steady hiving off of individual Jews, political leaders
and scholars, trade union leaders and workers, artists
and philosophers, into the general Gentile community.
Again it is impossible to speak of this phenomenon
in terms of apostasy or by uttering general condemnations of assimilation. For, as on the previous occasion,
these developments have had their roots deep in Jewish
values. In this case, when the heart of Jewry was usually an
orthodoxy which had become rigid and unadaptable, it was
also the assertion of the right of the diaspora, using its
experience in its Gentile environment, to profit by that
experience, and to pass judgment upon a separatism which
had lost its way, and which sought distinction and division
where no moral purpose was served. There was an argument
for separating Jews, at any cost of exclusiveness, from the
corruptions of a decadent paganism ; there was no justification for excluding them from the adventures of modern
science and scholarship, or the struggles of modern social
reform. For Jews were inherently sensitive to such adven-

tures and struggles, whether nineteenth century scholars found them mentioned in the Talmud or not.

* * *

It is time to draw together the threads of the rich and varied pattern which has been unfolded in the previous pages. The central truth that emerges from their record is that Jewish history cannot be understood by magnifying one element at the cost of others. Unless we are content with a partisan view, then we have to accept that it arises from, and continually involves, the tension between universalism and separatism, and that it is fully expressed only in the creative interaction between the centre and the diaspora, and between the diaspora and the Gentile world around it.

It is a partisan view to claim that the only link which binds Jews together is religion, if by religion is meant the particular beliefs about the universe of each individual. For the expressed intention of the Sinaitic revelation was to create a nation, albeit a nation of priests. Moreover, for those who do not accept the Divine authority of the scriptural account of Sinai, it is still obvious that all through their history the Jews have manifested themselves as a people, distinguished from other human societies in a way of life which involves an economic and political as well as a religious experience.

It is likewise an especially regrettable form of this partisanship when the orthodox of today attempt to claim that the foundations of the justifiably separate existence of Judaism as a religion rest on such matters as *shechita* or the strict observance of the Sabbath. Both these may be justified, and indeed held to be praiseworthy, by the argument that it is good to multiply opportunities for obeying a Divine law. But to put them in the centre of the picture is entirely to misunderstand what it was that enabled Jewish life to survive during the two thousand years of dispersion. That they do not qualify for such a position is shown by the recognition of the orthodox themselves that they are not obligatory on Gentiles, whereas the main reason for Jewish survival lies in those Jewish qualities which Jews recognised to be obligatory on *all* men, but found to be

161

better taught and practised within the Jewish fold than
outside. It is this which saved Jews from conversion to every
imaginable religion from China to Peru when every material
argument was in favour of it.

If it be partisanship to concentrate only on religion it is
equally partisan to concentrate only on the Jews as a nation.
Those Jewish qualities which justify the world—including
its Jewish inhabitants—in desiring that Jewry shall not
perish from the earth, are those qualities which are desirable
for all men. And it is this fact that Jewish survival is concerned with a moral, and not merely a geographical,
identity which has made the Jewish destiny unique. But,
even if it is unique, Jews are still human, with human
failings, and human reactions to the pressure of their
environment. The inevitable result has been that there have
been periods—and today is one—when Jews as a group have
failed to keep their universalism and their separatism in
creative equipoise, and Jews individually will incline to one
pole or the other. It is therefore again partisanship when the
nationalists denounce assimilation, or when assimilationists
denounce nationalism.

There has been a hysteria, an exaggeration, a vituperation
which has unhappily accompanied nationalist propaganda
and made Jews who are neither traitors to the traditions of
Judaism, nor degenerates, dissociate themselves from Jewish
separatism in the name of a universalism which is just as
distinctively Jewish. And when their Jewish environment
is monopolised by the separatism of either a narrow orthodoxy or a hysterical nationalism, this dissociation can be
driven, and driven by its authentic Jewishness, to complete
severance from the Jewish fold, in the name of a universalism which they find they can better practise outside it.

Even the condemnation of those who have thus hived
right off from the Jewish community, and become Christians,
Moslems, Marxians, or Humanists, is a partisan condemnation. It has as much validity as would have the condemnation
of the leaven which loses its own identity because it has an
essential contribution to make to "the lump." As long as
Judaism, and the Jewish consciousness, concern themselves
with moral values which are of universal significance, so

long will such hivings-off take place. But those nationalist or orthodox Jews who still desire to condemn them, and to label by opprobrious terms those who leave the Jewish community because, in their particular experience, these values are better observed in an environment which is not Jewish, must face the fact that if Judaism ceases to be a repository of such universal moral values, only the more stupid, inert and worthless Jews by birth will remain within a community whose distinguishing marks have been reduced to abstinence from pork or no abstinence from unrestrained propaganda and abuse.

The foregoing paragraphs have not been a thinly concealed argument in favour of progressive Judaism, conversion or agnosticism on the one hand, or of assimilation on the other. For exactly the same condemnation of partisanship can be levelled against those who see the Jewish past or future exclusively in terms of any one of these elements in the whole picture. The universal values inherent in Judaism would not have survived, had there been no such customs as *shechita* and the Sabbath. The ancient Rabbis were far in advance of their time in their understanding of group psychology. They deliberately made a daily life which should be distinctive, which should involve a certain complication of instruction and transmission, not that these things should display what was distinctively Jewish, but that they should be a fence within which the real essentials of Judaism should be maintained and developed. We must think of *shechita* in relation to the cruel killing of animals for sport which went on in the environing Gentile world, as well as the eating of unhealthy and tainted meat. We must think of the ritual of the Sabbath in terms of the family and of religion in the home itself, as well as in terms of the Sabbath rest in a life of continual strain and anxiety, if we are to get these observances in the right perspective. And then we have to confess that we doubt whether in any other way the values so safeguarded would have survived.

Likewise, it is a partisan view to see the story in terms of a finale of assimilation. We have to admit, of Jews as of Christians, that today there is an unhappily large passage from definite belief, or membership of a definite tradition,

163

to a vague "lumpen-proletariat" of mass-produced values without depth or colour; and we must recognise, Jews as well as Christians, that it will be a long and uphill struggle to substitute for these machine-made cultures something as compelling in the modern world as were our respective orthodoxies in an age which has passed. But it is not that kind of assimilation that I am thinking of, but rather of the beliefs put forward so frequently in the nineteenth century, that Jewish life in the diaspora should abandon all separatist Jewish values, national or orthodox, and yet remain Jewish. For the evidence is that such a solution is impossible, except at the cost of the total disappearance of the diaspora. Separatism is as fundamental an element in the Jewish story as universalism; and while there may be many different ways in which the consciousness of a need to maintain a separate identity may be expressed, it is not likely that parents will successfully transmit to their children something which they have themselves either rejected or never acquired.

I have spoken thus far of the partisanship of those who accept only one of the two elements, universalism and separatism, which make up the basis of Jewish identity. There is the same partisanship among those who elevate Israel at the expense of the diaspora, or see the continuation of the diaspora as independent of the continuation of Israel.

During the long ghetto period the underlying unity by which Jews could be identified as Jews, both by themselves and others in every dispersed community, whatever its cultural or economic level, made a visible centre such as Israel unnecessary. But from the moment when emancipation made possible, and indeed inevitable, the multiplying of varieties of Jews, when it became natural to be an English Jew, a Russian Jew, an orthodox, progressive or agnostic Jew, from that moment it became inevitable that there should be a movement demanding that somewhere, and in some way, it should be possible just to be a "Jew"—*somewhere* where all these varieties of personal attitude to life were enfolded within some larger mantle of Jewishness, *some way* in which the varied experience gained by the new intimacy of contact with different parts of the Gentile world outside could be stored, transmuted and redistributed within the ever changing and growing inheritance of Jewry.

But finally, it is equally partisan to insist that the centre is all that matters, and that the diaspora both can and will wither away without loss to the Jewish inheritance. There is, of course, a sense in which one can be "fully Jewish" within Israel more easily than in the diaspora ; but only in the sense that one can remain a Jew in Israel without exemplifying any Jewish values whatever, whereas in the diaspora, to remain a Jew involves some positive action, even of a minimal kind. One can be a Jewish criminal, a Jewish spiv, a Jewish black-marketeer in Israel, and still be a voting member of the Jewish community. In the diaspora, if one is any of these things, the odds are one is only a Jew by birth, and is not a member of any Jewish community. I do not think that those who laud the Jewish being of Israel at the expense of the diaspora have reflected that that kind of 100 per cent Jewishness, simply based on the fact of an Israeli passport, is not likely to ensure a useful future for Israel. Moreover, Israel today is the quintessence of diaspora experience and quite properly so ; and it needs to continue to be, at the same time as it develops its own peculiar Jewish qualities. For it must resume within itself the totality of Jewish experience, and that involves a continually sensitive relationship with that experience wherever it may be ; and much of that experience, by the universalism which is an inherent part of Jewry, will be experience of contact with the non-Jewish world.

It would be just as wrong for Israel to ignore all the experience of Judaism in emancipation and create a theocracy based on absolute conformity to the orthodoxy of the ghetto, as to ignore its religious history, and create a secular State on the basis of experience in emancipation. For Jewish experience in Israel and in the diaspora are inseparable ; and yet neither must dominate the other. For the same is true of the diaspora. If Zionists abroad attempt to create a political ghetto in every country by denying the full citizenship and the full Jewishness of Jews outside Israel, they are betraying the essence of Jewish history as completely as those assimilated Jews who see in Zionism nothing but a foreign nationalism, or those religious Jews who see in it nothing but a secularism which has gone far astray.

All these Jewish partisans of today are like children who have taken a watch to pieces ; and having put it together again to their satisfaction, find they have a number of apparently unnecessary wheels over! It is not some bits of the watch which will not go until those wheels are restored, but the very watch itself.

There are many wheels within the Jewish watch ; and *all* are necessary if it is to go at all. But all the pieces must be in true relationship with each other, if it is to show the correct time. And what is the correct time for Jewry ? One minute ahead of the time of us Gentiles.

NOTE TO SECTION III

I have not attempted in this section to deal with the situation as it is in the winter of 1967. I have written of Jews and Arabs in many other books and pamphlets, and do not want to repeat myself here. I refer the reader especially to chapters in End of an Exile *and* Antisemitism, *both published by Vallentine, Mitchell. The story of the three religions is told in much greater detail in my* History of Palestine from 135 to Modern Times, *published by the Oxford Press Inc. and Gollancz ; and the Jewish roots, which rest on much more than twentieth-century legal documents, in* Five Roots of Israel, *which was published by Vallentine, Mitchell, and which, in spite of the cataloguer of one public library, is not a kosher cookery book!*

IV

****
Theological Foundations
****

10

THE THEOLOGY OF TOLERATION

SIDE BY SIDE with the varied and delightful stories about Abraham to be found in the *Midrashim,* and collected by Louis Ginzberg in his *Legends of the Jews,* there is another of vast antiquity and uncertain origin which introduces the patriarch directly to the problem which we are considering now.

One evening Abraham was sitting at the door of his tent, looking out on the desert, when far away he descried a single figure trudging wearily towards him. Moved at once by those feelings of hospitality for which he was famous, Abraham rushed to meet the stranger and invited him in to share his evening meal and to pass the night. The stranger was reluctant, but Abraham pressed him until he agreed to come. The patriarch then prepared a tasty meal and set it before him ; and the wanderer at once fell to and began to eat. "Stay," cried Abraham, shocked to the depth of his being, "Are you not going to say grace and give thanks to God ? " "No," said the stranger, "I never say grace, and as to gods, I keep one here in my haversack who is quite adequate for all I need, but I have never thought of thanking him for my food." "No grace: no supper," said Abraham firmly ; and, when he proved obdurate, chased him back fasting into the desert. But in the night the Lord came to visit Abraham ; and, looking round the tent, asked the patriarch "Where is the stranger I saw you inviting in ? " "Lord," said Abraham self-righteously, "*I* prepared him a lovely supper and asked only that he should thank *You* for it. When he refused, I said that, in respect for You, I could not receive him as my guest. So I sent him back to the desert." And the Lord sighed, and replied: "For more than seventy years I have fed that man, have clothed him and sheltered him; and never once has he thanked me; and could not you, who are yourself not perfect, have looked after him just for one night?"

There is your theology of Divine toleration, and your human reply of intolerance. For there are two aspects of our quest. There is first our understanding of the relationship of the Creator to his creation, and of his attitude towards its imperfections; and there is secondly the attitude which we believe that men, seeking to serve and obey the Divine will, should take towards disagreement, opposition and wrong-doing.

When I was a younger and, perhaps, a rasher man, I once preached a sermon to a theological college in the form of a parable of a day of Divine audience. As in the last book of the New Testament, the Trinity was seated on the throne, and beneath it were those strange figures representing the four Gospels; and the angels of the Churches came to report the requests of their people. When angel after angel had said that all that their people had asked for was to be saved from hell, " the Father turned to the Son and said 'How often did you tell men to forgive their enemies, and do they really think that I shall never forgive mine?' And the four evangelists looked out from under the throne and blushed." So I began my sermon, reminding them that there was a great deal in the New Testament, as it stood, which presented what I believed to be an entirely unacceptable picture of the nature of God, and a division of humanity into black and white which had no basis in reality.

There is a great passage in Dr. Montefiore's commentary, *The Synoptic Gospels*, which it is wholly appropriate to quote here, not only because this is the tenth Claude Montefiore lecture, but because it is apposite to the consideration of Jewish and Christian thoughts on Divine toleration. I can commemorate nothing more splendid than the spirit of serene objectivity, humility and courtesy with which his commentary on the synoptic Gospels was written. Examining a description of the Day of Judgement put into the mouth of Jesus, and particularly the verse " Depart from me ye accursed, into the everlasting fire prepared for the devil and his angels," he wrote:

Such passages as Matt. xxv, 41 should make theologians excessively careful of drawing beloved contrasts between Old Testament and New. We find even the liberal theologian, Dr. Fosdick, saying: "From Sinai to Calvary—was ever a record of progressive revelation more plain or more convincing ? The development begins with Jehovah disclosed in a thunderstorm on a desert mountain, and it ends with Christ saying: ' God is a Spirit: and they that worship Him must worship in spirit and truth '; it begins with a war-god leading his partisans to victory, and it ends with men saying, 'God is love; and he that abideth in love abideth in God, and God abideth in him '; it begins with a provincial deity loving his tribe and hating its enemies, and it ends with the God of the whole earth worshipped by 'a great multitude, which no man could number, out of every nation and of all tribes and peoples and tongues '; it begins with a God who commands the slaying of the Amalekites, 'both man and woman, infant and suckling,' and it ends with a Father whose will it is that not ' one of these little ones should perish '; it begins with God's people standing afar off from His lightnings and praying that He might not speak to them lest they die, and it ends with men going into their inner chambers and, having shut the door, praying to their Father who is in secret" (*Christianity and Progress,* 1922, p. 209). Very good. No doubt such a series can be arranged. Let me now arrange a similar series. "From Old Testament to New Testament—was ever a record of retrogression more plain or more convincing ? It begins with, 'Have I any pleasure at all in the death of him that dieth ? '; it ends with ' Begone from me, ye doers of wickedness.' It begins with, ' The Lord is slow to anger and plenteous in mercy '; it ends with, 'Fear him who is able to destroy both body and soul in gehenna.' It begins with, 'I dwell with him that is of a contrite spirit to revive it '; it ends with, 'Narrow is the way which leads to life, and few

171

there be who find it.' It begins with, 'I will not contend
for ever; I will not be *always* wrath'; it ends with,
'Depart, ye cursed, into the everlasting fire.' It begins
with, 'Should not I have pity upon Nineveh, that great
city?'; it ends with, 'It will be more endurable for Sodom
on the day of Judgement than for that town.' It begins
with, 'The Lord is good to all, and near to all who call
upon Him'; it ends with, 'Whoever speaks against the
Holy Spirit, there is no forgiveness for him whether in this
world or in the next.' It begins with, 'The Lord will wipe
away tears from off all faces; he will destroy death for
ever'; it ends with, 'They will throw them into the
furnace of fire; there is the weeping and the gnashing of
teeth.'" And the one series would be as misleading as
the other.*

The story of Abraham with which I began was a story of
Divine tolerance and human intolerance. The passage I have
read from Claude Montefiore reflects a concrete example
of human tolerance in its delightfully witty and good-
tempered reply to a statement which might be regarded as
one of infuriating and inexcusable ignorance. Dr. Montefiore
does not turn the other cheek; with delicate irony he
extracts his opponent's teeth and shows them to be false!
He convinces because of his serene refusal to be annoyed
by one of the commonest examples of intolerance—the
ignorant comparison of one's own rightness with the wrong-
ness of other people.

One way of treating the subject would be to build up
more carefully the way in which, in fact, the two religions
have deepened their understanding of the nature of God
and of His laws, as it can be unravelled from the records
of many centuries. That could be a fascinating task, and it
would result in a picture totally different from that drawn
by Dr. Fosdick. They would be shown to have been
captured by the subject with the same moral earnestness and
intensity, with the same differences of individual temperament between optimism and pessimism, and with a common
conviction that

* *Op cit.* Vol. II, 1927, p. 326.

. . . the love of God is broader
Than the measure of man's mind.

There would be differences, arising, for example, from the much greater interest in the Christian tradition in the conditions of a future life, or from the situation of Jews as minorities in Christendom and Islam debating to what extent they could morally accept that "the law of the land is law." But the whole Fosdickian conception of superiority and inferiority would be absent from such a treatment of the subject.

Instead of this historical method, I want to approach the issues before us from the standpoint of a common liberalism in the middle of the twentieth century. Inevitably there will be moments when we turn attention to Jewish and Christian differences, some of them very important. But I want first to put forward what seems to me the inevitable approach of a liberal in the English tradition, whether Jew or Christian, to the doctrine of Divine tolerance.

Traditionally, whatever our emphases, both religions have accepted an ultimate division into sheep and goats, into righteous and unrighteous, into black and white. It is here that I believe that the liberal outlook asks for a profound breach with the past. As liberals I believe that we are bound to bow to the psychologists, anthropologists and biologists who tell us that the whole creation is a single inextricable unity; and that one fate inevitably embraces the whole of it. There is no point at which any such absolute distinction can be drawn between man and man that there is an absolute break in our mutual responsibility and dependence. There is no point at which an "I" can be damned while a "You" can be saved. I am just so much an individual, just so much a separate person, as is necessary in order that I may fulfil my purposes, exercise my talents, and understand my responsibilities. But I am at the same time continuously dependent on others, from the womb to the tomb, and so continuously a part of others. I am in inextricable debt to both heredity and environment; and if these are stripped away, that which is left is no longer me. I do not thereby deny the fundamental Christian doctrine of the value of human personality, nor do I deny the uniqueness of every person. But I am saying that this uniqueness, this personality, cannot be seen in isolation, or judged as a completely separate unit. Am I to be condemned because at a moment when I could draw myself up only by your help, you would not help me ? Is not the experience and belief of every happily married couple true that, separated from their partner, they are but half of themselves ? It is isolation, not uniqueness, that I am denying ; it is lack of responsibility to and for others, whether for good or ill, that I am asserting to be less than human.

Moreover, we cannot say that we appear thus blended with each other because our views are incomplete, whereas God will see each man clearly so that He can judge him rightly and separately. It is the opposite that is true. It is because of my imperfect vision and my limited knowledge that I appear quite separate from, and independent of, you ; in the vision of God I exist in my uniqueness only because of the link with Himself and with His whole creation. All—not just something—of what I am I owe.

This rejection of the whole concept of a final judgement, in which God exhibits His ultimate intolerance, finds support in this argument also. As liberals we may differ about the characteristics of a future life, but we cannot accept the idea of a purely static perfection which alone would give a final judgement either meaning or validity. We cannot readily accept that there can be life without growth, or the fulfilment of a Divine purpose which at the same time is a dead end, even if that end be called eternal bliss or the Beatific Vision.

In *The Paradox*, one of his greatest poems, Alfred Noyes wrote :

" I am the Lord.

I am the end to which the whole world strives :

Therefore are ye girdled with a wild desire and shod
With sorrow ; for among you all no soul
Shall ever cease or sleep or reach its goal
Of union and communion with the Whole

Or rest content, with less than being God."

174

I cannot conceive that the goal of "union and communion with the Whole" could be static!

Instead of a division into sheep and goats, we have the conception of a bond between Creator and the whole of His creation ; and a picture of Divine responsibility which replaces that earlier stage of liberalism which sought to lighten the picture of hell, or diminish the number of its permanent residents. The growing picture of a Divine love which had no pleasure in the death of a sinner, such as we find in the great liberals of all ages in both religions, played an important part in destroying the image of a vengeful God which was present in far too many traditional pictures of the deity. But today that kind of theology of toleration has passed into a theology of responsibility. By the very act of creation the Creator holds the whole indivisibly in His hand.

This does not destroy the idea of a theology of toleration ; but it shifts the field in which we seek to understand it. We are no longer concerned with the possibility of a wider margin of Divine tolerance than would be readily conceded by human conventions of religious respectability, but with a Divine toleration which must comprehend the whole of creation. Instead of asking how far the toleration of God extends, we have to ask how it enfolds the immense variety of human religions, and how it meets the most profound human sin and error. Neither Jew nor Christian would be willing to accept the solution that all religions were alike to God, or that there was no difference between truth and error as they were manifested in this world. That would not be toleration, but indifference. It would not enrich man's understanding of God ; it would so impoverish the idea of Deity as to make it meaningless and ineffective. For Jew and Christian, then, if God *tolerates* variety and error, it is because Divine toleration will bring variety into unity and error into truth. And the question becomes then to understand the conditions by which this can be achieved, and the measure in which human co-operation is possible or even required. For that will be the measure and manner of human toleration also.

So long as men believed in a selected salvation, or a

PRELUDE TO DIALOGUE

selected Divine choice, they could combine their assertion that their religion was true and of universal validity with particularism, because they did not expect all men to be acceptable to God, and so were not troubled by the disbelief of many. Those who disbelieved were those whom God had not selected. But if there is a common destiny for all humanity, then there is a common relationship of God to all human striving to understand the Divine nature. This does not mean that all human solutions are equally true, but that whatever truth God has revealed to man is accessible to all men, and so to all religions. Jews and Christians believe that certain historical events are true and of universal significance. If this be so, then the events themselves can be understood through all the channels of man's search for God, not alone by the channels along which Jews and Christians have historically caught the vision of them.

This truth is, I believe, becoming increasingly clear to Christians because of the complete change in the position of Western churches in Asia and Africa. Seventy years ago it would be universally expected that Africans or Asians should accept the proper forms of religion from European priests and teachers. Forty years ago it began to be appreciated that Africans and Asians might themselves rise to the highest places among these ministers and teachers. Today, we are beginning to see that the resulting forms of Christianity may be something quite different from the European originals, and that African and Asian may find truths in the life of Jesus of Nazareth, and interpretations of the Christology which arises from it, which have never been seen so clearly or appreciated so deeply by the West.

To take two examples nearer home : I hold firmly to the Christian doctrine of the Incarnation ; and I find the utmost enrichment to my understanding of God in the doctrine of the Trinity. If there are universal truths enshrined in these doctrines, then I believe that they are as relevant to Jews as to every other people. But it is the universal truths which are universally relevant, and not their interpretation through the particular inheritance of the Christian Church. I doubt whether Jews—or others—will ever express their beliefs in that typically hellenistic form which I have inherited, and with which I can quite happily find God. In what way Jews will express it, only they can tell; as to when they will express it, I do not know. But I can see that the complete disavowal of antisemitism and anti-Judaism by the Christian Church is a necessary preliminary. What happens after that will arise out of the Jewish and not the Greek manner of thought, and out of Jewish freedom to decide whether to accept the event itself or not.

In the same way I believe that the God revealed at Sinai and in Jewish history (for Sinai is a continuing event) is a God speaking to all nations through the creative discipline of law and the continuous interpretation of law in righteousness and mercy. I believe that rabbinic Judaism rightly developed these truths into a religion of *mitzvot* ; and that this conception has universal significance. But that does not mean either that I think that all Gentiles should accept the rabbinical *mitzvot* or, indeed, that the existing orthodox tradition is the necessary and unique Jewish implication of the truth of Sinai.

Now Judaism did develop an interesting form of toleration of differences by accepting that there was Sinai for Jews and the Noachic commandments for Gentiles. It was this distinction which made it possible for a Jewish theologian to say, much earlier than a Christian one, that the righteous of all nations shall inherit the world to come. But is this the final toleration ? More for some, and less for others in the demands of God and the response of man ? I doubt whether it be more than a noble landmark on the way ; and I believe that the goal will be to see the truths of Sinai as equal in significance to all men. For the toleration of God is not of different levels of truth but of different approaches to it.

The sense of equality between the religions which has been consequent on the decline of the West is, I believe, an admirable feature, many though be the problems and heart-searchings it creates. For the Deity cannot be protected by the refusal of criticism, or a religion proved to be true by its ability to silence its opponents. The total responsibility of the Creator involves the total freedom of response of the creation.

If that be the Divine toleration towards the world's

religions, what of the world's sins ? If there is no hell, then what is the Divine method of meeting and overcoming evil ? It is not a new question. Let us turn back to yet another story of Abraham, this time to *The Testament of Abraham,* a late Jewish pseudepigraphical writing of about the first century B.C.E., which has been preserved in various languages by the Orthodox and Eastern Churches. In it God permits Abraham to be taken by the Archangel Michael to survey the whole world before his death. Abraham is shocked by the amount of wickedness he sees, and, beholding a band of robbers, cries out to the Lord:

> Lord, Lord, hear my cry and bid that wild beasts come forth from the thicket and devour them. And even as he uttered (the word) there came forth wild beasts from the thicket, and devoured them. And in another place saw he a man with a woman committing fornication with each other, and he said: Lord, Lord, bid that the earth open and swallow them up. And immediately the earth opened and swallowed them up. In another place he beheld men digging through an house, and robbing the goods of others, and he said: Lord, Lord, bid that fire may come down from heaven and devour them. And at his word, fire came down from heaven and devoured them. Then straightway came a voice from heaven to the chief-captain, thus saying: "Michael, chief-captain, bid the chariot to stop, and turn away Abraham, that he may not see all the world. If he sees all that are living in sin, he will destroy every existing thing. For behold, Abraham has not sinned, neither pities he sinners ; but *I* made the world, and will not destroy any creature from among them, but I delay the death of the sinner, until he repent and live."

The main criticism which I would offer of the reply of the Lord is that the time scale is too short. We know, alas, that there are many who do not repent before they die, to whatever age their life is protracted. It may appear a curious inversion of expectation, but I would suggest that it is the wicked, and not the righteous, who provide an irrefutable argument for the continuation of life beyond physical death ;

an argument which can only be ignored on the basis of denying the personality or the goodness of God. And that seems to me much too high a price to pay for the convenience of scepticism.

If this life be all, then, however highly we may rate human responsibility for the evil in the world, we are left, as I have already said, with a God whose main quality is not toleration, but indifference—a fact on which humanists readily seize. I, with my more than sixty years of pleasant living, may have no ground for complaint if death be the end ; but what of those all around me who have not had my advantages—and through no fault of their own ? Of course the humanists, like Sir Julian Huxley, may be right. There may be no God ; all that humanity can do may be to lift itself as high as possible by its own shoe-strings. But if there be a God even faintly mirrored in the noblest that men have imagined of Him, then no theology of the Divine tolerance can be built except on some doctrine of immortality, some doctrine of growth beyond the grave.

But if such a doctrine be accepted, then the problem of evil can at once be seen in terms of that unity of creation of which I have already spoken. In one sense evil may be isolation, self-isolation, but it can never be complete isolation. The evil man can never be wholly unmoved by the cords which tie him with others into the bundle of life.

Curiously enough, while Christianity has often seemed to exaggerate the importance of the future life, and has certainly talked a great deal of nonsense in contrasting this vale of tears with the bliss of heaven, Judaism has gone to the other extreme and, while officially accepting its existence, has manifested singularly little interest in its conditions. The strong sense of the continuing community of Israel is partly responsible for this ; but the little interest of Judaism in systematic theology is a still more fundamental reason. For it is in considering God and not man that the belief becomes compelling. There is no theological explanation of evil which does not include it within the toleration of God ; but there is no theology of Divine goodness which does not include a victory over it ; and we live in daily evidence that this victory is not of this world.

179

It is here that Judaism and Christianity, in spite of the
differences between them, stand firmly against the many
dualistic faiths of the East. These explain the existence of
evil by positing an evil force in almost exact balance to the
force for good, and so they evade the problem of a good
God and a world full of suffering and evil. But if Judaism
and Christianity stand together on this issue, they are deeply
divided as to the method of the Divine conquest. Orthodox
Christianity sees, as it has always seen, that victory in the
Cross ; and it is an interesting speculation whether it was
not its conflict with the Church, and its repulsion from
various doctrines proclaimed by the Church, which resulted
in Judaism having little substitute. For, after all, the whole
of the Christian doctrine of redemption through suffering,
of which the Cross is the centre, arises from the vision of
Deutero-Isaiah in the Servant Poem in Chapter 53:

> He had no form nor comeliness, that we should look
>   upon him,
> Nor beauty that we should delight in him.
> He was despised, and forsaken of men,
> A man of pains, and acquainted with disease,
> And as one from whom men hide their face:
> He was despised, and we esteemed him not.
> Surely our diseases he did bear, and our pains he carried ;
> Whereas we did esteem him stricken,
> Smitten of God, and afflicted.
> But he was wounded because of our transgressions,
> He was crushed because of our iniquities:
> The chastisement of our welfare was upon him,
> And with his stripes we were healed.
> All we like sheep did go astray,
> We turned every one to his own way ;
> And the Lord hath made to light on him
> The iniquity of us all.

The Synagogue was not unmoved by the power which it
saw in Christian preaching of the Cross to Greco-Roman
society, for in the third century Rabbis began to speak of
the sacrifice of Isaac, the Akedah, as of equivalent value
from the Jewish point of view ; and so deeply did the need

for an implementation of the vision of Isaiah become that in many passages the author quite forgets that Isaac did not, in fact, give up his life, and speaks of his redeeming death.

I do not know whether the Jewish attitude to the world's sin and suffering, evil and failure, is more interesting to the student of comparative religion or to the student of psychology. For those in every continent whose common faith is Judaism have experienced more suffering through the sins of others than the adherents of any other religion. Compared with the bitterness and hatred which we find, for example, in the periods of persecution endured by Scottish Covenanters, there is very little bitterness in traditional Judaism. There is likewise very little of that obsessive concern with sin which has impressed—and still impresses —so deep a mark on Christian theology. But Christian liberalism, thank God, revolts as vigorously as Judaism against the appalling exaggeration of a doctrine of total depravity. There is obviously no explanation in rabbinic indifference to the distinction between good and evil, for there is no difference between the basic ethics of Judaism and those of Christianity. I suspect that the real difference lies in the innate Jewish conviction that God will, in the end, guide the creation to the haven, He destined for it, and to the optimism inherent in that belief.

Yet the bitterness of the Judeo - Christian hostility has undoubtedly impoverished Jewish theology; for the idea that human suffering does not leave the Deity unmoved is common to psalmist, prophet and Rabbi. But it has not received a systematic theological expression, and so tends to be dismissed as a charming and poetical image typical of the writers of *Midrash,* the composers of Chasidic anecdotes, and the makers of folk-lore in general. I have written elsewhere that I believe that lack of a theology is the greatest Jewish misfortune today. Here I would only say that this realisation that a Creator is responsible to and for His creation has a profound theological base.

It is important, not merely because it is a necessary link between the realities of Creator and creation, but because it is the source of the human attitude to evil which is the second part of my subject. A theology of toleration includes

G

not only the toleration of God of which I have spoken, but also the human toleration based on that theology. For a true understanding of the right attitude of man to sin and evil arises from the belief that man, as a responsible being, has a necessary part to play in the Divine activity for the perfection of creation.

Here we come to a point where it has been an advantage to Judaism not to be tied by a systematic theology. This has been so particularly in these recent decades when we Christians have been dominated, at any rate in the non-Roman world, by the anti-rationalist antics of Dr. Karl Barth, and his insistence that God is wholly other and wholly unintelligible. For the Rabbis never had any doubt that God and man were inextricably intertwined in the work of creation and redemption. It was no Jewish Satan and his band who spent their time debating

Fixed fate, free will, foreknowledge absolute
for Jewish thinkers just took the paradox in their stride and went on to the practical matters which interested them much more deeply.

It is precisely this practical aspect of the problem of human toleration that I want to talk about theologically. For a good deal of nonsense is talked about a supposed difference between Jewish common sense and Christian utopianism on this score. The Rabbis are supposed to be much more realistic about human nature, and to have eschewed the extravagances into which the utopianism of the Beatitudes and other passages in the Sermon on the Mount have misled the Christian Church. Now in their approach to the problem of evil and of the religious attitude to it there are interesting differences of perspective and approach between the two religions; but the opposition between a supposedly realistic Judaism and a supposedly idealistic Christianity is one of those myths whose exposure would delight the scholar whose memory we recall tonight. Indeed the whole of his commentary on the Sermon on the Mount is well worth reading for its balance, its generosity, its wide reading and its deep spirituality.

For the liberal Jew and Christian alike God's toleration of evil posits man's co-operation. For if God tolerates it because

THE THEOLOGY OF TOLERATION

His creation is a unity, the successful realisation of that unity implies the coming to His perfection of all of us who are parts of that creation. Because God regards the sinner as within that unity, man must also so regard him. That is not utopian but realistic. From a theological standpoint this insistence on an attitude to evil based on its redemption, and not on its exclusion, is the fundamental issue. Traditionally both religions believed that, even though God was long-suffering and patient, there would be a limit to that patience, a final judgement after which those rejected were consigned to some form of annihilation, or to extreme agony in hell. It may be that Christians have been more obsessed by interest in sin and its punishment than Jews, but in their attitude to the final destiny of the individual wicked man there was little difference.

To regard the sinner, the enemy, as within the unity is, likewise, not a distinctive Christian virtue as opposed to a less noble and spiritual Jewish attitude. It is to be found in various places in the Jewish Scriptures, and is exquisitely expressed in one of the greatest of the apocryphal works which crowd the centuries immediately before the birth of Christianity. *The Testament of the Twelve Patriarchs* dates from the Maccabean period, and *The Testament of Gad* (vi: 3ff) contains this profound understanding of the problem:

> Love ye one another from the heart ; and if a man sin against thee, speak peaceably to him, and in thy soul hold not guile ; and if he repent and confess, forgive him. But if he deny it, do not get into a passion with him, lest catching the poison from thee he takes to swearing and so thou sin doubly . . . and if he is shameless and persist in his wrong-doing, even so forgive him from the heart, and leave to God the avenging.

Apposite, too, is a saying in *The Testament of Dan* (ii, 2):

> Anger is blindness and doth not suffer one to see the face of any man with truth.

On the other hand, one has to admit that the New Testament, while it demands of man that he should love his enemies, contains few examples of the manifestations of that love towards either Pharisees, or Judaisers, the enemies *par excellence* of the first Christian century. Both Jew and Christian have found this counsel hard to follow, just for the reason which Dan explains to his children. It is natural that we should regard such a man as Hitler with anger, and anger blinds a man. But the advice itself is realistic. If it be true that it is the redemption and not the condemnation of a Hitler that we should seek, then a Hitler needs our prayers and blessings and not our curses. For if there be spiritual power in blessing or cursing, if there be reality in prayer, then surely a Hitler needs more prayer than a saint, and the little good in him needs more encouragement by blessing than the much good of his neighbour.

That we should pray for a Hitler is, however, only the beginning, not the end. It still leaves unsettled the decision as to what more one should do, and so opens the way to the whole debate about resistance to evil, about Christian pacifism, about the difference, if difference exists, between a public and a private enemy. It is a debate into which Jews have only recently been brought; for it is a debate about the use of political power, whether internally to a country or in foreign relations. But it is a subject into which the Jewish world has now been plunged in an extreme form with the creation of a State of Israel in defiance of the united hostility of the Arab world.

I have discussed pacifism at some length in *Common Sense about Religion,* a recent book produced under my war-time *nom de plume* of John Hadham, and I have likened the pacifist movement there to a tug whose task it is to nose, cajole and push a great liner into port. It is not for men on the tug to spend their time and strength in persuading the passengers on the liner to abandon their vessel and all climb aboard the tug; it is to get all the liner's passengers safely into port, where the task of marshalling them and seeing to their safe disembarkation will be organised by men with many different functions and parts to play. None of them, it is true, would be able to succeed unless the tug nosed the liner safely to the quayside; but neither could the tug disembark the passengers by itself. I am convinced that the difference between the religious pacifist and the religious man, Jew or Christian, who is not able to take the complete pacifist position, has been greatly exaggerated. In part this has been due to the prominence in much pacifist activity of action directed *against* war rather than the much larger, but less visible, action *for* peace. There are, of course, many pacifists who are not Christians, but so far as Christians are concerned, it is certainly due in part to a feeling that victory by defeat, which they see in the Cross, is determinant of the response to evil of the individual Christian. I find it a tragedy that they regard it so often as impossible to co-operate with Christians of different views in the attack on actual evils. For I believe that the great dividing line is the one I have already indicated—between those who see the whole creation as a unity and those who see the ultimate destiny of mankind as a division into sheep and goats.

Those who are at one on that fundamental will still attack a concrete evil, will treat of actual wickedness, in as many manners as there are organs in a body. The discussions which are going on at present about juvenile delinquency seem to me a very fair example of what I mean by toleration. No responsible person regards the juvenile delinquent as anything but a member of the community who must, as effectively as possible, be restored, or brought, to creative "social" membership of the body from which he is at present isolating himself. But there are various different opinions as to how that agreed object is to be attained; and it is more than probable that many elements, including both punishment and forgiveness, active resistance and non-resistance, will need to work together before we make a real impression on the equally varied juveniles.

It is obvious that the sense of urgency, of fear of betrayal, of passionate conviction, is much stronger when we are faced with disaster as appalling as nuclear war. But even so I doubt whether the right line to victory is to insist in advance that this or that line of advance must be denounced and excluded from fellowship, as John Collins wished to do in opposing the acceptance of Robert Stopford as Bishop of London. For toleration should be surely an active partner in the relations between those who are attacking evil, as it has to be at the deepest level between God and man in the attack. I had almost written "between those who are attacking evil and the evil to be attacked"; and indeed in the right perspective that is a right statement. Just as men engaged in the battle with juvenile delinquency recognise that the co-operation of the delinquent is absolutely essential to his successful reintegration into society, so men engaged in the battle against international war must recognise a common humanity with their potential enemies; and all their actions, whatever they be, must be under the discipline of that common humanity.

Those who are agreed on the fundamentals will not wish to perform any action which they believe, or recognise, will make it less likely that the redemption of the outsider will be achieved. If they resist, or punish, they will still act within this limitation. Resistance and punishment will have a redemptive purpose. And, to go back to my analogy, those manning the tug will at all points work together with those manning the liner.

Many years ago now I had a profoundly moving experience of the richness of unbroken fellowship in action with those who were as convinced that they could not follow my path as I was convinced that I could not follow theirs. It was while I was still a secretary of International Student Service. In 1932 we had accepted the invitation of our chief German collaborator and oldest friend in Germany to hold our next annual conference in Bavaria. When the time came for the final planning of the conference, he had already been murdered by the Nazis among his own students and, of course, no Jew could attend the conference. There were four of us. Two refused to go to Germany and accept a conference from which our Jewish members would be excluded; two said that our only chance of still being some influence in German universities was to go. Neither group thought of excluding the other. In the end the conference was held half in Germany, half in Liechtenstein, but all of us shared without any inhibitions in the planning of the whole and all of us agreed afterwards that in no other way, in the political circumstances of the time, could

186

the conference have been so impressive a demonstration of where International Student Service stood.

I began with a dreadful example of prejudice against Judaism which came from a distinguished Christian scholar. Let me balance it with a superb naughtiness about Christianity from an equally distinguished Jewish scholar. I refer to the late Rabbi Milton Steinberg, the lucidity and depth of whose thought it is always a delight to read. On page 168 of the posthumously published *Anatomy of Faith* he writes:

> Professing no gods who are yet man, no vicarious atonement of sins, no trinities that are somehow unities, no justification of one man and damnation of another, though both are equally sinners, professing in sum none of the paradoxes of Christianity, we Jews are subject to little of the motivation of Christians to the glorification of the unintelligible.

How truly delightful as coming from one whose religion symbolises the entry into a national relationship of unique responsibility with the Creator of the universe by a primitive physical mutilation, which indulges in violent religious controversy over the culinary destination of the pig, which splendidly refuses to abandon a combination of intense particularity with the most comprehensive universalism, which combines a history of the longest and most dreadful persecution with the most illogical belief in human perfectibility, which, in a word, exhibits in glorious confusion all the paradox and unintelligibility to outsiders to which any ancient and living religious tradition is necessarily heir.

I am convinced that at no point have I delivered the lecture, or treated the subject, which was expected of me. I do not know whether it is that I have been a Hellenist in a world of semitic thought, or an antiquarian among the moderns ; but in either case I crave the toleration of which I have spoken, for the world has need of both heritages, and many others besides.

11

A THEOLOGY OF THE JEWISH-CHRISTIAN
RELATIONSHIP

I AM GOING to be largely autobiographical tonight, because I want to explain, not merely what I believe, but how I came to believe it and to reject the more familiar attitudes of both Jews and Christians to each other. But I must warn you at the beginning that my concern with some aspect of the Jewish question goes back now for forty-five years, and that it has been my central interest for more than thirty. I by no means pretend to be infallible or even correct; but it is no good asking me, for example, how I reconcile my views with those found in the Epistle to the Romans. I don't; and I long ago discovered that the question is irrelevant. In St. Paul's day, neither developed rabbinic Judaism nor Nicene Christianity existed. But it is with these we have to reckon today.

I must, however, acknowledge that I started with entirely conventional ideas. I read theology at Oxford, and left the university convinced that St. Paul had said the last word on the subject, and that nothing survived of Judaism but an arid and formal legalism once it had been rejected by, and separated itself from, Christianity. That means that the views I now hold have been forced upon me by actual experience, and will need very good evidence to dislodge.

My opening contacts with things Jewish raised no question of religion. At Oxford in 1921, I founded an International Assembly as an activity of the League of Nations Union; and Class A Mandates were members. We had a pair of Iraqi brothers, and we had a keen Zionist from Palestine. I don't remember a Syrian, but our Moslem and

Arab representatives accepted that it was fair that a Jew represented Palestine. Then, when I was a member of the Executive of the English National Union of Students, I was rapporteur on the attitude to be taken to the application for membership of the international body by the International University Jewish Federation. So I was plunged into the question of "what are the Jews?" Are they a nation or a religion? I took the attitude that they could not be full members because in the international body nationhood had to be expressed by independence. On the other hand, since they were recognised by international minority treaties as a nation, they should be accepted in some form of associate membership.

The third issue in which I became involved was antisemitism in the European universities. This was towards the end of the twenties. I was at the time secretary for cultural co-operation of International Student Service; and plans and travel were continually interfered with by antisemitic riots causing universities to be closed. I proposed, and held, two conferences between Jewish and antisemitic student organisations: for there were problems on both sides, and it gave each a unique opportunity to meet the other side—which they never could do in their own universities. It was as a result of these conferences that the problem gradually became a whole-time occupation, and led to my resignation from International Student Service in 1934 and my return to England in 1935 so that I could devote my whole time to it.

I had already written a short study of Jewish relations with the non-Jewish world in 1930. It began, reasonably enough, with the massacres in the Rhineland which accompanied the First Crusade in 1096. But the question was always at the back of my mind: Why these massacres of a long-established Jewish population, which had lived for centuries at peace with its Christian neighbours? I very quickly discovered that it was useless to try to engage in scholarly work in Europe and the United States without acquiring a doctorate. So I thought I would kill two birds with one stone by making the subject of a doctoral thesis the answer to the question: Why the massacres of 1096? The result was *The Conflict of the Church and the Synagogue.*

The central and overpowering, indeed horrifying, impression which that research brought me was the total responsibility of the Christian Church for turning a normal xenophobia into the unique disease of antisemitism. The book begins with a study of pre-Christian Greek and Roman hostility to the Jews, and makes clear how different was this attitude from the theologically-based hatred disseminated by patristic theology and Church Councils. It is very important to add, especially when speaking to Israel, that this tragic verdict was later completely confirmed by my studies of Islam, and of the history of Jews in Islamic countries. Much nonsense is talked about a pretended ideal relationship between Jews and Moslems. But, while Jews suffered a great deal from the ignorance, contempt and intolerance of their Moslem neighbours, they never suffered the sustained theological denigration and the conscious falsification of their history which they had to endure wherever they lived in a Christian environment.

As the book developed, I found that, for the first time, I had to understand post-Christian Judaism. Even the names of men like Johanan ben Zakkai or Akiba were previously quite unknown to me, and all that I had acquired from my Oxford theology was a grotesque caricature. Needless to say, I had absolutely no knowledge of the Talmud.

It was bad enough to discover the denigration and falsification of Judaism in men like Justin, Ambrose or Chrysostom: but I could not in honesty reject the evidence that the first seeds of patristic hostility lay in passages of the New Testament itself. I met Claude Montefiore in this period, and had many discussions with him. He gave me his three volumes on the Synoptic Gospels, which I read with care. I was also brought into close contact with the late Herbert Loewe at Cambridge. Between them I began a new study of the Gospels and of St. Paul. The result was a short book, *Jesus, Paul and the Jews.* In it I tried to show the growing hostility as we pass from Mark to Matthew and then to John ; I examined the different meanings of the word *nomos* in St. Paul's letters ; and I tackled the paradox between the evidence of the letters and that of his defences in the last chapters of Acts.

After the publication of *Jesus, Paul and the Jews* I carried forward the history of antisemitism into the Middle Ages. Though the war ended my medieval studies, this was not before I had made the uncomfortable discovery that every one of those false accusations which had led to the execution and massacre of tens of thousands of Jews had come from a Jewish convert to Christianity, whose authenticity was accepted by the Church of the time. The accusations of ritual murder, of poisoning the wells, of plotting to destroy Christendom, all came from converted Jews, the first from one who had become a monk in Cambridge, fourteen miles from where I was doing my research in my home in the village of Barley.

I must confess that this discovery not merely horrified me, but was the basis of my questioning the whole attitude of the Church to Judaism. I had grown up in an atmosphere of acceptance of the missionary obligations of the Church. As a secretary of the Student Christian Movement I was wholly working in a missionary environment. I *knew* there was nothing parallel to this appalling truth in the relations of Christianity to any other religion. Dr. Aggrey of Africa, Dr. Datta of India, Kagawa of Japan, and a similarly outstanding Christian from China, T. Z. Koo, were all known to me personally. They were all outstanding friends of their countries, outstanding interpreters of their diverse spiritual and cultural heritages. Nor did the records of the past, when tolerance was admittedly narrower in its interests, offer any parallel. If the convert was not an interpreter, at least he was not an enemy, a denouncer, and a false denouncer at that.

Here is one of the roots of my present conception of the relation of the two religions—the conviction that the missionary relation, based on the traditional idea that the truth was entirely on our side, and that all we had to do was to convey it to those who did not have it, did not cover our relations with Judaism. Missions to the Jew have been cultivated more assiduously, and for a longer period, than any comparable missionary chapter in the history of the

Church ; and its results, in spite of many sincere converts, have been appallingly tragic.

While my research work was producing these puzzling results, an event took place which still further disturbed me. A Rabbi, well known to most of you, came stampeding down from London one night — no lesser word would describe it—with a demand that I do something about a Jewish boy, child of orthodox parents in Prague, who had himself just become barmitzvah. He had been brought to England by a missionary society, when his parents were desperate because Hitler had just occupied Prague. They had signed a document in English whose purport they had not understood, in which they agreed that their son should be brought up as a Christian, and they were in despair when they discovered what they had done. The Rabbi, as well as his Jewish relatives, had been refused all access to the boy, and could not even discover where he was.

I do not wish to name either the Rabbi or the missionary society. But there followed three months' intensive work, in the course of which we found twenty-eight more orthodox Jewish children, removed from all contact with their Jewish relatives in England, and being brought up as Christians. Gradually most of these were restored to their relatives. But again I had to ask myself whether a policy which could lead to such results as this could possibly be the Divinely intended relationship between Judaism and Christianity.

When the Second World War came, my attitude to the Jewish-Christian relationship was a huge question mark ; but I had reached the conviction that the right answer to this question was more important than any sociological or political studies.

I must now retrace my steps to describe a quite independent development. Like many of my generation who had fought in the First World War, I came out of the army more concerned with the problem of peace than with any question of my personal career. I founded the League of Nations Union at the university—it had previously been just a local town branch—and the International Assembly I have already mentioned was its public activity. It was one of the best attended and the most interesting gatherings in the Oxford of the early twenties. It led to my being invited to become international study secretary of the Student Christian Movement. But it did not lead to my discovering that there was any consistent or thought-out Christian attitude to politics and international relations.

From 1923 to 1930 I was perpetually occupied with the morality of politics and of international relations. I had as many national as international contacts. I spent a considerable part of each year up to 1928 in Europe. After 1928 I lived in Geneva until 1935. During that period I not merely came to realise that there was nothing central in the Christian tradition which could be called a doctrine of the natural community, both in terms of its policies and in terms of its relations with other natural communities, but that there was a strong and uninhibited Christian tradition which denied the relevance of the Christian insight to the political field, and even relegated ethics themselves to a completely secondary place of importance.

It was, therefore, of fundamental importance to the development of my theology that I gradually came to see that the main distinction between Judaism and Christianity was that the one was the Divine imperative to an elect nation, and the other a similar imperative to the elect from every nation. The natural community was the subject of Judaism, and all descriptions of Judaism as a *church* were completely false. On the other hand, Christianity was, from its very beginning, a body *called out*—which, after all, is what *ecclesia* means—from the natural community of which each person happened to be a member. What I slowly came to realise was that the religion of a natural community was inevitably concerned with every aspect of the life of a natural community, its social life, its economics, its politics and its relations with other natural communities.

I had already discovered in my studies of Jewish history that Jews had always been concerned with these things in the full measure of the possible. Sometimes they possessed considerable freedom, sometimes they were restricted within the narrowest boundaries. But they were always concerned with practical things, with the attainable.

This perspective threw a new light on the passage from

the period of the prophets to that of the scribes; and I
began to realise that, so far from there being a steady
decline beginning with Ezra, it was with Ezra that there
began a consistent attempt to embody the great declarations
of the prophets in the daily life of the people. A natural
community cannot live by generalisations however elevated
and splendid. It lives by the principle of " here a little, there
a little " in concrete daily decisions. Ezra, by arranging for
the weekly reading of Torah, by training a body in its interpretation, and by setting in motion the steps which made
of the Jews the first literate people, was, as the Rabbis
declared, truly a second Moses. I realised how absurd it was
to term a period of decline a period which saw the beginnings of the three fundamentals of the three contemporary
monotheisms of Judaism, Christianity and Islam. The three
were: regular religious worship wherever there was a community, universal religious education, and the selection and
preservation of a canon of sacred writings.

What Ezra began, the Rabbis continued. One cannot
approve the work of Ezra and condemn the work of the
Rabbis of the Mishna and the Talmud. There is no break in
the chain of development from the one to the other. I
realised how meaningless also was the conventional Christian
criticism which contrasted the magnificence of the prophets
with the pedestrian ordinariness of the Rabbis. Those of you
who know Dr. Charles's volumes on the Apocrypha and
Pseudepigrapha, will remember how he sets down the text
of *Pirke Aboth* in order to point out how inferior it is to the
Gospels. But the comparison is utterly unfair, for the objectives of the two are completely different. One sets a level
of perfection to be reached by the few who can enter in
by the narrow gate; the other is concerned with what is
attainable by a total community.

This is not a criticism of either alternative, nor does it
allow of a comparison claiming one to be better than the
other. On the one hand, none of my studies of Judaism make
me deviate from a relatively conservative Christian orthodoxy. But, on the other hand, I realised that Judaism was
not an incomplete Christianity but a different religion,
stemming from the same roots in the religion of ancient

Israel, but meeting the reality of the human situation at a different point.

All thought of a comparison claiming one to be better than the other vanishes before any objective consideration of the task which confronted each religion during the same formative centuries—from the second to the fifth of the Christian era.

Christianity, with its mission to the elect of every nation, confronted all the philosophies and religions of the ancient world. It drew its converts from the widest range of those philosophies and religions. How varied and difficult their backgrounds were is well pictured by the moral and domestic problems which confronted St. Paul in the single community of Corinth. It was not merely inevitable but right that Christianity developed an elaborate and well reasoned theology, carefully distinguishing between legitimate and illegitimate interpretations of the historic events on which it rested. Hierarchical organisation and a clerical caste were both necessary means for its preservation and expansion. Throughout it recognised the existence of a world outside, the object of its evangelism and its charity, but not the determinant of its theology.

The task confronting the leaders of Jewry was totally different. No central organisation, religious or political, survived the war with Rome. The people were dispersed all through the Mediterranean and western Asiatic world. On the other hand, their missionary interest was much more peripheral than that of the Christian Church. Their real concern was with the Jewish people themselves. *Vis-à-vis* the Jews they could never appear as a Church, separated from the nation. They might abuse the *amme ha-aretz* to their hearts' content. But they had to win their allegiance or fail in their responsibility. For the covenant of Sinai was with a people, not with those called out from a people.

So while in those same formative centuries the leaders of the Church were devotedly accepting the responsibility laid on them, and moulding a Christianity which spread from China to the Atlantic, and captured the Roman Empire itself in less than three centuries, the Rabbis were tackling with equal devotion their completely different task. The first thing that strikes the outside student is the almost complete lack of theological interest. It is not merely that there is no definition of theological orthodoxy, but that there is no attempt to define and deepen prophetic monotheism. They retained an inextinguishable sense of the nearness of God; but with that they were content, and went on to concentrate their minds on the life which He called on His chosen people to live.

Christians have condemned Judaism for not conducting the same kind of mission as they themselves know to be inherent in Christianity. Only ignorance can explain, though scarcely excuse, a Christian for condemning the Jew for not doing what his Christian ancestors readily put him to death for if he attempted to do. For almost the first law of Constantine which recorded the victory of the Christian Church punished a Jew with death if he sought to convert a Christian. The last man to die in England for a religious offence was condemned to death in the reign of James I for converting to Judaism. But the condemnation itself is based on a misunderstanding. The mission of Israel, conducted whenever Jews had the opportunity, is not the conversion of Gentiles individually to Judaism, but the spreading of justice and righteousness in the community which has admitted them as equal citizens.

It was only the tiny Western Jewries who had the opportunity of exercising their mission in the century and a half which followed emancipation; and they had to exercise it against a rising tide of antisemitism which finally overwhelmed them. It is important to emphasise this, for no passage in the Old Testament anticipates the New Testament call to preach and teach every nation. Whether in Deuteronomy or in the prophets, Jews are called to loyalty to Torah, and told that it is the demonstration of this loyalty which will draw the nations to the God of Israel.

If there is much misunderstanding about the mission of Judaism, there is equal Christian misunderstanding about its nature. Judaism is not, like Christianity, a religion of salvation. During a lecture tour in the United States a dozen years ago I was constantly posed this kind of question by clergy of different denominations: " We know that we are saved in the name of Jesus Christ. In what name do Jews preach salvation ? " To which I had to reply that Jews did not preach salvation : they preached a way of life which fulfilled the will of God. In the same way I was challenged with the Pauline doctrine of justification by faith, and asked whether I was not bound as a Christian to condemn the Jewish belief in justification by works. To which again I had to reply that Judaism does not believe in justification by works because it has no doctrine of justification. It is true that the sacrifice—or rather the willingness to be sacrificed —of Isaac hovers on the periphery of Judaism, but it never moved to the centre. It is likewise true that God's judgement of a man is connected with his obedience ; but it is the obedience of the heart for which the Rabbis called, not the external conformity to a set of works, an attitude which they condemned as heartily as Jesus condemns it in the Gospels.

So, then, I found myself confronted with two different religions, neither of which was an incomplete example of the other ; and I had to move to the next stage of the problem : what was the right relation between them ?

I had various possibilities to consider. The traditional missionary approach was impossible, since it was evident that there were much needed virtues in Judaism which were absent, or belittled, in Christianity, so that the world would lose if all Jews became members of the existing churches. The natural community, the nation State, was not only still with us, but much more powerful than in the time of the separation of the two religions. Man needed, even more than he did then, to understand the Divine action in politics and international relations ; but it was also true that the State was penetrating more and more into the private life of every citizen. And before this encroaching power, the churches seemed impotent. On the other hand, I had no intention of denying the qualities peculiar to Christianity —its profound theology, philosophical and mystical, its doctrine of the Atonement, its pastoral understanding, its healing mission, its teaching about the life to come. There was no solution in all Christians becoming Jews.

There was the view of the Swiss Protestant, Leonhard Ragaz, that Judaism possessed the Messianic age, while

Christianity possessed the Messiah, and that this formed the basis for a synthesis. There was the view popularised by Rosenzweig that Judaism was the Divinely intended religion for the Jews, and Christianity for the Gentiles.

I came to the conclusion that there were two fundamental points which had to be accepted for any solution. The first was that Jews and Gentiles formed a single humanity with the same needs. The solution of Rosenzweig would therefore have worked had the two religions been identical in character. Since they were not, there was either something which each missed, or each possessed something which was erroneous or superfluous. If the former, then each ultimately needed the other ; if the latter, then they could combine by each dropping what was peculiar to themselves. This latter seemed to me an impossible solution. I was prepared to assert of both religions that they contained human imperfections and errors ; that both could still grow and develop. But I was quite certain that neither could surrender what made it different from the other, and showed as its essential identity and quality. I was definitely not going to give up my belief in the Divinity of Christ or in the doctrine of the Atonement. I was equally sure that Jewry would not surrender its doctrine of Torah and of the covenant relationship between God and Israel.

What prevented me from leaving the matter there, and compelled me to go on to my present position, was my lifelong concern with the world of the natural community, the world of politics and international relations, and with my disillusion with the typical Christian attitude thereto. And it was in these fields that I had discovered the strength of Judaism.

When I speak of the strength of Judaism it must be borne in mind that I am a historian. Modern orthodox Judaism, like much of modern orthodox Christianity, seems to me a sorry shadow of its true self. There is more excuse for Jews than there is for Christians, for centuries of denigration and active persecution force a religion to be conservative and even reactionary. Nevertheless, there seems to be a tragic loss of values when *shechita* and rules of Sabbath observance are made to play so central a role in the preservation of the

198

meaning of Sinai; and when an inexhaustible memory of past decisions becomes the main basis for the understanding of totally new problems.

I am, then, moving through the centuries in selecting what seem to me the essential qualities on which rest Jewry's immense understanding of the Divine imperative in the natural community. I have already mentioned one: the continuous concern with the attainable, which is in such contrast with the perpetual surge of idealistic movements among Christians. An obvious example is the disastrous forcing of prohibition on the unwilling American public. Another is the sad ineffectiveness of the Christian pacifist movement.

Of equal importance with the pursuit of the attainable is the selection of the pursuers. It is not for a clerical caste to decide on the attainable—especially in politics and economics—for an obedient laity. It is a task in which success will only come if representatives of the total life of the community are entrusted with the task. Such was the situation in the rabbinic academies which forged the Judaism that survived the centuries between the fall of Jerusalem and the establishment of Israel. The third is a quality not conspicuous in present-day Jewish orthodoxy. It is the willingness to accept constant reinterpretation to meet changing conditions and new demands. There is no passage in the Gospels which bears more clearly the mark of an evangelist's misunderstanding, than that in which Jesus is made to side with the Sadducees, and condemn the creation of "the traditions of the elders." A static religion is a dead religion, especially if it be a religion concerned with the everyday life of ordinary men and women.

There are clearly qualities and characteristics in rabbinic Judaism which owe their existence, or at least their emphasis, to the artificial and unique life which Jewry led for a millennium and a half. For a multiplicity of widely scattered minorities, bound by no hierarchical obedience, marks which distinguished ordinary Jews easily from their non-Jewish neighbours were extremely important. The fence about the Torah was very necessary when each little Jewish community was a minority surrounded by a hostile, a seductive, or an apathetic majority. We easily forget that even in the first century Gentile cites were scattered about Judea and Galilee. But today, I doubt if there be anybody who will be drawn to Israel by the fact that they eat pork only *sub rosa,* or that they do not open their refrigerators one day a week. The challenge to Jews today, both in Israel and where they are free citizens in the diaspora, is to a renewal, in concrete and twentieth-century terms, of the message of Deuteronomy and the prophets. And it is because the Jewish response to that message is so clear and so world-wide that I am convinced that the power which flows through Sinai was not arrested, nor replaced, by another power when Jesus of Nazareth was born.

But this does not mean that I deny or belittle the power which flows from the life and death of Jesus of Nazareth. My solution is not to challenge either, but to challenge the traditional use of the great Catholic doctrine of the Trinity. I admit that from a fundamentalist point of view, my interpretation is impossible. But I am not a fundamentalist, and I do not hold that every definition in the New Testament must be embodied in our dogmas and liturgies. The Gospels and Epistles make a trinitarian definition of the Divine nature inevitable but they are not themselves fully trinitarian. They describe a kind of Divine bureaucracy by which one member delegates tasks to another, or performs them through another. This seems to me quite untrue. On the other hand I fully accept the clauses of the Athanasian Creed which define clearly that the three equal persons are not interchangeable.

If we use the word " channel " in place of person, I believe that power flows from one unknowable godhead through three equal channels, and that each channel reached its fullness at an appropriate moment in the history of creation. I believe that the first such moment was at Sinai. The second was at the Incarnation. Consequently I hold the right relations between Judaism and Christianity to be a creative tension within a single trinitarian theology.

Just as man as social being lives in perpetual tension with himself as person, so the power which flows through the channel of the Incarnation is in tension, creative or destructive, with the power that flows from Sinai.

This concept of a Divinely intended tension in revelation may seem strange until we face the fact that this tension exists continuously in human life, and that it is by accepting tension, and making it creative, that every step forward is achieved. The religion of man as social being is a religion of the attainable as clearly as the religion of man as person is the religion of the unattainable. No statesman can build a policy for his nation on the basis that " here we have no abiding city." No person can ignore the words of Jesus that we should lay up our treasures in heaven.

In stating the relation of the two religions in terms of the Trinity and in terms of creative tension, I may be innovating; but I am completely orthodox in refusing to recognise inequality within the Godhead. Judaism and Christianity are to me equal partners in the task of bringing mankind to the Messianic age, and neither can replace the other. This means, of course, that I hold the Atonement wrought on Calvary to be of equal significance, whether they accept it or not, to all men.

And this brings me to my last point. In stating that the Atonement comes to all men, including especially Jews and Christians, our subject at this moment, through the one act of Jesus Christ, I am stating something which, at present, Jews cannot accept, and indeed find repugnant. I think they are in error, just as I think those Christians are in error who are convinced that they possess everything which can be offered by Judaism. I believe that for a long time to come, we shall have to accept that Jews will think like that, and that Christians will think like that. I am equally convinced that it is for Christians to take the initiative in every forward move, while making no attempt to force Jewish reticence or reluctance. They owe this to Jewry, because of the appalling history of Christian denigration and persecution. What both sides can do is to accept the other side as an equal partner in the work of God in the world, each making his own contribution, and rejoicing in the positive side of the contribution of the other. That which each of us condemns in the other, let us leave until we understand each other better.

12

THE BIBLE, THE WORLD AND THE TRINITY

THE BIBLE IS our ultimate source of information about how both synagogue and church began, but it is also constantly used as an ultimate theological authority. The traditional argument of both Jews and Christians for ascribing this authority to it is that it is the *Word of God*. If not actually dictated by God, it is so completely inspired by Him that it is without error in matters of faith and morals. That is one view, and it is astonishing how it still persists in liturgical and ecclesiastical usages. But there is another attitude: that the Bible describes *the activity of God,* as interpreted by men who with their whole heart believed in Him. But the men who wrote it were men of widely different under-standing, and of widely different time and environment. The literature they composed covers more than a thousand years of history.

If Christians adopt the first, the traditional, view, then they have to face a certain number of very difficult facts. They have to justify it in the face of the fact that these seven words *The Bible is the Word of God* have been responsible for more evil and cruelty than any other seven words in the history of the Christian Church. In the whole battle for humanising the law which raged over Europe, both Catholic and Protestant, from the seventeenth century to the nineteenth, the churches, Catholic, Anglican, Lutheran, Calvinist, all opposed reform again and again on these same grounds—the Bible is the Word of God, and you cannot tamper with it. This was the authority for burning witches, for maintaining slavery, for enforcing capital punish-ment for innumerable offences. In the argument today over apartheid the same words are heard. The Bible ordains that the sons of Ham shall be kept in subjection, and the Bible is the Word of God.

But it is not only the Old Testament which is involved. We have to keep a belief in hell, because the parables of the Gospels constantly terminate with a division of men into sheep and goats. We have to defend, as Christians, a demonstrably false picture of Judaism in its Pharisaic form, because of the words which are ascribed to Jesus in the Gospels. We have to accept that Jesus behaves in a way which, to contemporary moral standards, not merely denies that he is God incarnate but makes him a figure unworthy of our admiration. Without regard to any distinction between the innocent and the guilty, he damns whole classes such as the Pharisees or the rich ; he damns whole cities. Because "Woe unto thee Chorazin, woe unto thee Bethsaida" (Matt. xi, 21) was the Word of God—doubly so, because it is both a word of Jesus and in the Bible— whole cities were destroyed in the crusade against the Albigenses in the south of France in the thirteenth century. Every man, woman and child was killed on the orders of the churchmen who led the crusade. "Kill all," they cried. "God will know his own."

Alternatively one may believe that the Bible was written by men who agreed in believing that the central factor in history is the activity of God. But they were men of widely different sensitivity and outlook. It is urgently necessary to say that this belief is as profound, and as penetrating as the other. For believers in biblical infallibility constantly imply that this other belief belittles the Bible, is devised to blur the distinction between truth and falsehood, seeks to get rid of the challenge of religion, is privately known by its proponents to be untrue, and so on. All that is false. Critics *may* possess such views and such desires. But these are not the necessary consequence of refusing to accept the Bible literally as the Word of God.

The fascinating thing about the Bible is the common conviction of its writers that material power and intellectual activity are not the central dynamic of history, but that the real dynamic is the activity of God in His creation. Every writer interpreted the Divine activity in accordance with the knowledge of his time ; and there lies on us the responsibility to interpret it with the knowledge available in our own time. It will be for tomorrow to interpret it afresh in accordance with the knowledge of tomorrow. To me such an attitude to the Bible presents a far more compelling and attractive picture of the activity of God than those seven words " the Bible is the Word of God " could ever do.

THE NEW TESTAMENT VIEW OF JUDAISM

I have spoken of the consequence of deifying the biblical text from the standpoint of general Christian history. But it has direct bearings also on the attitude of the church to the synagogue. The Gospel attitude to the Pharisees is not the only disaster. All the apostolic writings imply definitely that a heritage has passed over from the synagogue to the church, that Sinai is *functus officio* and has been replaced by a new covenant. At times Paul implies that the covenant of Sinai was never intended by God to be anything but temporary and limited in its scope. The dynamic Pharisaic doctrine of interpretation is condemned in the Gospels as a substitution of the teaching of men for the revelation of God (Mark vii, 9), and is equally condemned in Paul's letter to the Romans as substituting a man-made righteousness for obedience to the Divine will (Rom. ix, 31). Jews are described as living under a curse (Gal. iii, 10 and James ii, 10), apparently by Divine intention. While one might argue—even if unjustly —that the Pharisees were condemned only because their Judaism had become a narrow and superficial legalism, the condemnations in Paul and James are condemnations of Judaism itself, of the whole conception of a way of life Divinely revealed at Sinai, and perpetually renewed by Divine inspiration.

When such a view of Judaism was a commonplace of apostolic preaching, one cannot be surprised that Christianity had separated entirely from Judaism by the beginning of the second century. In the fourth century, when the Roman Empire had become Christian, when the church had obtained power to embody its will in legislation, the

attitude to Judaism passed from disputation and verbal
controversy to increasingly violent anti-Jewish legislation.
By the end of the first hundred years of a Christian empire,
it had become a capital offence both for convert and con-
verter, if a man voluntarily adopted Judaism as his religion.
All this was on the authority of the Bible, which pronounced
that all Jews were forever guilty of the crime of deicide, and
that all the Divine promises had passed from the synagogue
to the church. One cannot escape, in tracing the history of
Jewish-Christian relations, from deciding one's attitude to
the Bible.

THE CENTRE OF THE CHRISTIAN REVELATION

If we look at the nineteen hundred years of Christian history
we can see that Christendom reveals certain strengths and
weaknesses. At its centre is its emphasis on *man as person.*
This runs all through the teaching of Jesus. It has provided
the dynamic of the Cross in every culture, civilisation and
century, through the conviction of each Christian that on
the Cross Christ died for *him.* It has flowed out in the
immense missionary activity of the church.

At the present moment, when two world wars in our life-
time have dishonoured Christendom, we are living through
a period when the rest of the world—Asia, Africa, the Com-
munist bloc—look with contempt on the Christian West.
It is a contempt which we deserve, and which we must live
through. But if we accept it, and seek to understand it,
there will come a time when from Malaysia, or Bali, or
Ghana, youngsters will be getting their Ph.Ds by studying
in the libraries and records of the Society for Promoting
Christian Knowledge, or the Church Missionary Society, or
the Society for the Propagation of the Gospel, or the forgotten Colonial Office, in order that each may gather material
on the lives of Christian after Christian who came to spend
his life in their particular part of the world. And by then
the nations of the world will be ready to accept, and embody
in their own history, the essential contributions which these
Christians from abroad once brought to them. For it is in
activity such as theirs that the strength of Christianity lay,
and still lies.

That has been the enormous contribution of the power
of the *living Christ* to man as person. There has been nothing
else like it. The missionary activity of Islam is quite different.
The missionary activity of Judaism, inhibited or prevented
for a millennium and a half by the other monotheisms,
has involved, where it was possible for it to function, the
transformation of society, not the going out to man as person
without regard for Jew or Greek, bond or free. The missionary activity of Christianity, common to all the Christian
churches, is an indisputable fact of history, and its consequences, once they can be seen in historical perspective,
will be more justly assessed by its beneficiaries than is at
present possible.

CHRISTENDOM AND SOCIETY

The picture is very different when we pass from the consideration of man as person to the understanding of *man as
social being*. The influence of the church in the transformation of society has been negligible. In the field of law, as
I have said already, it has been disastrous. And yet it is not
due to lack of opportunity. In the first centuries after the
victory of the church there were great Christian emperors
—Constantine himself, Theodosius the Great, Justinian, to
name only a few—and the empire itself lay at the feet of
the church for it to mould as it would. Yet there came
practically no change in the nature of political power, the
nature of political thinking, the attitude to crime and punishment, which can be traced to the influence of Christian
theology. When the centre of authority passed from Rome
eastwards to Byzantium or westwards to the Germanic,
Gallic, or Hispanic kingdoms, the same was still true. The
influence of Christianity on public life remained negligible.
When the medieval church reached the apogee of its
power there were some slight changes, some slight adjustments, such as the Truce of God which prescribed that you
could only go out and kill your neighbours on four days of
the week—I forget which days—instead of seven. But this
can scarcely be called a transformation of society. There is
a medieval German saying that " under the crozier one lives

206

well," meaning that there were certain advantages in living on the territory of a prince bishop and not of a secular prince. There were, of course, personal tendernesses and kindnesses because among the church leaders of every country and century there were men of saintly character as well as men simply accustomed to rule. But there is no basic change which can be traced to the Christian Church in the nature and structure of either political or legal power.

Today the lack is equally conspicuous. As soon as we pass from personal problems to political or economic issues, the voice of the churches becomes hesitant ; there is no common Christian tradition or authority ; and Christians end up by weakly accepting the idea that all kinds of mutually opposite policies are equally Christian.

CHRISTENDOM AND THE SEARCH FOR TRUTH

From the fifteenth century onwards a similar picture—or lack of picture—can be seen in another field as well. An extraordinary change was taking place in *the nature of authority*. It was a move of fundamental significance away from the medieval conception that authority resided in something which had been laid down in the past to the modern belief that it resides in the most accurate possible examination of the actual facts.

If you had gone to a medieval doctor with an ailment which you described to him, he would have looked up his Galen or his Herbal to discover what herb or frog or mouse he should pound up to cure it. But if you had gone to a doctor who did not fear excommuncation by the predecessor of the Royal College of Physicians—for doctors are collectively more conservative than the church—he would have taken out a queer little wooden trumpet and begun by listening to your heart. He would probably then have extracted something from some part of you and examined it under a microscope.

A change, affecting every part of our relationship to the material universe, was taking place in those centuries, a change from reliance on already existing authority to the immediate search for truth. It was the change which led to the birth of Humanism.

The church behaved toward this change in exactly the same way as the synagogue had once behaved towards the church. The church now excommunicated the new seekers after knowledge on the ground that their findings contradicted, or were not sanctioned by, biblical and other tradition. The new seekers became "Humanists," agnostic or atheist, simply because the church had no place for them or their discoveries.

In both excommunications there was disastrous loss to both sides. For in each case the excommunicated party retorted in similar vein. The church had pronounced that the Jews must be preserved as witnesses to the gravity of the crime of deicide, preserved with every humiliation which human imagination and ingenuity could devise. Now the Humanists retorted as the church had done. They dismissed Christian dogmas as medieval superstitions or as wishful thinking. And the result of all this is that we are in the state we are in today. Among the many unfortunate phrases which are current in contemporary discussion, the most unfortunate is to describe the present age as being both happy and adult. I doubt whether man has ever lived in a less happy, less stable, society with less understanding of his environment, with less passion to make life worth living, and behind all, with the threat of nuclear war. It is absurd to call it happy. Nor is it adult. There is not a single political, social, or human problem which it has begun to discover how to solve, or has even created the preconditions for examining objectively. Ability to fly round the moon may make man an infant prodigy. It does not make him an adult.

CHRISTOCENTRIC CHRISTIANITY

It was natural that in the first flush of excitement the early church thought that the acceptance of Christ was all that mattered. But it was unfortunate that the attitude persisted and persists. The outlook of the church is entirely christocentric, and an exclusive interest in Christ is accentuated by a doctrine of Divine activity in which Christ occupies not merely a central but an exclusive position. It was popular in my day at Oxford to use the cliché that we cannot know what God is like, but we could know what he was like from Christ. Liturgically we do not ask God to bless even our morning porridge except through Christ, or to listen to prayer unless it is passed first through him. What he was not interested in, the church is not interested in ; and if it be something to which men devote their lives, then they must still ask for a Divine blessing on it, or invite Divine aid in its performance, only through Christ. As for the Holy Spirit, he is simply Christ's main executive officer for governing the Christian Church. In London, the *Times* and the *Daily Telegraph* publish weekly sermons in their Saturday issues. Quite recently, in I forget which newspaper, it was explained that the Holy Spirit was governing the church " since at his Ascension Christ had returned to his place at the right hand of God."

In spite of the evident failure of that area of the world which we call Christendom to give the world the blessing of peace, it does not seem to occur to the spokesmen of Christianity that anything can possibly have been inadequate in the basic content of their message. In spite of empty churches, it does not seem to occur to ecclesiastical authorities of any denomination that it is their basic message which may have failed to meet men's needs. No. The church always *has* preached that Christ is the solution to every human problem ; and, in spite of the obvious evidence to the contrary, it has no intention of asking itself whether that is, in fact, the whole truth.

This exclusive christocentricity has had another, and equally unfortunate, effect. The church has attached so much importance to the phrase " salvation in Christ " that during long centuries of its existence it has denied that the immense majority of men have any eternal destiny except the flames of hell. Again and again, even in the history of different denominations within the church itself, Christian has excommunicated Christian and damned him to a lower hell than that inhabited by the heathen, or the man who lived before Christ was born ; for they could, at least, plead ignorance. The inevitably universal responsibility of a Creator has been forgotten, the existence of holiness within other religions has been ignored. The Thirty-nine Articles

of the Church of England, which a foolish covey of ecclesi-
astics wishes to fix still more firmly upon us, actually proclaim
(Article XIII, *Of Works before Justification*) that God considers it to be sinful if any man perform a good work, save
through faith in Jesus Christ.

It is surely time that the churches faced the fact that a
christocentric gospel has not only led them into deplorable
beliefs and activities, but has failed, of itself, to meet the
whole of human need.

An Alternative Approach

Now there is an alternative. Little exploited by the church,
quite incomprehensible to the synagogue, despised as
antique phraseology by the Humanists, it is the doctrine of
the Trinity, the most majestic, creative and enthralling conception of God and His relations to man available to any
religion.

Those who enjoy exploring the beauties of our countryside
and its ancient buildings—Suffolk is our own happy hunting-
ground—will find from time to time two different medieval
representations of the Trinity. One is nearly always in stone.
It consists of a large and bearded figure which represents
God the Father. He holds on his knees a very much smaller
God the Son on his Cross; while somewhere about—
presumably where the carver had a piece of stone available
—is a dove representing the Holy Spirit. This is the Trinity
according to the New Testament, and I believe it to be
entirely false and misleading. But there is another common
presentation on the subject. It is sometimes in stone on fonts
or corbels, but more often in stained glass. It is the triangle
represented on the next page.

In it, as distinct from in the other representation, Father,
Son and Spirit are equal manifestations of one Godhead, and
the Godhead is equally manifested in each. But the Father
is not the Son or the Spirit, the Son is not the Spirit or the
Father, the Spirit is not the Father or the Son.

There is none of the subordinationism which there is in
the New Testament. The Father is not identified with the
Godhead in a way in which the Son and the Spirit are not
so identified; and there is not the pathetic Divine bureau-

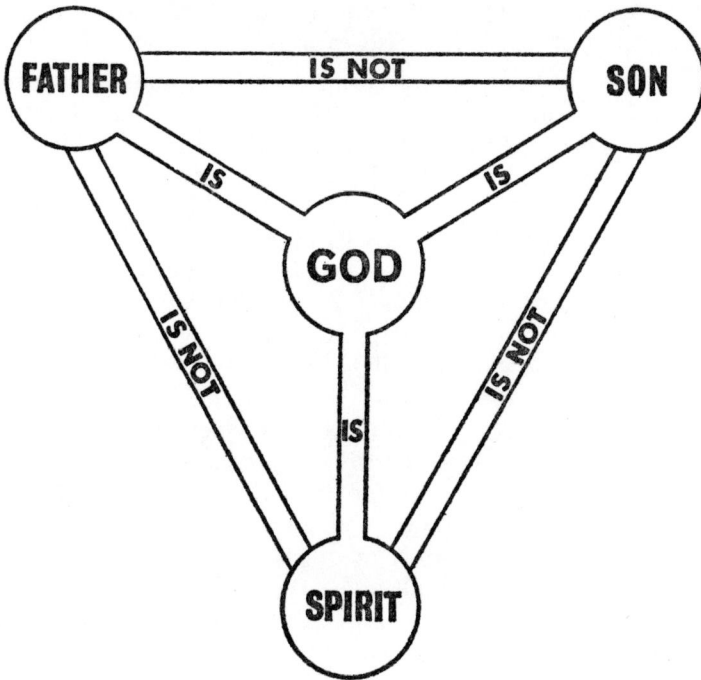

cracy by which one member of the Godhead is perpetually
sending or directing another, or acting on behalf of or
through another, instead of behaving in his own unique and
irreplaceable quality.

It is fascinating to find that this representation of the
Godhead circulated at the same time as the other, without
anybody apparently objecting to their evident inconsistency.
But the same is true of the creeds of the church. Those in
common use carry the implication of subordinationism and
bureaucracy. But the Book of Common Prayer has also a
creed giving precise definition to the triangular representation. It is known as the Athanasian Creed, though it has
nothing to do with the saint of that name. It was originally
a theological formula expressing the development of
Christian belief, and defining the heresies to be rejected.
When it was turned into a creed two appalling verses were
added at the beginning and end, saying that this was the

Catholic faith "which, except a man believe faithfully, without doubt he shall perish everlastingly."

Now, one of the very few sermons which I remember from my undergraduate days was preached by W. R. Maltby precisely on the Athanasian Creed. This was on a Sunday when all the college chapels were saying the Athanasian Creed, and Maltby was preaching at Mansfield. He had a high, squeaky voice, and he began his sermon by saying that it was a Sunday when all the Anglicans would be saying the Athanasian Creed. He said: "People get very angry about the Athanasian Creed, but the Athanasian Creed's all right— there is only one word left out—whosoever will be saved, it is *not* necessary that he hold the Catholic faith "; and he then went on to deliver the most magnificent sermon on the Catholic faith which, after forty-two years, I still remember. "What is the Catholic faith ? It is the experience of men and women of every culture and civilisation to which the church has penetrated over nearly two thousand years. And you, poor little man, think you have got to hold the whole of that to be saved. If you even get an idea of the most minute fragment of it, it will be enough for you, and as much as you can possibly take."

Setting it aside, then, as a creed, we still have its precise and significant definition of the Godhead:

The Godhead of the Father, of the Son, and of the Holy Ghost, is all one: the glory equal, the majesty co-eternal. Such as the Father is, such is the Son, and such is the Holy Ghost. The Father uncreate, the Son uncreate, and the Holy Ghost uncreate. The Father incomprehensible, the Son incomprehensible, and the Holy Ghost incomprehensible (the word means "that which cannot be contained or limited "). The Father eternal, the Son eternal, and the Holy Ghost eternal. And yet there are not three eternals ; but one eternal. As also there are not three incomprehensibles, nor three uncreated ; but one uncreated, and one incomprehensible. . . . And in this Trinity, none is afore, or after other ; none is greater, or less than another ; but the whole three Persons are co-eternal together, and co-equal. So that in all things, as aforesaid: the Unity in Trinity, and the Trinity in Unity is to be worshipped.

Contemporary teaching about God is usually inhibited by this word " Person." It is a block excluding Judaism on the one hand and Humanism on the other. The pathetic thing is that it is a mistranslation. It is simply an Englishing of the Latin word *persona,* which does not mean what the " person " conveys to any twentieth-century hearer. It is difficult to get a single term which fully explains what the original authors were getting at, but at least we know what they were rejecting. They were rejecting, on the one hand, the idea that God, the infinite and unknowable, communicated with man, the finite and concrete, by a hierarchy of beings, each one of which was a little less spiritual and more material than the last, until they had reached the state where communication with man was possible. This is the kind of picture one gets in various forms of gnosticism and mysticism, Jewish, Christian, or other. But, on the other hand, they were also rejecting the idea that the ultimate reality was an entirely characterless and impersonal force, the prime mover which is itself unmoved, of Aristotle. So they insisted, first, that the communication with man came from God himself, and secondly that within the Godhead was what man understood as personality and purpose. God might be much more than man meant by personality. But he could not be less than personal.

There is another word in the New Testament account of the activity of God which is similarly liable to confusion, if we insist on taking the New Testament as an ultimate theological authority. That is the word " spirit." The Old Testament is concerned to insist that God is spirit. He is not a particular material entity like pagan idols. It is because he is spirit that he is omnipresent. In the New Testament the reference to spirit may be sometimes simply a continuation of this traditional usage, but at other times it is attached exclusively to one of the three *personæ* which the early church saw in the Godhead. That one of these *personæ* was also called " the Holy Spirit " simply added to the confusion.

H

For not every reference to a *persona* of God as spirit is by any means concentrated on the third person.

Finally, modern discoveries about the many immaterial forces in the universe, and their immense power, have given wholly new emphasis to the meaning of the word "spirit" as descriptive of God. In at least two fields it is more creatively linked to ideas of ultimate reality which are impersonal, than to ideas which are expressed in personality. For we are becoming accustomed to immense fields of activity which are not just mechanical or automatic, but in which there is a natural and rational response to moral or intellectual initiative from the human side. All the forces of radiation are more naturally understood in relation to an immensely disciplined but impersonal reality ; much of the activity of communication of human minds and spirits, whether in the Divine-healing movement or in telepathy or in extra-sensory perception, are to be as much explored through the understanding of the more subtle laws of the universe as of the "personal" will behind those laws. For there is nothing arbitrary in their functioning.

That there was within the Godhead not one *persona* but three *personæ* the early church deduced entirely from the Bible, and it is because of this biblical origin that biblical language still dominates the liturgy, as well as much of the theological thinking, of the church. The practical consequence of this biblical domination has been, as already said, that the church in its teaching and activity, has been exceedingly christocentric, and has certainly not given equal emphasis to the other *personæ*.

We can, perhaps, see this most easily by considering man, for we can draw a similar triangle presenting the position of man in the world, a position imposed on him by the nature of the world he lives in, not one which he can accept or reject at his own pleasure. In the central circle would be MAN, and in the three outside circles would be

SOCIAL BEING   PERSON
SEEKER

Man cannot help being a social being, for he cannot live independently of his fellows. He cannot help being a unique

214

person in himself. There is that within him which he can neither share, nor control, nor communicate, that which Francis Thompson describes in " The Fallen Yew " as

> The hold that falls not when the town is got,
> The heart's heart, whose immurèd plot
> Hath keys yourself keep not.

But equally man is obliged to be a seeker in a world which never stands still, in which he must either advance or go backwards. And here also the " is " and the " is not " are equally valid. The same man is *equally* all these three things. But man as person is not man as seeker. Man as seeker is not man as social being. Man as social being is not man as person.

It is easy to illustrate the reality of these distinctions. A person becomes a judge, a Member of Parliament, a governor. In these capacities he has to become impersonal. In his personal relations it is for a man to forgive those who offend him ; as person he is specially related to his family and his friends, and has special obligations to them. But if he is a judge, his task is not to forgive all those who come before him, or to favour his family and friends, but to administer the law, to administer justice, in the most objective, most impersonal way he can.

Even so he is not the same as man as seeker. Let us choose an example — a ridiculous example, if you will — of the demands of research. Let him be working on the diseases of chrysanthemums. He has always believed that these diseases were due to a bug which came up from the ground. He has built up an immense apparatus of research activity, with sprays, dusting powders and special fertilisers, on the basis of chrysanthemum disease being due to a bug which rises from the ground. Then he suddenly discovers that it is due to a gnat which flies down from the sycamore tree. All his decisions are invalidated, and he must start again from scratch. He cannot keep bits of it on the grounds that they cost him much in time or money. If the premises are false, the consequences deduced from them are of no further value.

Look now at the problem of research for man as social being. Let us imagine him a high official in the Ministry of

Health in a society as complex as our own. Someone comes
to him and says: "You know, it would have been far better
if, in designing hospitals, the Ministry had done so and so."
He may say, "Bless me! So it would!" But he cannot order
all the hospitals to be destroyed instantly, and just start
again. He can only ask "Well, what do we do with the
hospitals we've got?" He has all the time to compromise,
to discover the limits of the possible.

There is yet a third way in which we can use the diagram
of the triangle. The essential quality which relates God in
his triple revelation to man in his triple situation is not
single and identical. If to man as person God is Love, to
man as social being God is Righteousness or Justice, and to
man as seeker, God is Truth. And again we may say that
God is equally Righteousness, Love and Truth. But
Righteousness is not Love, Love is not Truth, Truth is not
Righteousness.

THE HISTORIC TRINITY

All our three uses of the triangle we can relate directly to
Judaism, Christianity and Humanism. And in this relationship
we can see also the interdependence, as well as the distinction, of the three corner circles. It is, perhaps, clearest in regard
to the three qualities. It is evident that truth, righteousness and
love are not synonyms for the same quality. Yet is is equally
evident that they are not in opposition to each other. There
cannot be love which is based either on injustice or on a
lie, and it is the same with the other two. But if they are
neither interchangeable terms, nor opposing terms, then the
real relationship between them is a creative tension which
recognises on the one hand that all are separate parts of a
single whole, and on the other that the whole would be
incomplete without the separate contributions.

So I believe it is with the three expressions of the
experience of man in Judaism, Christianity and Humanism.
They are as related to each other as are the three circles
of the Trinity, circles which I believe it is more fruitful to
relate to the Divine mystery as "channels" than with the
traditional word of "persons." The term is not perfect, but

it is less misleading to speak of three equal channels from one Divine essence, three communications from what in itself is incommunicable and indefinable, than to use the language either of celestial genealogy or of bureaucratic relationships by which one element operates "through" another.

JUDAISM

The centre of Judaism is the natural community. Its whole emphasis is on man as social being, related to other men through righteousness and justice. It insists on human responsibility, on definable and achievable objectives. Yet it would be absurd to pretend that Judaism is unaware that man is person, and that the relationship of persons is through love, or that man is seeker and that what he seeks is truth. But Judaism has not developed these possibilities with the same intensity, and the emphasis on the way of life of a community does not lend itself naturally to that development.

CHRISTIANITY

Christianity has its evident centre in man as person. It is aware that man is a social being, but it has consistently tried to subordinate this to the personal aspect of life. It subordinates righteousness and justice to love. It coins the obviously insufficient phrase that the community exists for the individual. And it has very late and very reluctantly interested itself at all in truth. It has fought against every attempt to challenge what it proclaimed to be "revealed truth" as manifested in the Bible. The battle for the freedom of the spirit has not been fought under its banners. On the other hand it cannot abandon the link between its overwhelming concern with man as person and its absolute conviction of the essential power of the Incarnation and the Atonement, doctrines inextricably interwoven into its affirmation of the Trinity in Unity. Sophisticated critics may wax sarcastic about the narrow, or even intellectually ridiculous, dogmatism of preachers and proclaimers of salvation in the Blood of the Lamb, but they can show nothing from their own resources to equal the devotion which those who hold by such doctrine have poured out in blood and treasure in all the dark places of a cruel world. Nor can they pretend that it was not the compulsive power of religious belief which provided the motive force for the lives which resulted. And the centre of this belief were the three words that "God is Love."

HUMANISM

Thirdly, there is the Humanist, rightly proclaiming that man is a seeker, and that the only ultimate objective of his search is Truth. He is impatient with man as social being, always compromising to achieve the attainable. Man as person he dismisses as a sentimentality. He tends to be the most intolerant, perhaps because the youngest, of the three.

The dominant feature of our present situation is, surely, his complete failure to provide any positive and creative substitute for the systems which he has so contemptuously dismissed. He has not made man adult by his discoveries, and has failed, like his predecessors, to cope with his total situation, or give him any basic security or sense of belonging in the world in which he lives—a failure of particular signficance because he has deprived him of any expectation of a life beyond this one. The exclusive search for Truth has not justified itself any more than its predecessors.

THE ATHANASIAN TRINITY

It is at this point that we can realise that the Athanasian formula is right in insisting that "none is greater or less than another." It would provide a good Christmas game, but nothing more serious, to attempt to arrange the Divine channels or the human situations or the abstract virtues, in a hierarchy of importance.

Of course, the traditional Christian will be tempted to say that man as seeker and man as social being, as politician and citizen, belong to this life and to the demands of this world, whereas man as person has an eternal destiny. But it all depends on our belief as to the nature of life beyond the grave. It seems to me odd to think of it as being so sub-human that the angelic choir consists exclusively of soloists, incapable of co-operation and orchestral music, or that life beyond death is neither social nor capable of any further understanding or more exciting discovery of reality. As long as man is identifiably man, he will remain with the three fundamental qualities, though the tensions among them may be other than they are here.

There is a point here that I am bound to make clear. In this formulation I am definitely departing from the accepted tradition of the New Testament and the Church that " the Holy Spirit was given at Pentecost." I am not rejecting Pentecost, but I am not accepting that when Jesus said, as St. John records, that there were things that he could not tell them then, and that the Spirit would come and lead them into all truth (xvi, 13) he was referring to an event which was to take place in fifty days, and be confined to the small group to whom he had already revealed himself. I believe that the overwhelming experience of Pentecost was the experience—or realisation—that Christ was still living in them and among them, and would continue to lead and guide them as in the days of his earthly life. We are bound, whatever our interpretation of the New Testament, to recognise that its different writers were exceedingly vague as to the nature and functions of the Holy Spirit, that they would in succeeding paragraphs define the same activity as being due to the Holy Spirit and the Spirit of Christ.

The Apostles' Creed proclaims belief in the " Holy Ghost," but without any further statement about him. The " Gloria in Excelsis," the concluding hymn in the Anglican Communion service, is a very early one, and it adds the Holy Ghost as an after-thought. The first paragraph deals with the Father, the second with the Son, and it concludes with these words, addressed to Christ:

" Thou only art holy, thou only art the Lord, thou only, O Christ, with the Holy Ghost, are most high in the glory of God the Father."

The impression is overwhelming that, being obliged to include the Holy Spirit as a Divine manifestation, because of the words of Christ, those responsible were then hard put to it to allot him a special activity, and still harder put to it to claim that this activity was equal to that of the first and second persons of the traditional Trinity. And the same vagueness is true today in circles which attempt to base their doctrine on Pentecost and the New Testament.

I would add that, while this is a novel and original point of view, I find it difficult to see at what point it could be condemned as heretical, except, of course, on the grounds that any rejection of the verbal inspiration of the Scriptures was heretical, or that there could be no fresh discovery as well as interpretation of Christian doctrine.

THE TRINITY OF TRINITIES

In any genuine and total " existentialism," really considering the whole of our human situation, is it not evident that men need what is expressed in all three words—that *the same man* in the same life, needs all three ? The same men, at all times, have perpetually to deal with the tensions created by the competing demands of justice, of love and of truth. It is no help to dismiss any of the triad. It is no solution to concentrate on getting one right first. They cannot be arranged hierarchically. None of them can be served " through " another. They are permanently equal, provocatively non-interchangeable. And we cannot choose whether to recognise their existence or not. Their demands are inherent in the world we live in.

This is surely a situation in which the doctrine of the Trinity—if the church would but use it—presents a conception of God's relation to His world which is adequate to our total needs. In the march of time Judaism naturally came first, for man develops as social being first. It is only within the ordered community that man can develop to the full his separateness as person. So the first channel which reached its full flow came through Sinai. Within the Sinaitic community in the fulness of time the second channel was expressed in the Incarnation. What of the third ? In the same way, when men had fully explored the power which flowed from Sinai, when the medieval church was passing from being an instrument of exploration to becoming one of repression, the time was ripe for the filling of a third channel, the channel of truth for man as seeker.

In treating this development historically, we must bear in

mind one important point. In the measure in which man was capabale of receiving it, power has been flowing along all the channels from the very beginning. One channel does not succeed another. The revelation of Sinai did not come into a world which knew nothing of dynamic social order, but into a world full of complex social systems. Nor has the Incarnation brought the natural community to an end. Human and Divine love were not born first with Jesus of Nazareth, but have been manifested at least ever since creatures turned from the production of self-hatching eggs to producing their children alive. So also with the third channel. The pursuit of truth, and the understanding of the world in which they lived, occupied men through all the arts long before they expressed it in any of the sciences, though the tensions between the channels developed only as their full character began to be made manifest.

*　　*　　*

And so you get what seems to me the most majestic, most dynamic, and at the same time, most fluid conception of God in His relation to man, a conception which can be understood in terms of our present manner of thinking as deeply as in the centuries in which it began first to be formulated. It is a conception giving an equal place to the Jew, the Christian and the Humanist, challenging all of them not to sacrifice their own integrity, but to discover a relation of creative tension with each other. To the three together this view gives a central place in the world's understanding of its nature and purpose. But it is not a centrality which condemns all other religions as evil, or foolish, but which is open both to give and to receive contributions, as men everywhere discover righteousness, love and truth in the concrete realities of life in the inmost recesses of the human capacity for thought.

Index

Remnant, The, 5, 7, 21, 24
Revelation, 96 ff, 176
Riccius, P., 75
Ritual murder accusation, 76, 80
Rehovoth, Institutes, 129
Romans, Epistle to the, 188
Rosenzweig, F., 198
Roth, Cecil, 71, 72
Rufeisen, Oswald, 78, 81
Ruppin, A., 126

Sabbath, 161, 163
Sabras, 134, 135
Safed, 121, 126, 156
Saladin, 116
Salvation, nature of, 28 f, *see* also
Death, survival of
Samaritans, The, 98, 117
Schleiermacher, F., 38
Scientific outlook, the, 137
Shechita, 161, 163
Sheep and goats, 173
Schwaben, D., 75
Scribes, 8
Scriptures, the, 8, 21, 24; Jewish
interpretation, 25; Christian
interpretation, 21 f, 63
Scholars, Jewish, 51
Selden, John, 48, 74
Sephardim, 133 f
Servant Poems, The, 180
Sharett, Moshe, 89
Shechita, 42, 198
Sheep and goats, 185, 203
Silberg, Mr. Justice, 83 ff
Sin and forgiveness, 65
Sinai, revelation of, 6, 143, 177;
interpretation of, 94; relation to
Incarnation, 62, 200, 204, 220 f
Sinner, within unity of creation,
182 f
Slavery, 202
Social Being, man as, 206
Society for Promoting Christian
Knowledge, 205
Spät-Judenthum, 6, 7
Spinoza, B., 72
State capital, 140
State, the, 11
Steinberg, Milton, 187
Stellvertrer, Der, 78
Stopford, Bishop, 185
Storrs, Sir R., 128, 131, 134

Surenhuysen, W., 47, 74
Synagogue, origins of, 8
Syriac civilisation, 98

Talbot, E. K., 17
Talmud, The, 73, 101, 102
Tension, theology of, 16 f, 53, 200
Testament of XII Patriarchs, 183
Theobald of Cambridge, 76
Theodosius, Emp., 206
Thirty-Nine Articles, The, 209 f
Tolerance, Divine, 173, 175
Torah, meaning of, 22, 40, 96;
eternal validity, 66; human
responsibility, 68; interpreta-
tion, 194; reading, 8; *see* Fence
Toynbee, Arnold, 43, 48 f, 92 ff
Traditions of the Elders, 199
Trinity, The, 67 f, 73, 96, 200;
and Judaism, 67 f, 176; bureau-
cratic view, 200, 210; channels
from, 200, 216 f; equality with,
218; Persons in, 213
Truce of God, 206

Ugolini, B., 75
Ussishkin, M., 135
Union of American Hebrew Con-
gregations, 20
Uniqueness of Jewish history, 48 f

Victorians, 155

Wadham College, marriage of
warden, 70
Way, Lewis, 75 f
Weizmann, Dr. C., 129, 131
Wells, poisoning of, 81
West, collapse of, 95
Wisdom Literature, 147
Witches, 202
World Jewish Congress, 160
World Zionist Organisation, 160

Yom Kippur, 65

Zionism, 103; European origins
of, 103 f, 126, 127, 164
Zionists, 131; early, 139; Eastern
European culture of, 134 f; and
Arabs, 129